MAN BUYS DOG

MAN BUYS DOG

A Loser's Guide to the World of Greyhound Racing

David Matthews

headline

First published in 2005
by HEADLINE BOOK PUBLISHING

10 9 8 7 6 5 4 3 2 1

Cataloguing in Publication Data is available from the British Library

ISBN 0 7553 1171 X

Typeset in Cochin by Avon DataSet Ltd,
Bidford-on-Avon, Warwickshire

Printed and bound in Great Britain by
Clays Ltd, St Ives plc

Headline's policy is to use papers that are natural, renewable and
recyclable products and made from wood grown in sustainable forests.
The logging and manufacturing processes are expected to conform
to the environmental regulations of the country of origin.

HEADLINE BOOK PUBLISHING
A division of Hodder Headline
338 Euston Road
London NW1 3BH

www.headline.co.uk
www.hodderheadline.com

For Tunis Matthews and Bunmi Daramola

Acknowledgements

I would like to thank the following people for their help, support, encouragement and/or guest appearances: Juliana Foster, David Wilson, Helena Towers, Jane Butcher, Ian Marshall, and the Headline Syndicate; Julian Alexander and LAW; Linda Jones and everyone at Imperial Kennels; Corrina Faith; John Watt and Ray Jones; Big Al; Tamara Adair and Brian Coleman; Ann Aslett, Tracy Cooper and the staff at Walthamstow Stadium; Vince, Paul and John; Ginger and Romford Phil; Luca, Mum, Dr Paul, Wayne Jordash and Owen Clegg; Anna Lovegrove and Johanna Beumer deserve special praise for their commitment to the welfare of retired greyhounds; maximum respect is due to Danielle for putting up with me and my idiosyncratic behaviour.

And finally, to Kevin: thanks for the ride. It's been emotional.

chapter 1

I cracked open beer number four: just another day at the office. The traps flew open, and six scrawny-looking mutts sprang to life like a canine jack-in-the-box. The one dog, the four dog, the three, the five . . . Bleary-eyed I watched them scamper round the first bend through a hailstorm of sand in pursuit of a polyester bunny. Silly fuckers. They'd never catch that Day-Glo hare in a million years. Still, the dogs were not the only ones chasing a dream that night.

Ten feet away from me, lurking in the shadows, a man with pork pie fingers riffled through a thick wad of dirty cash. I rubbed my eyes, looked again and the dogs had passed the post, the crowd roaring its time-honoured approval like so many Romans. But empty vessels make the most noise. For every vocal, lucky winner, there are ten fated, muted losers. I wondered, in that moment of glory, how many fortunes had been won and lost; how many hopes and dreams had been flittered away in the night air; how many children would go without new shoes or pocket money thanks to a father's whim and £300 on a thing with four legs, two balls and no chance.

Soon enough I was introduced to Lennie Knell, a shifty trainer with a story to sell, albeit unintentionally. He seemed eager to please, eager for sleaze: a small-time cheat with a big mouth. 'You can't ever mention that however,' he muttered. Mention what exactly? 'I mean, obviously what I'm doing is illegal.' I was confused. I took a gulp of Red Stripe and crushed the can cos I could, cos I can. Ah . . . lager, lager, lager . . .

Suddenly, an equally indiscreet and well-fed character added with a cheeky grin, 'It's all a fix. It's all a twist.'

Hustlers hustle and rustlers rustle and so the world turns. Greyhound racing, by anyone's stretch, is a racket: man's best friend takes on man's second worst enemy,[1] i.e. greed, generating an electrifying £1.6 billion in revenue every year. Somebody somewhere is getting fat. Why, I wouldn't mind a lickle piece of that action myself. But if I was looking for an easy touch I had another think coming. It would not take long for me to find out that the only dead cert in greyhound racing is the hare. Everything else is a lottery. Or, as Winston Churchill had put it, 'animated roulette'.

Blindfolded by drink, tired and groggy, I was whisked away from the track on another diversion. I saw the shovels go to work. Bones were uncovered. A skull peered at me in the mist. Sweet Jesus, I'd been led to a mass grave. These old dogs, whose twisted remains lay rotting in the earth, had learnt a new trick all right: win or die. But how and where did this sort of thing go on? Where does a man kill a dog with a bullet to the back of the head: a farm, a clearing in the woods, the allotments up the road from Albert Square? Whatever. Location is immaterial at this point. I'd seen enough to be sucked in. Like an eighteenth-century duellist, I demanded satisfaction. I wanted more information, more dirt, more secrets and lies to satiate my lurid curiosity. I didn't have long to wait.

I could feel myself sinking. *Concentrate, concentrate*. I heard a voice say, with more than a touch of English relish, '*Tonight*, we chase down the criminals, *at the dogs*.'

Fade to black.

I came round, slowly. On the floor was half a can of beer. In my lap was a half-eaten pizza. In my mind was a half-baked idea.

---

[1] Fear is arguably man's greatest enemy but greed runs a pretty close second.

It was the usual tedious, suicidal winter night. December 2001. Slumped on a sofa in front of a portable TV in a dingy little flat in Paddington, west London, I had watched most of *Kenyon Confronts* – a BBC exposé on corruption in the world of greyhound racing – before drifting into the Witching Hour and then a 1a.m. resurrection. I call these moments of alcoholic, mindless inspiration 'research'. This is how I get all my best ideas, by eating pizza, getting trashed and crashing out in front of the telly.

From what I'd seen, or from what I thought I'd seen in the opening sixty seconds of the programme, the 'voice' a.k.a. eponymous hero Paul Kenyon, had managed to trip the light fandango through every conceivable stereotype and cliché of greyhound racing imaginable. Cheeky chappies, doping, snuffing out lame dogs, race fixing, you name it, the boy Kenyon had it all there bar the pencil line moustaches, camel hair coats and Arthur Daley.

But if you're born and raised in a place like the East End, which I was, and you'd had the odd, shall we say, 'run in with the authorities', which I had, then you take it for granted that a little bit of skulduggery is all part of life's rich tapestry. A bit of hooky gear here, a 'favour' there . . . As Grandmaster Flash and the Furious Five broke it down on their seminal 1981 hip-hop anthem, *The Message*, '. . . you gotta have a con in this land of milk and honey'.

For instance, we all know that greyhound racing is bent, right? Like the man said, 'It's all a fix. It's all a twist,' is it not? How many times have you heard the one about a dog being fed a Mars bar or a bowl of porridge before a race to slow it down, or heard that greyhounds have mustard shoved up their choccy lockers to make them, literally, hot to trot? Then there are the puppy-dog tales of pumping a greyhound with gallons of water in order to bloat it to a standstill or 'ringing' – switching a slow dog for a fast one by disguising it with a false beard and moustache so that no one would recognise the poor bugger. Or how about putting a dog on roller skates with a nitrous oxide injection unit tied to its back so it could R-O-C-K-E-T its way to the finish line.

On a more serious note, in the summer of 2001 the Irish Greyhound Board, the Bord na gCon, had come down hard on doping in the sport by banning the use of Viagra. It had transpired that a number of unscrupulous trainers were using the love drug on their animals as a performance enhancer. Whether Viagra works on the track or not is debatable but I'm sure one or two dogs (and possibly trainers) have got more than they'd bargained for back at the kennels.

So there I am in my west London pad; still half-cut, still strung out on the sofa like a row of broken beads. I watched the tail end of Kenyon's investigation with heightened curiosity: he nailed Lennie Knell and his buddy Colin West offering to fix a race by over-feeding a dog at Catford track in south London; he also captured West on film boasting that the dynamic duo had once made eleven grand from a bent race. What a win-double! I had to take my baseball cap off to Kenyon for exposing these halfwits. Knell, West and their ilk had got their karma for being greedy little shits, for trying to cheat the system rather than beat the system.

An exposé by its very nature doesn't leave much room for balanced reportage. But to be fair to the thousands of honest Johns involved in greyhound racing, Kenyon had taken a cynical, one-sided angle, casting an even darker cloud over a much-maligned sport. I know all too well how easy it is to pull off a 'sting' or make a bad story fit a good headline. Muck-raking, stereotypes, clichés, demagoguery . . . this is my stock-in-trade. Heaven knows, as a journalist, I have fingered enough people in my time in pursuit of 'the truth'. Whatever that is.

As the old Fleet Street maxim goes, 'never let the truth get in the way of a good story'. I had a hunch there were many truths about the dogs that do not involve confectionery, cereals or amphetamines. Despite its bad press, greyhound racing is still Britain's second most popular spectator sport (football is number one) in terms of attendance. On any given day or night of the week, practically 365 days a year, there is dog racing at most of the 34 tracks licensed by the National Greyhound Racing Club (NGRC) – the sport's governing body – totalling around 68,000 races.

Either there are trailer loads of very gullible people out there, or these characters know something that the likes of Kenyon and I don't. Could there be another story to tell, another truth to reveal? Shock, gasp, horror: could it be that greyhound racing is not so bad after all? I suspected the dogs were a victim of the 'chav' witch-hunts of the early twentieth century, the marginalisation of the white-bread working classes and their associated 'end of the pier show' lifestyle. But there was only one way to find out for sure: it was time to put on the greasy trilby, the dirty raincoat and the cynical charm, and start sniffing around my local dog track.

chapter 2

After the festive season had crackerjacked its way out of sight and out of mind I trundled off to Wimbledon Stadium in south-west London to experience a night at the dogs. I badgered my woman Danielle and our friend Wayne into coming along with me. Danielle, who I affectionately nicknamed 'Margot' because of her penchant for the good life, knows more about foxhounds than greyhounds. That's not to say she's a toff. It's just that she was brought up with gymkhana, ponies and the thrill of the chase while I was dragged up with Jim Beam, Ford Escorts and the thrill of joyriding.

As for Wayne, he's a barrister and a 'brother' who, like me, had made his way 'across the tracks' in search of a career that didn't involve flesh-coloured pantyhose, a sawn-off shotgun and a getaway driver called Camp Freddy. Wayne is a cosmopolitan kind of guy and he leads a far from sheltered life; but it's fair to say that any relationship he was likely to have with the world of dog racing would be a vicarious one: i.e. via a character like me.

Anyway, as impromptu acid tests go, if a couple of left-leaning lounge lizards like Margot and Wayne could handle the simple pleasures of Wimbledon Stadium then maybe there was truth in the rumour that the trendy classes were now going to the dogs in their droves.

'Is this it?' said Margot frowning as the stadium came into view.

'I guess so,' I said.

Wayne looked at the pair of us and laughed. The Lady and the Tramp. I turned the corner into Plough Lane, passing a smattering of racegoers, then swerved Margot's Polo into a dimly lit car park. The exterior of Wimbledon Stadium is an unimpressive mix of crumbling brickwork and corrugated iron. It has the air of a makeshift penal colony. As we drove in, I noticed a sign dangling precariously on the wire perimeter fence advertising a car boot sale the following weekend. Class.

Apart from the dogs and boot sales, Wimbledon Stadium also doubles as a stock car and speedway venue. However, following the closure of White City Stadium in 1984 it has become synonymous with the English Greyhound Derby, the premier event in the dog-racing calendar. Sponsored by high-street bookie William Hill, the race runs every June and is now worth a cool £75,000 in prize money to the winner. The Derby is what 'dog people' dream of — be it breeding, owning or training a winner. But, on this particular night, the top prize was no more than 160 quid. Nevertheless, it was the start of the New Year and the dog-racing public, like the rest of us, was still nursing a headache after the excesses of the holiday season.

The three of us ambled up to the main entrance. A young couple were having a tiff in the car park. From the sounds of it, Boyfriend had spunked all his dough at the track already, so Girlfriend would have to settle for a video and chips, instead of The Ministry and a curry. Aw, young love . . .

'C'mon. It's not that bad,' I said, trying to humour Margot as we sashayed through the turnstiles. I gave her arse a squeeze.

'Can we get food in here?' asked Wayne.

'I'm sure you can,' I replied. 'Whether it's edible or not, I don't know.'

For a moment I felt like a mean old man, forcing his teenage children to get involved in some terminally boring adult experience while they whined, 'Do we have to?' I often took it for granted that despite my lofty pretensions as a hack writer and pseudo-academic, I inhabited for the most part an everyday world that many of my chattering friends were blissfully unengaged with: football, boxing, car boot sales, beanos, drug smugglers, ragamuffins, jerk chicken, pie and bloody mash and now, the dogs. If the truth be known, yeah I love slumming it, if only to reaffirm the fact that I still know how to cross the tracks every once in a while, and be comfortable with the view on either side.

Which was precisely why, theoretically, greyhound racing was something I could get into. Born in Hackney and raised in a mixture of E-numbered postal codes, I'm sociologically hardwired for such activities, much in the same way that I'm genetically hardwired for flat feet, baldness and a beer gut. But could the bourgeoisie 'get' into the dogs in the way that they had eventually 'got' football? As the comedian Frank Skinner once opined, 'Football's not the same since women and the middle classes got involved.' What Skinner meant was, to accommodate the fairer sex and the chattering classes, straight, predominantly white, working-class men have had to modify their behaviour at football matches to such an extent that they are now practically indistinguishable from Homo sapiens. Apart from football grounds, pubs and of course dog tracks, the British working class was running out of places to socialise en masse in, er, stereotypical working-class fashion. Political correctness had effectively banned smoking, boozing, belching, farting, swearing, fucking and fighting from public life. The personal freedoms of the common man were under threat. The only sanctuary regular Joes had these days was on the toilet seat at home with a jazz mag and a roll of Kleenex for company.

The way that I look at it, women and the middle classes have an appreciation for the finer things in life that blue-collar guys simply do not have. Fish knives, dental floss, keeping your elbows off the dinner table, yoga, getting in touch with your feelings, calling a napkin a napkin not a serviette, paying taxes . . . this kind of stuff just isn't part of a working-class guy's remit. Now consider hunting knives, gold teeth, sticking your elbows in an opposing footballer's face, sex, getting in touch with your drinking buddies, calling a spade a spade not a bloody garden implement, paying your gambling debts . . . that's more like it.

For people like Margot and Wayne the dogs are . . . well, they were a couple of greyhound virgins, too sophisticated for such a Runyonesque pastime. But wait. What am I talking about? When I listen to myself waxing lyrical like this about class and race and blah blah blah I can hear distant voices echoing from the Dick Van Dyke School of Cockney. As a social chameleon I have become obsessed with class and race and blah blah blah. It tempers my view of everything I do and everyone I meet. I sound like a champagne socialist who's had one too many. What the fuck do I know about the sociology of greyhound racing? Before Wimbledon, I hadn't been to a dog track in nearly twenty years.

My initiation into greyhound racing came after I had started my first job, as an apprentice electrician. I'd left school with the bare minimum of qualifications, intent on earning a living and escaping the drudgery of a parochial existence. An awkward and gangly youth, apathetic yet highly excitable, I wasn't really interested in much of anything except my own teenage angst, scrapping, loafing around and getting laid, or more to the point, losing my virginity.

I worked with an old boy who (for the sake of a libel writ), I'll refer to as 'Monty Wright'. Monty was a compulsive gambler and a sociopathic liar. He was also very fat and very lazy. On Thursday afternoons, we would skive off work and head for Hackney Wick dog track, leaving broken central-heating systems, busted lights and dissatisfied tenants in our wake.

Monty was born and raised somewhere in Hackney but he'd done all right for himself so like anyone with half a brain, he moved out to the 'burbs in readiness for retirement. 'Fuck the council,' he used to say, trying to justify the paltry effort he put in for the maintenance department. 'What have they ever done for us, eh?' I could've told him that they'd given us a job and a steady income for starters but I didn't want to rain on his parade.

DAVID MATTHEWS

As an apprentice, I did as I was told, most of the time. I was at Monty's mercy. As much as I hated work, I wasn't into goofing off at a dog track. I wanted to learn how to be a sparks, make a few quid, do a few 'privates' now and again, buy a little gaff somewhere on the outer reaches of Zone 3, maybe shack up with some sister called Beverly or Sandra. Then I could goof off where I wanted to, like down the snooker hall on Leytonstone High Road or the Thai massage parlour in nearby Stratford.

Like most teenagers, I was narcissistic and vain. Going to the dogs was naff, especially at a dump like Hackney Wick Stadium. Once upon a time, it had been a prosperous dog track and speedway venue but now it was nothing more than a concrete wreck on the edge of Hackney Marshes. Its dog days had ended unceremoniously in 1994. Nowadays, for its sins, it was best known as a sprawling Sunday car boot sale, ringed by a phalanx of shifty pikeys who lived in unbelievably ostentatious caravans while dressed in tacky rags that were greasier than a mechanic's jockstrap.

Anyway, as Monty's protégé, where he went I went, which meant frequent trips to Hackney Wick Stadium. More often than not, I would sit in the smoky atmosphere of the main grandstand supping on half a lager and reading the *Daily Mirror* while Monty, as we like to say in the East End, 'did his bollocks' on the dogs.

'Fucking stupid mutt,' he would say, screwing up his fat face, before sticking it faithfully back into the race card in search of yet another loser. Not being a gambler, I'd snigger at his misfortune and amuse myself with the goings-on: loudmouthed bookies; irate losers; tic-tac men with white gloves and funny little hats, waving their semaphoric arms around like air traffic controllers on crack; old hags trying to double up on their pension money; care in the community cases having minor psychiatric episodes . . .

At the time, Hackney was reputedly the poorest borough in Britain, so there was never any shortage of toe-rags, skivers and dole bludgers hanging around the track. Where, and more importantly how, these people found the money to gamble I will

10

never know. Did they not have jobs to go to, mouths to feed, and addictions to be treated?

Most of the punters at the track were small fry, Monty included. He was an habitual gambler but too stingy, or perhaps too smart, to wager meaningful amounts. There were other punters, however, particularly the hardcore professional gamblers, who bet with *real* financial conviction. They were all called Bill or Terry or George – the land of middle-aged likely lads who drove black cabs, owned pubs or 'businesses' that only handled cash and knew someone who knew someone who used to know the Kray twins. They would stroll up to the bookies, chests puffed out, shoulders back, barking shit like, 'A bottle on trap two,' or 'I'll have a monkey on the five dog.' A monkey: five hundred smackers! On a DOG?

The majority of these high rollers were thick as thieves with the bookies, so they never handed over their dough when they placed a bet. The bookie *trusted* the bet. Likewise, these punters did not need a ticket as proof of purchase, as the mugs did. Business was done on trust. Five hundred pounds *trusted* on a dog. In those days, back in the early eighties, £500 was a month's wages to me; or alternatively, twenty visits to that Thai massage parlour in Stratford . . .

Against this backdrop, I never saw the sense in greyhound racing. Put simply, like most forms of gambling, I considered it a waste of time and money. As a yoof I had played a little three-card brag or pool with my mates for shekels, but for the most part I thought gambling on the dogs was bullshit. The utter sense-lessness of it all seemed compounded by the fact that week in week out grown men and women wagered millions of pounds on an animal whose only talent was that it could outrun a Reliant Robin. Oh, and lick its own gonads: though unfortunately for the *Daily Sport*, not at the same time.

Two decades on and inside Wimbledon Stadium Margot and Wayne were as underwhelmed as I had once been. The track was too common for their liking. I tried to explain to them that its simplicity was part of the charm, the Zen if you like, of greyhound racing, but my argument was a waste of time. After walking through a carpeted façade, which offered a brief taste of style and modernity, we followed the signs to the bar through a grey, concreted anteroom. The interior of the bar was reminiscent of a bingo hall or a working men's club: hideous fluorescent lighting, a mishmash of primary colours splattered on the floor and the walls, enough plastic fittings to give Barbie and Ken hives, all scented with the stench of tobacco smoke and booze and dead things frying.

The poor weather had forced all but the headstrong into the bars and dining areas of the track. Corporate types and those going for the big night out headed for the relative glamour of the 'Broadway' and 'Star' restaurants or an executive box. We opted for the common or garden bar at the foot of the main grandstand. It was busy inside. Most of the patrons were men and white, many of them old enough to have lived through a couple of world wars. I ordered up two gin and tonics for Margot and Wayne, and a pint of Guinness for myself. A number of TV screens flickered with betting information on the Tote: forecasts and trifectas, theoretical wins, elusive promises of improbable prizes.

The next race was at least ten minutes away. Several overweight men and pallid old codgers were looking at replays of the previous race on a large screen, offering each other animated 'expert' analysis. I noticed Margot and Wayne scanning the bar, the punters and the décor, trying to reconcile their presence with this chavvy new environment. I could tell they were both wondering why they had agreed to go to the dogs with me. We found a table smeared with fag ends, half-eaten chips and empty plastic beer glasses and sat down.

Wayne grinned impishly, eyeing the posters of greasy burgers and meat by-product hotdogs at the takeaway concession. I spread out, pretending to study the form in the race card. Why does junk food smell so appetising? *I could murder one of those airbrushed quarter-*

pounders with chips. Well, the least I could do was have a nibble, in solidarity with Wayne of course.

So I bought a burger with chips. 'That looks *disgusting*,' said Margot, as I bit into the grease, meat, processed cheese and cardboard bun. It was *extremely* disgusting. Margot was right: women always are. My burger was so rare I thought it was going to eat *me*.

'I'm going outside to take in the atmosphere,' I said, picking my teeth, leaving Margot and Wayne at the bar.

On the track, several hurdles were wheeled out for the next race. The hurdles looked like giant wallpaper brushes turned up on end; they struck me as more of a novelty than a genuine obstacle. In front of the main grandstand was a narrow terrace with a series of steps that offered a decent view of the action. This was occupied by a number of coughing and spluttering old men, so I ventured over to the other end of the main grandstand where there was a small betting ring flanked by half a dozen or so bookmakers. It was just like I remembered Hackney Wick Stadium: suited and booted bookies in big dark overcoats with slicked-back hair and tangerine perma-tans, each with their own coterie of tic-tac men, clerks and tipsters helping to oil the machinery of bookmaking.

'I'll take 2–1 the favourite,' hollered one of the bookies in the far corner of the betting ring. 'TOODA-ONE!' The bookie's name was Tony Morris, the grandee of Wimbledon Stadium I learnt later. Tony M was real old school, a little guy with a big nose and an even bigger wallet. He was perched high on a stepladder or a stand of some sort, looking down at the throng of punters. He wore immaculately polished loafers, a well-cut single-breasted navy suit – bespoke I would say, none of that ready-to-wear muck – and a pair of gold-rimmed glasses.

'FIVA-TOODA-FIELD,' cried another bookie, this one with silver hair and a suit to match. The new market info sent the betting ring into a minor frenzy. Punters looking to back the favourite rushed from one side of the betting ring to the other to get the better price, pushing and barging each other like old girls at a jumble sale. While the punters waved their wads of cash at the bookie, he reeled off a series of numbers to his clerk sitting incognito in the background. Apart from the regulars, of course, when the bookie called the numbers, he handed out a ticket to each punter representing their bet: a simple yet effective system. Bingo for big boys. In sixty seconds these brightly coloured bits of card would be the difference between success and failure.

'Six dog: £175 for 50. Ticket 17,' cried the Silver Bookie. 'Two dog: £100 for 20. Number 18. Six dog: £120 for 40. Ticket 19. Six dog: £75 for 30. Number 20 . . .'

The bookie kept reeling off number after number as his clerk scribbled furiously, marking up each bet on a large ledger. Sweating, impatient, anxious men (for the betting ring is exclusively male, save for the most intrepid woman), continued to push and shove each other in order to place a bet. Prices moved constantly on each bookmaker's board, reflecting the intensity of the action in the betting ring. Suspending reality for a moment or two, here was a microcosmic futures market, a Stock Exchange for Joe Public.

No sooner had the punters gone crazy for the lengthened price on the favourite, than one competing bookie's flunky (who was keeping a beady eye on the proceedings) shouted, 'Johnny's gone a bottle on the bottom. You're out on your own.' With that, the bookie rubbed '5/2' off his board and marked up '2/1'.

And so the prices ebbed and flowed in the run up to 'the off' . . .

Added to their armoury of tic-tac, mobile phones and walkie-talkies, the bookies communicated with each other through a crude but unique nomenclature, which was utterly meaningless to the uninitiated, apart from the odd term that transcended the betting ring and made it into the cosmopolitan patois of modern Britain.

These gold-plated moneymen filled their leather satchels with a Noah's Ark of cash: 'monkeys', 'ponies', 'cockles' and 'bull's eyes'. In bookmaking parlance, words and phrases are an enigma and like any slanguage they act as a 'keep out' sign to those who aren't in the know. The bookies' lexicon is full of bent-out-of-shape, customised and redesigned words, which could be *converse* as much as conversed. 'Enin', for example, means nine (or alternatively 9–1) just as 'neves' stands for seven (or 7–1). There are expressions of etymological mystery like 'carpet' to express 3–1 (or 300 quid) or 'bottle' for 2–1 (or 200 quid).

There were now under thirty seconds to go before the next race. I had already missed half the card, but as I had no money I didn't intend to gamble anyway. Once again I looked at the race form, and once again, just as when I looked at the ever-changing Tote screens dotted around the track, the words 'arse', 'elbow' and 'don't know' sprang to mind. Form, statistics, the names and breeding dates of greyhounds meant nothing to me. I couldn't even pick a winner in a one-dog race.

I watched the kennel hands parade the dogs for the last time in front of the expectant crowd, and then load them into the traps, gently nudging them by their backsides into the tiny boxes, which were no bigger than the dogs themselves. No wonder they didn't hang around once the hare came calling. I was just thinking that the kennel hands probably earned less than the dogs did when Margot and Wayne appeared with another round of drinks.

'Aye, aye, Dave, what's the score?' said Wayne.

'I'd say bookies six, punters nil. Cheers.'

We headed through the betting ring for the stands to get a better view of the action. A wire mesh fence, some ten-feet high, ran along the perimeter of the track in front of the stands to stop the crowds from pelting the dogs with missiles. The lights around the stadium dimmed as though a 10,000-volt electric chair on Wimbledon's Death Row had been levered into action. A bell rang signalling the start of the race. A garbled voice over the PA announced, 'murmur murmur murmur, hare's approaching' and then *Pow!* six dogs exploded out of the traps, pounding their way down the home straight towards us, their paws drumming an allegro beat in the sand and gliding over the hurdles like they just weren't there.

The crowd followed the rapid progress of the dogs along the home straight with a Mexican wave of sound, the cheers climaxing then stalling as the tightly bunched mass of fawn, black, white and mottled coats, resplendent in their multicoloured satin jackets, hit the first bend at some 35mph. The two wide runners on the outside of the pack collided with each other leaving four dogs now with a clear run to the second bend some fifty metres away. They rounded the turn, galloping into the back straight, bounding effortlessly over the hurdles, then broke into Indian file as the lead dog, a big brindle machine, kicked on, racing to the third bend unopposed, leaving the field a tiring ragtag of also-rans.

The crowd roared again, urging on the lead dog, which took the fourth and final bend a good five lengths clear of its nearest rival. It flew over the last two hurdles and won comfortably. The winner, and the field, kept running until the kennel hands emerged from the other side of the track at the 'pick up' with the lure – a ragged cuddly toy used to compensate the dogs for not catching the elusive plastic hare. For just under thirty seconds of work I calculated that the winning dog had earned an hourly equivalent of £19,200, making it theoretically one of the highest paid breeds of athlete in professional sport.

Down in the betting ring the cabal of winners were having it large, back slapping, laughing, high on the rush of success. Meanwhile the losers, the silent majority, consoled themselves that they had nearly picked the winner, ripping up their tickets and throwing them into the air like confetti.

'Is that it?' asked Margot.

'Well, yeah,' I said. 'What were you expecting?'

'Well, it was over so quickly.'

'Yeah Dave, it was over so quickly,' said Wayne sarcastically. 'What you gonna do about it?'

The garbled voice returned to the PA announcing, 'uh, uh, wobble, wobble, rhubarb, rhubarb twenty-nine point wobble,

wobble seconds.' Strange. I could've sworn that I'd only had two pints. As the dogs were led off the track and through the entrance to the kennels under our enclosure, a small crowd gathered to congratulate the victor, not that he'd understand much, being a dog and all.

'Hey, let's have a butchers,' I said, beckoning Margot and Wayne. We went down to get a closer look at the winning animal, muscling our way past a group of small girls who were petting the panting, wistful creature. His name was Gift Trader. Not that this meant anything to most people. In horseracing, the gee-gees have names and personalities; in dog racing, greyhounds simply have numbers. Ordinary punters refer to dogs as 'the one dog, the two dog' and so on. For the average Joe, a greyhound is a commodity, a proposition, a living, breathing poker chip distinguishable only by the 1, 2, 3, 4, 5 and 6 of a red, blue, white, black, orange or monochrome jacket.

Up close and personal, Gift Trader did not seem as anorexic or yappy as I expected a greyhound to be; in fact he was poised, lean yet solid and muscular. Wide-eyed, frantic and muzzled when racing, they look psychotic, possessed, but as I stroked this dog's smooth Jaffa Cake coat and felt his tiny heart racing he was no more dangerous than any poodle. His tongue hung out of his head, dripping with saliva, as he caught his breath repeatedly. Even as the young girls mauled him, jockeying each other and giggling all the while, the dog remained impassive, majestic even.

'D'you wanna buy him? He's for sale you know.' I looked round and a nondescript middle-aged bloke was beaming at me.

'Really, what do you want for him?' I asked straightening up, not that I had money to burn on a greyhound.

'Ah, I'm only kidding,' said the man giving the dog a brisk rub. 'He's not for sale. I wouldn't sell him for the world.'

'Shame that. I was gonna make you an offer you couldn't refuse.'

'Ha. Beautiful dogs aren't they? I've got five of 'em you know. Got another one running here tomorrow.' The Dog Man leaned forward as though he had a great secret for sharing, but only with me. 'Her name's . . .' he whispered something like Tunbridge Cyclone or Maidstone Hurricane. ' 'Ave a few quid on her . . . she should win.'

'Cheers,' I said. 'Will do.'

'What was all that about?' asked Margot.

'I just got a hot tip from that bloke,' I said, hunching my back, giving it a touch of the Arthur Daley. 'I got connections here you know.' Margot looked at me sympathetically and laughed.

We went back into the stands, took in another race and stood there for a while shooting the breeze. A small tractor driven by a sullen man crawled round the track, smoothing the sand in readiness for the next race.

'I'm cold. Can we go now?' said Margot.

'What are you talking about?' I said. 'We've only just got here.'

'Don't look at me,' said Wayne, raising his arms in faux surrender.

Margot shrugged her shoulders and started walking towards the bar. 'Let's go back inside then.'

'Yeah, let's get another drink,' I said, throwing her the car keys. 'You can drive. I'm over the limit.'

I looked at Margot, gave her a cheesy grin and a gentle squeeze of her arse. We went back to the bar and I ordered another round of drinks. She looked bored.

Maybe the acid test had failed.

chapter 3

You get two things from a tip: small change and rubbish. Dog Boy said that Tunbridge Cyclone, Margate Tornado or whatever it was would win, but it didn't, did it? It came absolutely nowhere. Still, what did I expect? Relying on a tip from a stranger at a dog track was no smarter than Jack and that funny business with the beans. Which is why I did the right thing: I passed the information on to a buddy of mine and let him lose his shirt at the bookies instead.

Nevertheless, my descent into the wonderful world of greyhound racing had begun. Well, sort of. Perhaps it was inevitable that someone who has lived most of his life 'shooting from the hip', 'flying by the seat of his pants' and 'sailing close to the wind' would one day wind up as a human cliché by 'going to the dogs'.

It was actually a couple of months before the Wimbledon situation that my luck had really started to run dry. I had lined up in Sportspages, a pokey little bookstore off Shaftesbury Avenue with four other writers to contest the William Hill Sports Book of the Year Award, a.k.a. the 'Bookie Prize'. My entry, *Looking for a Fight* – the tale of how I'd transformed myself from a 15-and-a-half-stone slob into a 12-and-a-half-stone professional fighter – was drawn against a tome on sailing, the biography of a dead American horse, another book on boxing and the bookies' favourite, something about an Irish footballer nobody had ever heard of.

In the event, the dead horse won it: Laura Hillenbrand's *Seabiscuit: Three Men and a Racehorse* scooped the ten grand prize and all the bits and pieces that came with it. The book was later made into a movie that grossed over $100,000,000 within a couple of weeks of its release, which was of little consolation to me. For being pipped at the post by a necrobiotic nag I pocketed a grand in cash and a £750 complimentary bet from the sponsors. I didn't win the big one, or get a movie deal. But I wasn't bitter. Early retirement would just have to wait a while.

It didn't take me long to blow that grand, but the free bet voucher spent several weeks burning a hole in my pocket. Then the dog thing happened. I'm not sure how or why it happened. It just did. I know Paul Kenyon and that stupid bloody TV show had something to do with it; but the last time I saw *Only Fools and Horses* I didn't go out and buy a hundred and fifty remote control blow-up dolls, so I can't blame television for this one. Perhaps it was something I ate. Maybe it was delusions of grandeur or whispers in my mind. Who knows? Temporary insanity notwith-standing, for someone who is generally *compos mentis*, buying a greyhound was, er, an odd thing to do.

My previous 'hobby' of professional boxing had left me with a cauliflower ear, occasional dizzy spells, several pug-nosed enemies, and a libel suit from a well-known promoter. I was flat broke and fed up with being punched out for my art; fed up with all that struggling artist crap. There had to be an easier way out there to make a buck without actually doing any work. All I had left to my name was seven hundred and fifty smackers to wager on a dream – seven-fifty to parlay into a slot machine on legs. It seemed like *a good idea* at the time. Man buys dog. Man races dog. Man makes money for old rope. Man, I had taken too many punches to the head.

At the bottom end of greyhound racing, i.e. my end, I found out that I could buy a young unproven puppy for a monkey or a race-ready older one for around a grand. Kennel and training fees were about a fiver a day plus VAT, which could be covered in part by prize money. For a fraction of what a racehorse cost, I could get a dog that could run just as fast and would take up less space.

I had it all figured out: the costs, the benefits, everything. It's amazing how life always seems to work out right on paper. Finding a sure thing, however, was easier said than done. Picking a winner, even with someone else's money isn't easy. Bookies know the odds are stacked so much in their favour that free bets are nothing more than an act of fulsome generosity. So what do you do with a £750 free bet? In a moment of madness I considered whacking it on a 100–1 shot at Kempton but a one-off bet of such magnitude couldn't be staked on something as fleeting as a horse race, let alone a dog race.

In the final analysis, after careful consideration of football, cricket, athletics, snooker, darts, bowls and the World Shove-Ha'penny Championships in Billericay, I decided to go for England to win the Six Nations tournament. At 3–10 the odds were skin tight, but the market and the 'experts' suggested an England win was a *fait accompli*. Ireland, Scotland, Wales and Italy did not have a prayer, leaving France as the only viable threat. What did the French know about rugby anyway?

On January 31st I called William Hill and placed the bet: 750 sovs on England to win the Six Nations. I was about to learn my first painful lesson as an unprofessional gambler. Two days after I'd struck the bet England got off to a flyer: Scotland got whacked 29–3 at Murrayfield . . . *Swing low, sweet chariot*. One down, four to go . . . Two weeks later Ireland were annihilated at Twickenham 45–11 . . . *Coming fo' to carry me home*. Two down, three to go . . . Going into the game against the French at the Stade de France, England were still odds-on favourites. The French had creamed Italy 33–12 in their opening game, but the following week *Les Bleus* went to the wire with Wales, narrowly winning 37–33 in Cardiff. France v England was the match that would decide the eventual winners of the tournament.

As I watched the game at home on TV, the French methodical, disciplined fashion closed down England chipping away at them like master stonemasons. If you don't want to know the score look away now: the French, everybody's favourite enemy, took England to school, winning 20–15. As the final whistle went, so did my £975 windfall. France now only had to overcome Scotland and Ireland to win the tourney. Even if you discounted the fact that the French were far superior to either team, history dictated that neither would do England any favours and actually try to win, even if it were humanly possible. France eventually beat Scotland 22–10 and battered Ireland 44–5 to complete the Grand Slam and lift the Six Nations trophy. *Merde*.

Having squandered my free bet, my dog days were over before they had even started. I had shot my big mouth off to all and sundry about my bright idea and was now in danger of winding up with ego all over my face. Professional sport, the bookies, the *system*, had all conspired against me, robbing me of what was rightfully mine. Mine, mine, mine, I tell you! To hell with England, William Hill and common sense. In the words of Iron Mike Tyson, 'I refuse to lose.' I *knew* I could beat the system. It was time to even the score, time to take on the big boys at their own game, time to score a blow for the little guy. So I went cap in hand to my publisher . . .

This was the deal: in return for salacious tales of dodgy deals, drugs, gambling, corruption, animal cruelty, celebrities and sex (I lied about the sex) my publisher would invest two grand and take a 50 per cent stake in the dog. Fair enough. They would also bankroll £1000 to cover initial expenses. OK. Of course, I would get a suitable advance for delivering a juicy manuscript in twelve months' time . . . Once the year was up I would get rid of the dog, for a profit, natch, and everything else would slot into place, including the Bookie Prize I had been so cruelly denied. With the money I earned I would go to Cuba and have a back-street plastic surgeon reconstruct my cauliflower ear for a hundred bucks and a year's supply of refried beans. Sorted.

A couple of months passed and the dough was in the bank. Damn. I was living large again. This was the easiest score I'd had in ages. My old man always said I had 'money counting hands'. It was now May and while the bulk of that fat cheque from my publisher marinated in its own juices at Lloyds TSB, I set aside two Gs and started looking in the obvious places for a bargain Derby prospect, chiefly the *Racing Post, Greyhound Star, Greyhound Monthly, Fiesta, Loot* and Battersea Dogs Home. The latter two turned up nothing of note, but I did get a great deal on a Sony Minidisc. *Fiesta* was simply a good read.

As you can imagine, the greyhound press was an oasis of dogs but without really knowing what I was doing, my lack of knowledge betrayed me every time I made an inquiry.

'What are you looking for exactly?' said the man in a thick Irish brogue.

'Er, a greyhound, er, that's, er . . .' I mumbled.

'Well, I know you're looking for a dog otherwise you wouldn't be calling would ya? What d'you want? D'you want an open racer, a grader, a sprinter, a stayer . . .? What d'you want? I got the lot you know.'

The ad in the paper said the man had 'Bitches For Sale'. I liked the sound of that. Bitches. Maybe he'd take one of my ex-girlfriends in part-exchange.

'I want something fast,' I ventured. Crackle crackle. It was a bad connection. 'How about . . .? Why don't I come and see what you've got?'

'What? What was that? Listen, this isn't a fekking car show-room you know! I got no time for timewasters!'

Brrrrrrrrrrrrrrrrrrrrrrrrrrrr.

'Hello? Hello? *Hel-lo?*'

Ignorant fucker. Subsequent calls were no more helpful. Breeders and dealers could spot a bullshitter a mile off, even down a phone line. One woman even said, with a mild hint of sarcasm, 'You're not that Paul Kenyon fella are ya?' after I intimated I was on a mission to find the 'inside track' on greyhound racing. I wasn't doing an exposé, so I wanted to be as upfront as possible with anyone I dealt with. Having been busted for ticket touting, spat at by tramps, hexed by a witch doctor and made to smoke crack cocaine, all in the name of investigative journalism, I'd long since given up on undercover reportage.

Sooner or later I had to get off my fat arse and spend some money, so I hit the road and headed for the greyhound sales at Perry Barr racetrack in Birmingham, which offered the discerning mug an unenviable selection of bargain-basement dogs. Over the years, regrettable purchases of clapped-out motors, snide antiques and job lots of salmonella foodstuffs have taught me that an auction isn't the best place to go shopping for quality goods. Buying a greyhound at a public sale was therefore a very risky business. Nevertheless, fortune occasionally favours the reckless as well as the bold so I decided to take a chance.

The Perry Barr sales were a treat for anyone brought up on Galton and Simpson sitcoms. Every fat, balding, incontinent, polyester-wearing, middle-aged man from the West Midlands seemed to be there, either propping up the bar and ruminating over the auction catalogue or gobbing scornfully at the track as the dogs went off in ones, twos and threes during the pre-sale time trials. It was a crisp spring day in Britain's second city, given lustre by a cinnamon glow of sunlight. But the punters weren't there for the weather. After a short nap in the Polo, I returned to the dark, dank atmosphere of the bar-cum-auction room to find the action underway.

'Eight hundred . . . eight hundred over there. Eight fifty, eight fifty, eight fifty . . .' The auctioneer was a chalky-white, elderly Irishman in a funereal suit. To the right of him on the dais was a weaselly little fella in his mid-forties clad from head to toe in synthetic sports leisurewear. Rub shoulders with him and sparks would fly. Throughout the bidding Synthetic Man whispered conspiratorially in the auctioneer's ear, to which the old man would utter some indistinguishable sales pitch such as, 'She's got bags of staying power, a gutsy little bitch,' or 'She was the 2002 All-Ireland Guide Dog Champion, trained at Barbara Woodlouse's Walkies School of Canine Excellence.' The crowd would grunt at every titbit of information then continue coughing and spluttering and murmuring their disdain as dog after bitch after mutt staggered on to the stage.

'Eight fifty, who'll give me eight fifty? Eight fifty. Nine hundred. Nine hundred. *Nine hundred* . . .' To the left of the stage, near the exit, stood a spotty-faced teenager with lot number something or other: a shivering, quaking mess of a dog, dazed and confused at his sudden fifteen seconds of infamy. I stood rigid by the exit door determined not to make any gesture that could be misconstrued as a bid. 'At nine hundred she's being sold. Nine hundred. *Nine hundred*. NIIIIIIINE HUNDRED POUNDS. Selling her away at nine hundredddddddd . . .'

A thousand pounds seemed to be as good as it got; many of the greyhounds on offer went for nothing more than chump change on a sliding scale of incontinence: the cheaper the dog, the weaker its bladder. For £200, you could buy a dog with its own aerodynamic colostomy bag; £100 bought you one with a year's supply of nappies; and for a score you got your very own Portaloo on legs. Some of the dogs were so old and piss poor they'd need a Zimmer frame to get round the track. This was not the place to find the next Mick the Miller or Scurlogue Champ, especially if you didn't know what the hell you were looking for. I decided that the only bid I would put in at this sale was a farewell one. As auctions went, ebay was more up my street.

For a chicken-shit greenhorn like me the safest route to take was to follow the advice of an advertisement I had seen in the Wimbledon race card. 'Why Not Become An Owner?' it said invitingly, with just the hint of a knowing wink. *Go on . . . Why Not Become An Owner, eh? Go on . . . you know you want to. Go on sucker . . .* The ad listed a number of trainers who would be 'pleased to advise' on buying a dog. This was more like it.

Aside from coursing greyhounds, which run round rural Britain terrorising hares, rabbits and city dwellers, there are basically two types of racing greyhound: open racers and graders. Open racers are the better class of dog. They travel from track to track (with the aid of a trainer and the obligatory white transit van) taking on allcomers for the best prizes, the ultimate being the Derby, followed by an array of Grand Prix and 'classics', many of which are named after famous horse races, such as the St Leger, the Oaks and the Grand National.

The majority of racing dogs however are graders, which compete on a sliding scale of ability based on recorded times and results. Graders are usually ranked from 1–9 with the A9 grade being for puppies and 'scrubbers' (or mediocre animals) to A1 for high quality dogs some of which may be good enough to moonlight occasionally as open racers.[2]

Another feature of professional greyhound racing is the use of selected or 'attached' trainers at each track. Major league promoters tend to have up to ten approved trainers under contract to provide a regular number of graders for race duty on a rota each week. Being attached is not an exclusive arrangement; it does not stop a trainer from taking his or her best dogs to other tracks. It just means the promoters can guarantee that their race cards are always full thanks to a revolving door of graded animals.

Race meets more often than not have a mixed ability of grades and distances. The first couple of races are usually for the lower grades and, as the card progresses, so the quality of dog improves. I was aiming for a good, young grader with bags of potential who could move up in class rapidly and then compete for the big money open prizes. I also hoped that the Easter Bunny, Santa Claus and the Tooth Fairy would give me six winning Lotto numbers. As the writer, Charles Bukowski once said before throwing up into a beer glass, 'Lack of hope makes a man discouraged.'

---

[2] Grade prefixes for greyhound races are as follows: 'A' for 475 metres; 'B' for 435 metres; 'D' for 275-metre sprints; 'S' for 640-metre stayers races; 'M' for 840-metre marathons; 'P' for puppy races; 'OR' for open races; 'H' for hurdle races; and 'HC' for handicaps. Trial races are denoted with a 'T'. Distances vary from track to track.

Now that I had a basic idea of what I was after – namely a dog that ran fast – I had to find a track from which to operate. Geographically, Wimbledon was the nearest track to my home so it would have been convenient to buy a dog through a trainer based there. Spiritually, however, Walthamstow Stadium, a.k.a. the Stow, was closer to my heart as I had spent much of my misspent youth on the streets in and around it.

In the early nineties, on the advice of the Pet Shop Boys, I decided to 'go west' and turn my back on Walthamstow and a life of sewing mailbags/drug addiction/insanity. Largely through my own recklessness, misfortune and bad company, at that point my twenty-five years as an East Ender had been a living horror movie rather than a cheery soap opera. In the event, the furthest west I had made it was Shepherd's Bush. Going back to Walthamstow after all these years would be like a homecoming of sorts, a way of rediscovering my darkened roots. I would become the Alex Haley of dog racing.

Sprawled across a drab, featureless part of the city and reclaimed from the surrounding marshes and encroaching forests, Walthamstow is a working-class area in the most traditional sense, one of London's last remaining hinterlands. To the north-east is Chingford, gateway to Essex and green pastures, and to the south is Hackney, a concrete cockney jungle. In some parts of Walthamstow, elderflower, rocket and fennel grow along with blackberries and wild strawberries; and in others, if you know where to look, you can also find magic mushrooms, khat and hydroponically cultivated strains of skunkweed.

Walthamstow has none of the gentrified 'artists' quarter' nonsense of Shoreditch or pretension of Islington; there's no Bo-ho Brixton or Hoxton hippy chick shit in these parts. Walthamstow is the original 'crap town', condemned in 1998 by *Midweek* magazine no less as 'one of the five worst areas in London'. Around the same time, a kangaroo poll voted the local football team, Leyton Orient, the worst for catering in the Football League. That is the worst out of *92 clubs* in the entire country.

In their greedy pursuit of virgin realty, estate agents have now dubbed Walthamstow and its environs 'the new Islington'. As if. Apart from being home to Europe's longest street market and the birthplace of nineteenth-century artist, poet, decorator, printer and socialist William Morris, Walthamstow has nothing going for it; it is little more than a conduit between sexier inner London and sassier Essex. It is a soulless dump. However, it does have one redeeming feature: the Stow.

On the border of Walthamstow and its relatively more salubrious neighbour Chingford, the Stow is an impressive venue, a suburban coliseum. Its façade, which is also the exterior to the track scoreboard, is a sight to behold: a white art deco monolith festooned in pink, orange and red neon and punctuated by a huge black illuminated greyhound leaping through a googolplex-megawatt sign that roars, **'WALTHAMSTOW STADIUM'.** At night, this larger than life slab of concrete and lights is a seductive beacon, a siren luring punters into an arena that harks back to the mythical good old days of greyhound racing. For over eighty years the dogs has been a quintessential part of British working-class life. God knows what it must have been like in the roaring thirties and forties, the sport's heyday, when crowds of up to 25,000 would be drawn to the stadium like pilgrims heading for Mecca.

A temple of glass and repro furnishings, the Stow's numerous bars and restaurants transcend the average night out in the East End. It even has a nightclub adjacent to the track called Charlie Chan's, a plastic plant and mirror ball throwback to the 1980s, replete with penguin-suited bouncers of the 'your name's not down, you're not coming in' variety.

The Stow is the vanguard of British greyhound racing. It has the largest attendance and gambling turnover of any of the NGRC tracks, with an on-course market turnover of around £50 million per annum and off-course bets generating nearly £300 million a year. On Saturday nights, it shifts over a thousand meals in its restaurants. No wonder the greyhound-racing community voted it the 'Racecourse of the Millennium'. From what I had seen so far of the competition, it would take a thousand years for them to catch up with Walthamstow Stadium. When media whores or movie directors want an archetypal dog track for their commercials and Brit flicks, this is where they come. There is no speedway or stock car racing here, mate, no car boot sales or caravan sites. The Stow is the Madison Square Garden of dog racing. This is the Big Time, baby.

chapter 4

I headed for the Popular Enclosure (the cheap seats) on the southern side of the stadium. It was a Tuesday night, warm enough to leave the jacket at home, cold enough to make you wish you hadn't. I was looking for a guy called Vince, an unassuming local in his early forties; we had met a couple of weeks earlier through an associate at the National Union of Journalists. Vince worked in the NUJ's accounts department, so he had a way with figures, which I guess was useful for an habitual gambler.

'I used to come here every night once upon a time,' said Vince, peering through his heavy specs over the smattering of grey faces in the stands. 'That was before the missus started getting the hump. I was so into the dogs at one point that buying a greyhound seemed like the natural thing to do.' Vince had once bought a greyhound for a few hundred quid with a couple of mates, which they had raced at the Stow. The dog had won a few and lost a few more but was forced into early retirement due to injury. The experience had left him somewhat jaded.

'Bloody thing,' he said ruefully. 'The others didn't want to know once it stopped racing. I was the mug who had to take it home. It sat around all day doing nothing. Most expensive pet I've ever had.'

'I'm after a greyhound myself,' I said. 'Got any advice?'

'Don't bother,' said Vince looking up from his race card. 'They're more trouble than they're worth.'

I laughed off this remark and allowed myself a temporary distraction from Vince's sermonising: the sight of the gleaming chrome and leather of a Harley Davidson perched behind the bar of the Classic Diner. It was the one concession to glamour in the otherwise dreary enclosure. Vince smiled and gave me 'the look'. You know the one I mean. The ocular tut tut tut. He carried on marking his race card. I carried on drinking and soaking up the over-familiar smell of fried food, second-hand tobacco smoke, BO and farts.

On Tuesday nights, entry to the Popular Enclosure is just £1 (including the price of a programme). Consequently, many old gits, misers, families, loners and Luddites hang out there in preference to the comparatively ritzier and more sociable Main Enclosure. Tuesday nights are strictly for graders and the top prize is usually no more than £120, which makes it a low-key event. On a quiet Tuesday night such as this one, the Stow would attract maybe a thousand or so punters.

Thursdays have a mix of graders and open racers, with top prizes running into several hundred pounds; it attracts a slightly livelier, pre-weekend crowd. Saturday nights, though, are the big money nights, where the top open racers can compete for several thousands of pounds in blue riband events. The atmosphere and timing of Thursday and Saturday meets pull in a lot of office parties, stag do and hen night types and the infamous 'six-packers'.

Six-packs are all-in-one deals consisting of, surprise surprise, six different elements: admission, scampi or chicken and chips, two alcoholic beverages and two £1 Tote bets, all for £13.50. The British Greyhound Racing Board (BGRB) had come up with the six-pack as a way of attracting casual punters to greyhound racing – the kind of people who see the dogs as just another night out rather than a means of supplementing their income.

Until the 1960s, greyhound racing only contended with football, the cinema, radio and the emerging goggle box. But in today's leisure-obsessed society, punters have an embarrassment of pastimes to titillate and amuse them. To keep the wheels from falling off the industry, race promoters, like all hucksters, need to get new blood through the turnstiles, so they have to offer more than packs of dogs running round a track and a free race card.

Like all modern leisure industries, greyhound racing is marketed as 'A fun day out for all the family'. Vince often took his two young daughters with him to the track, to give his wife a break. One of them was about five, the same age as my daughter, the other about ten years old. They would roam around the Popular Enclosure freely and hang out in the adjacent playground, occasionally bobbing up with requests for a Coke or a bag of crisps. Both were effervescent and playful; they seemed content to marvel in their own little world, blissfully disengaged from the adults around them. They reminded me of how self-contained children are, how the juvenile imagination can make magic of any situation. The older one ran in the 100 and 200 metres for her school. From the cradle to the grave, man and beast are always running after or away from something.

Apart from his kids, Vince went to the track with Paul, a work colleague and John, a giant of a man who worked behind the counter of a high-street bookie. Vincent, John and Paul. I called them 'the Saints'. It raised a giggle. However, they could hardly contain themselves at the thought of me buying a greyhound.

'Sounds like you've got brain damage,' said John, exploding with laughter.

Confessing you are an ex-fighter, regardless of status or intellect, is an invitation to ridicule. Pity the Frank Brunos and Michael Watsons of this world then, men who for different reasons lack the brainpower to parry the banana sharp wit of life's smartarses.

'Do yourself a favour,' implored Vince. 'Don't waste your money. Get yourself a car, go on holiday, anything. Just don't buy a greyhound, they're trouble, mark my words.'

I shrugged off his warnings. What did I care? Easy come; easy go.

For everyday punters the dogs isn't just about gambling and making money; it certainly isn't about partying hearty and pissing it up with your mates. Yes, it is a social activity, but more importantly, it's about the competition, the challenge of taking on the bookies and trying to *beat the system*. Aside from his own financial limitations, a punter is up against the promoters, the bookies, the race manager (whose job it is to handicap the races), the weather, the trainers and of course the dogs themselves. In this jungle of variables, gambling, as reckless as it seems to the abstainer, requires a lot of concentration. A punter has fewer than fifteen minutes between races to analyse each dog's form, permutate possible outcomes and scenarios, consider the odds and come to a conclusion from which a sensible bet can be made.

In the era of the ever-increasing short attention span the quick-fix dog race is a compulsive gambler's wet dream. During the course of a three-hour meeting of up to fourteen races, an habitual, but not necessarily high-rolling punter, like Vince, could easily stake the equivalent of week's wages or more. With such little time to play with you have to keep your eyes on the prize. Idle chitchat can cost a lot of dough. Hanging out at the track reminded me of how difficult it was as a kid to get my old man's attention on a Saturday afternoon when the gee-gees were running and he had one eye glued to the telly and the other ensconced in the *Daily Mirror* racing form.

Vince, Paul and John bickered with each other constantly over how the dogs would run. 'I told you the six dog wouldn't make it to the first bend in front,' Vince would say. Or 'That five dog will never stay the distance,' he advised. Of the three, Vince was undoubtedly the best judge. Six or seven times out of ten he got the pattern of the race right, if not the winner. He could predict the outcome of a race with frightening, almost clairvoyant, prescience. If I could learn what he knew about the dogs I'd be rolling in it; but at this stage I was more interested in the theory of gambling rather than the practice of it. It had been a while since my bank balance had been as flush as it was now. I wanted to keep it that way.

Nevertheless, Vince gave me a crash course in how to read the race card from an analytical perspective, i.e. a perspective I had previously ignored. Short of being 'in the know' with every trainer of every dog in every race, the race card is a punter's primary source of information.

The race card or programme contains information on each dog's last five starts (and at some tracks, six). It details the date and venue of races, distances, trap numbers, sectional times (i.e. the dog's recorded times at the crucial first bend), their positions at each bend, finishing positions, winning and/or losing distances, the name of each winner, winners' times, the going, weights, starting prices, grades and finishing times. It also gives an abbreviated review of each race, indicating for instance if a particular dog had been bumped, was slow or quick away, or ran lame in a previous race. These comments, coupled with the rest of the card's information, provide punters with vital clues as to what *might* happen in a future event.

The number one performance indicator in greyhound racing however is that most precious commodity: time. All things being equal, if greyhounds are made to race down a straight track, barring a mishap, the fastest one will win every time. But if you're aiming to pick winners based on time you have to make two assumptions: one, is the fastest dog on paper in a physical and mental condition to reproduce its best times; and two, what's the likelihood of some donkey impeding his run?

It is the fact that greyhound races run on an oval track (and always anti-clockwise) that makes the races competitive. It is also a fact that greyhound tracks, like the people who patronise them, are idiosyncratic. Walthamstow is known for its tight bends, which cause many dogs – particularly those unfamiliar with it – to baulk or 'check' when speeding into a turn. Whereas Hove, for instance, is a galloping track, characterised by longer straights and looser bends.

On such a tight circuit as the Stow, theoretically, dogs on the inside or the outside have a slight advantage over those in the middle. The middle traps are known as the 'coffin boxes' on account of the tendency for the middle runners to get boxed in and buried by traps one, two, five and six on either side, particularly at the first bend. Whatever happens at the first bend can make or break a race. If a dog has early pace and can get to the first bend in front and 'on the bunny' it stands a good chance of getting a clear run to the finish line by avoiding the scrimmaging and rough-housing the pack endures in the battle for the lead.

Conversely, a dog with a lot of 'early' pace might not necessarily have the stamina to maintain his lead over the distance, in which case a stayer or a finisher with a bad start, particularly a wide runner, can close the gap in the latter half of the race and steal a victory.

However, picking winners is not an exact science. All the data, indicators, inside info and *Daily Star* horoscopes may suggest a trap four win, but dogs are people too. Sometimes, they just do not perform to type; though an animal not known for its mental agility is generally easy to read. 'In most graded races there's only around thirty spots (30 tenths of a second) between the fastest dog and the slowest one,' said Vince. 'Greyhounds are very predictable animals. A railer's always gonna run on the inside and a wide runner's always gonna go wide.'

Some dogs only chase the tails of those in front, even if they have the pace to overtake them. Some dogs are simply prone to trouble and others are flyers, i.e. dogs that run and run and run. Greyhounds are simply creatures of habit. Unlike in horseracing, where a jockey can manipulate a horse's speed, save for a few rare exceptions, a greyhound does not hold anything back in a race. It will maintain an even speed, tiring only at the end of the race. Greyhounds buckle only from physical affliction, not emotional fatigue. This simple fact is probably the most important difference between man and dog. Dogs always try their best. They do not subscribe to work to rule, unions, cultural stereotypes, or laziness. This is why we love them, because they are dumb enough to keep on going regardless. Dogs have a level of tenacity that man often tries to facsimile but rarely achieves.

Apart from the odd occasions when something or someone is thrown on to the track, if you're going to nobble a greyhound race you've got to do it before the off. Another reason why punters like Vince prefer the dogs to horseracing is that the probability of human interference *during* the event is low. Every other sport that attracts a betting market, theoretically, is corruptible well in advance of the contest or during it; and in the case of professional boxing, given its history of dubious tinkering with scorecards, after the event too.

Just before the end of the evening, I decided to split and leave the Saints to spin the wheel of misfortune. 'How you getting on Vince, are you winning?' I asked. 'Getting there,' he mumbled. I was in no hurry to lose my shirt so I kept my money in its rightful place, i.e. my pocket. After all, I had bigger fish to fry. Vince gave me another warning about getting involved in the dogs. Perhaps it was to ease his conscience more than anything, as he seemed genuinely concerned for my financial well-being.

'Look, if you're serious about buying a dog, Linda Jones is the top trainer over here,' said Vince. 'She won the championship last year . . . top trainer in the country. I get a few winners from her dogs now and again. Then there's John Mullins – he's all right too. His mum used to train here but now he's taken over the business. Then there's . . .' Vince pointed to their numbers in the race card and suggested I call the ones he recommended. There were ten trainers under contract at the Stow including Jones, Mullins and Gary Baggs, who handled ex-footballer and Hollywood hard man Vinnie Jones's dogs. 'Good luck,' said Vince. 'See you again,' I said and left the track on the long journey back to west London, no richer or poorer but slightly wiser.

chapter 5

The following Tuesday I was back at the Stow in the Popular Enclosure with Vince and the Saints, trying my luck on the Tote. The Tote, short for 'totaliser', is a dog track's biggest earner. Punters stake their money in a pool from which the promoter takes a cut, which in the Stow's case is around 27 per cent. The balance is paid as a dividend to each winning punter, in proportion to their stake. Each dividend (to a ten pence stake) is displayed on the multitude of TV screens around the track. Ten pence is the minimum you can bet at the Stow. The low unit stake thus attracts punters in all financial shapes and sizes; the downside of the Tote however is that a few relatively large bets can change the odds dramatically.

Unlike with the bookies, whose minimum stake is a fiver, you don't know what price you're actually getting when you back a dog on the Tote as the computer-generated odds change rapidly in response to the market. The most popular bets are forecasts and trifectas. In the course of a fourteen-race card, even if you only have 'fun' bets of a few quid a race, your pockets soon empty if you hit a losing streak. As the rails bookies only take straight bets, even punters who favour fixed odds betting will have a flutter on the Tote if they fancy a forecast or a tricast, or the bookies' odds are too short for a bet on the nose. If you are only into small stakes of a couple of quid, the Tote is the ideal, affordable and accessible way to nurture a gambling addiction.

'Hello, love', I said, rummaging through the change in my pocket. 'I'd like a 50p reversed forecast on traps one, two and five please.'

'Three pounds please,' said the woman in the Tote kiosk punching away at a computer keyboard. She was chewing gum and nattering away with another old bird at the next counter. This is the Stow's equivalent of garden-fence gossiping.

The Tote kiosks are staffed mainly by women, young, old and in-between, the sort of disaffected checkout types, much like those who work in the high-street bookies. In between races they do their make-up, file their nails, gossip or simply stare at the ceiling. At no point do they ever seem the slightest bit interested in what is going on down at the track. They have a detachment that invites the uninitiated, the naïve and the clueless to gamble, which is probably a conscious marketing ploy on the Stow's part. The last thing they want is pseudo bookies behind the counter smoking cigars, swearing and putting off the six-packers and coach parties.

Once, I'd seen a Tote scam on *Derren Brown: Mind Control*, a TV show about this guy who walks around the streets hustling mugs with cod psychology and mental magic tricks. In one episode he went to the Stow and apparently managed to get money out of a Tote kiosk by banging on the counter and saying to the woman behind, 'This is the winning ticket.' I tried it twice. The first time the woman just looked at me and laughed. The second time another broad told me to stop acting like an idiot or she'd call security. So much for mind control.

Too much thinking leads to uncertainty and self-doubt. 'Paralysis by analysis,' my old boxing trainer Howard Rainey would say in response to my over-philosophising. I had to make a decision. Was I in or out, out or in? In out, in out, shake it all about . . . I had been shuffling around the dog track for a couple of weeks, trying to pick up scraps of information. One thing I learned was, while two thousand pounds seemed like lot of money for a dog, it was not excessive. Top dogs regularly change hands for up to £20,000 and more, but knowing this did not make me loosen my belt any quicker. I grew up in a household where everything was recycled; even the patches on my trousers had patches.

In the back of my mind, I knew owning a dog, let alone spending two grand on one, was an utterly ridiculous idea. Having signed on the dotted line, in Faustian fashion I had sold my soul, dear reader, for your delectation and my wallet. However, to get this freak show on the road I needed a dog, and I needed one fast. Time was marching on. Then fate, or should I say 'Faith' called on me . . .

Corrina Faith was a young, idealistic documentary filmmaker. Her latest project was a programme for ITV on men and plastic surgery and she had heard about my cauliflower ear. She got in touch with me and asked if I would be interested in being a contributor on her show. I thought if I played my cards right I could blag a free ear job. Howard Rainey called me a wimp for wanting rid of it. 'What d'you wanna get rid of it for?' he would growl. 'It's a fucking trophy!' To me this 'trophy' was fuel for my hypochondria, not an heroic souvenir. Corrina's boss however didn't think my ear was the right kind of prize meat for the show.

'Sorry, David, I'm afraid we've got someone who's keen on having a penile extension,' she told me. Alas, my lame lob had lost out to a shrivelled penis; nevertheless, Corrina and I met for coffee in one of those overpriced caffeine peddlers on Baker Street for a spot of 'relationship marketing'. Over a grande mocha with whipped cream she told me her ambition was to make pro-grammes that meant something. I told her mine was to find a greyhound that made money.

'You should talk to Linda Jones then,' she said.

'Linda Jones, eh?' This sounded promising. 'Do you know her?'

'Yeah, I know Linda. I made a programme on her for *Pet Rescue*. She's a lovely woman, very sweet. She's the top greyhound trainer in the country.'

'Linda Jones . . . I've heard a lot about her . . .'

'She's really sweet and loves her dogs to pieces. I'll give you her number.'

I already had Linda's kennel number, along with those of several other trainers, from the Stow race cards. Now, armed with her mobile number and mutual friend Corrina, I felt more comfortable and 'in the know' which made taking the next step a lot easier . . .

Linda Jones is the queen pin of greyhound racing. She had been champion trainer in 2001 and was well on the way to doing the double in 2002. She had a column in the *Racing Post* every Wednesday and is one of the most respected figures in the game. I had no concerns about the animal rights lobby but I was mindful of the heat I was generating among my anti-racing friends and acquaintances, so I thought it best to do the right thing and find a kennel where the flies were on the dog shit, not on the trainer. I arranged to meet her at the Stow the following Thursday night, so that we could chitchat and check each other out.

I arrived at the track a couple of races into the card. A dour-looking security guard ushered me through the main entrance; a sharp right turn took me outside to the track and I made my way through a swamp of boozy wide-boys, peroxide blondes, big tits, cockney accents, office parties, stag dos and excited German tourists. Thursdays, particularly on balmy nights like this one, were the new Fridays – a night when short-sleeved and mini-skirted six-packers came out to play at the dogs, all of them ready, willing and able to lose their money in the name of 'entertainment'.

The race steward appeared in front of the traps in a white shirt, a pair of tight black jodhpurs and a black bowler hat. He looked as camp as a row of pink tents. A loud bell rang out: the muezzin called and the faithful scrambled frantically to pay their respects to Tote, God of Gambling. I noticed a sign by the finish line as I jostled my way through the betting ring: 'Flash photography strictly forbidden'. If only the same could be said for flash clothing.

Another bellowed: 'DANGER! KEEP OFF THIS RAIL!' I heard the track come alive as the hare went on its merry way. The lights dimmed. I stopped in my tracks and turned to face the traps. I knew the routine now. Programmed like Pavlov's dog, I responded instinctively to every sight and sound, smell and touch that this twilight world had to offer.

I could see Linda in the terraces in front of the Main Enclosure, surrounded by a group of largely overweight men. I recognised her instantly from her picture by-line in the previous day's *Racing Post*, where she beamed out of the page with an ear-to-ear smile. As I walked past the Main Enclosure through the betting ring, I saw her leap down from the terrace to the side of the track screaming frantically at the dogs. I neared her and could see the veins on her neck bulging, her face reddening as the crowd yelped and yawed behind her. She clenched her fists as though she were trying to squeeze a pip out of a grape. At one point, she looked like she was in a trance. Linda had the dog thing bad.

'Go on boy, go on, that's it, go on, go on, go on,' she cried. 'Yeaaaaaaaah!'

'Hello Linda,' I said, slipping through her coterie. 'I'm David.' She was breathing heavily, wide-eyed and grinning like a Cheshire cat; for a moment, she looked like a tranquillised housewife, but she was simply high on success. Having just notched up another winner, she had a right to be pleased with herself.

'Hello, David, pleasure to meet you. Come and join us up here.' I followed Linda up a few steps into the stands behind a row of Tote booths. 'These are some of my owners,' she said, waving her arm like the Queen Mum across a group of identikit thirty- and forty-something beer-bellied geezers, all of them a Gary, a John or a Steve. I was not a Gary, a John or a Steve, but as a Dave, I could still pass the Swinging Sixties name check. The complexion would take some work. As for the beer gut, that was coming along nicely. It wouldn't do for me to look too healthy: being slim at a dog track would make me stand out among the dog-owning set almost as much as being black did. Linda loved holding court. All the owners hung on her every word. Her 'larger than life' bonhomie was matched only by her figure. I noticed her work the owners very subtly with the odd coquettish glance or flirtatious comment. I guessed she was in her late forties, maybe early fifties, but her obvious love of the dogs was a natural anti-ageing agent both physically and mentally. To get myself into the conversation I asked the thinnest owner in the group if he had a tip for me.

'Yeah, don't gamble.' Cue: raucous laughter. The old ones are always the best.

'What about you, Linda?' I asked.

'Take it from me, David, gambling's a mug's game. Personally, I don't get involved in it. I don't know the first thing about it. The money, the gambling . . . it doesn't interest me one iota. It's the winning that counts.'

At that moment, a small party, including a photographer and a member of the track staff, interrupted our conversation by beckoning.

'OK then,' she said. 'Come on, David, you're not getting out of this.' Linda grabbed me by the arm and led me away with the group towards the winners' podium by the finish line. The winning dog was Sekopats Fancy. The owner was not at the track, so I had the honour of standing on the podium with Linda for the trophy ceremony and customary photo call.

'There you go,' said Linda, handing me the glass trophy, which had the Walthamstow Stadium logo carved into it.

'You what?' I said, slightly embarrassed by the gesture.

'Go on, have it,' said Linda, thrusting the trophy into my stomach. 'I've got plenty more where that came from.'

The optimist in me was impressed: here I was collecting trophies and having my photo taken on the podium and I didn't even own a dog. The cynic in me, however, figured this was a shrewd bit of marketing on Linda's part. *Kid the chump. Butter him up. Make him feel like a 'winner'.* Nevertheless, like a sucker, I bought Linda's spiel hook, line and sinker.

'I love my dogs more than I love people,' she said. 'That's the buzz for me: the dogs. I also love the excitement of the game, you know, pitting your wits against everybody else. When you look after the dogs day in day out – everything from picking up their mess to grooming 'em and feeding 'em – at the end of the day, when you take 'em racing and that dog wins, the feeling you get is like no other. It's better than sex, drugs and rock 'n' roll.'

Corinna was right. Linda was not just affable and easygoing, she was mad about her greyhounds. Moreover, she didn't smell of dog piss, which was an added bonus. Crucially though, she had drive, an addiction to success. I just hoped I wouldn't wind up being shafted by her. 'Don't worry, I think you'll be safe with me,' she joked, much to the amusement of her owners.

As the evening rolled on, I sensed Linda was getting itchy feet. Being the top trainer in the country meant there were always places to go, people to see. She had had an entry in ten out of fourteen races that night and picked up five winners and a place; not a bad success rate. I left her to her owners and glory and arranged to visit her kennels to talk business.

chapter 6

I left the Smoke early, ran the gauntlet of rush-hour traffic across London, and hit the M11 on my way to Linda's Imperial Kennels. Ninety-odd miles later I was in the sleepy village of Eriswell, Suffolk, a stone's throw from the US airbase at Lakenheath. Square-jawed GIs in Chevys, Cadillacs and Ray Bans flashed by as I crawled through the sleepy backwoods. The streets were deathly silent. England was about to kick off against Argentina in the World Cup. It was wet and miserable, a typical English summer. What a glorious day to go dog shopping.

I hung a left at the faded cardboard sign nailed to a tree, just as Linda had directed, and cruised slowly up a winding, leafy lane. The path was muddy and waterlogged in places. To the right were a riding school and fields with mounds of rotting, smouldering carrots and potatoes; to the left was a pig farm. I meandered along the path, pausing briefly to watch a stream of jets overhead as they broke the sound barrier, and the idyll with it. Wild rabbits darted in and out of the hedgerows in front of the car, inviting me to run them over. The landscape was flat, almost barren, and sparsely populated by distant faces that paid me no mind. Someone had dumped a car in a pond just off the lane, its rusty rear end sticking up in the air like a baboon's arse. Maybe the local yokels had run a pesky journalist off the road . . . Going into the country always gave me the creeps. The Fens, as they call these parts, seemed like the ideal place to snuff someone out.

About half a mile down the lane, I could see my final destination. Dogs were howling and yapping, vying for an audience over the sound of jet fighters in the distance. A long mesh fence ran along the side of the path to a set of heavy wrought-iron gates. Two sleek black greyhounds, barking furiously, chased the car as I cruised along the fence and then they tailed off in pursuit of an imaginary lure. A sign read: 'Beware, security dogs on guard.' All that was missing were entry posts, a watchtower and the cast of *Escape to Victory*. Welcome to boot camp for greyhounds.

I approached the gates and saw two burly fellas busying themselves inside the compound. One nodded grudgingly, the other said, 'All right mate.' The padlock to the gate was unlocked so I slipped inside. Neither man was going to open it for me. 'I'm looking for . . .' 'Down there on the right,' said the smaller, stony-faced one. I followed the wall of what looked like an elongated outhouse down to a grimy wooden door. Two lurchers leapt at me from behind the fence to an adjacent paddock. Startled, I opened the grimy door and went inside. For a moment, I thought I had stumbled into Denis Neilson's kitchen. Flies hovered round lumps of unidentifiable meat which were coagulating in several large plastic containers. Linda and a couple of kennel hands were preparing dinner for her hungry charges.

'Hello, Linda, what's on the menu?' I said.

'Ooh, you're just in time,' she replied, grinning. 'I've got some lovely beef here, succulent breasts of chicken, rice . . .'

The food looked very appetising . . . to a dog maybe. Linda fed her little darlings on meat from a commercial butcher, supplemented with dog biscuits or rice, for their dinner; breakfast was cereal with milk. I decided to take a raincheck on her offer and opted instead for a guided tour of the kennels and an insight into the world according to Linda Jones.

'David, I'm very competitive,' she said, as we trudged through paths separating the numerous paddocks. '*I* go out there to win. I want every *dog* that goes on the track to win. I don't enjoy coming second or third or last. I'm in it to win it. We all want to be top of the tree, don't we? It's *all* about winning . . . about getting the dog over the line first. At the end of the day, when you go home with the big trophy, it's absolutely wonderful.'

As we were walking through the kennels, in a little caravan next to Linda's modest detached house on the site, I noticed three of the kennel hands, Mark, Kelly and Peter (the stony-faced one), watching the big game. I poked my head round the door just in time to see David Beckham curl in the winning penalty against the old enemy.

'Yes, yes, yes,' screamed Peter. 'Get in there. Fucking Argies!'

Linda's spread was no Hilton hotel, nothing more than concrete huts built on farmland, but it was well equipped and maintained. She had 'around forty-five or so' dogs kennelled at any one time although she was deliberately vague about numbers as the neighbours weren't too keen on her being there, due to the dogs barking and all. Linda keeps most of her greyhounds in male and female pairs in 4ft × 4ft cubicles. They live in 'mixed' accommodation to stop the dogs from fighting each other, apart from when a bitch is in season, in which case she has private digs.

The greyhounds spend most of their time lolling around on mats and sawdust in their little bedsits, which suits their temperament. Contrary to popular belief, greyhounds do not need much exercise. At Imperial Kennels they get a couple of twenty-minute walks up the lane or gallops round a paddock each day; one after breakfast at 8a.m., and another in the afternoon following lunch. During their racing career, the last thing a greyhound needs is strenuous exercise. As sprinters they exert so much energy racing just once a week, they would burn out in no time if exercised vigorously on a daily basis.

'I can't run,' said Linda as we ambled along. 'I'm absolutely useless at running. I can just about walk! My dogs do the running for me. If you look after them, they'll do their best for you. I give 'em the best feed, I give 'em lots of attention . . . I've got lovely paddocks here . . . they're treated with kindness and love and that will make them win for you.'

Once again, Linda gave me her 'sex, drugs and rock 'n' roll' line. Sure, I was convinced (against to my better judgement) that I too could lose myself in dog racing; after all, my modus operandi is to immerse myself with autistic fervour into my work. However, the day I believe *anything* is better than 'sex, drugs and rock 'n' roll' is the day I cosy up inside a pine box.

I sussed that Linda was full of it; but instinctively I trusted her more than I could trust any male trainer. With men, you have to contend with all that macho ego crap. At 6ft 2in, with a 44in chest, a fair dose of testosterone, adrenaline, self-confidence and, most importantly, a brain, I am always deflecting weekend warriors, wannabe tough guys and plastic gangsters who feel threatened by me. *Grow up guys*. Men . . . we're our own worse fucking enemies.

'I'm a London girl,' said Linda proudly. 'But when I was a kid, at school we were factory fodder . . . and that's all we were.' Linda and I had a lot in common, that's why I trusted her. Like me, she too had been 'a bit of a tearaway' in her youth, on the streets of Plaistow in the East End, a stone's throw from the Stratford–Leyton–Leytonstone–Walthamstow axis where I grew up. After leaving school with few qualifications, she turned her hand to hairdressing among other things before landing her first job as a kennel hand in the late 1960s with 'a mad Irishman', Paddy Keane (RIP), at the now defunct Clapton racetrack in north-east London.

'Paddy would buy a big side of beef from the abattoir for the dogs, and he'd say to us kennel hands, "If any of you take a steak out of that beef I'll take a fucking steak out of you."' Paddy's 'bark was worse than his bite,' said Linda but that didn't stop him intimidating her on many occasions.

'Once, I had to give the bitches season-suppression pills and one of them fell pregnant. Paddy went ballistic,' said Linda, before going into one of the worst Irish accents I've ever heard. ' "I fucking told you to give dem pills to those fucking bitches, now

she's gone and got up the effing gut. She's fucking pregnant!"'
She explained how she had pleaded with Paddy, insisting she had
administered the pills; but the old boy was having none of it.
' "You fat fucking bitch, you silly cunt," he called me. I went to
Paddy's wife and his mum at the house, crying my eyes out.
"You'll be no good to me if that's how you're gonna behave,"
Paddy said. But it was thanks to him that I toughened up to the
sport. He taught me not to take any shit from no one. That's
where I got my gob from!'

Linda eventually left 'the fucking big crook' after he punched a
dog that lost a race on which he'd wagered heavily. She floated
around in odd jobs, worked at the Stow and Romford track in
Essex, before branching out there with a handful of her own dogs
and then landing a contract as an attached trainer. After nearly
three decades in the game, she eventually landed her dream ticket,
a contract at the Stow.

'I've had some good jobs in my lifetime, but this one I've
excelled at. I used to be a kennel maid at the Stow when I was
nineteen . . . I'm a little bit older now, but I'm back at the track
that I love, with the dogs I love. And I'm top of the tree, so I don't
see any reason why you can't be the same.'

Winning begets winning. I liked the idea of that. Maybe some
of Linda's boundless enthusiasm and optimism would rub off on
me. I *used* to be happy once upon a time too. Then I grew up.
Jesus. Where had this cynicism come from? I wore it like a cheap
t-shirt.

Badinage was easy with Linda. She spoke with an effusive mix
of old school cockney charm and wit. I like a woman with a sense
of humour, and an inbuilt ego massager. I knew I was being
reeled in, softened up. Linda beckoned one of the kennel hands
and asked him to fetch Twotone, a.k.a. 'Twoey'.

'Right, David,' she said, leading me towards one of the empty
paddocks. 'I want you to take a look at this dog: he's called
Twotone, which I think is quite apt for us as you're black and I'm
white.'

'Very apt,' I said, laughing along with Linda.

'I don't suppose you get many greyhound owners who are black, eh?' I asked.

'Do you know what?' said Linda, pausing for thought. 'In the eighteen years I've been a trainer I've had one black owner.'

We walked over to the wire fence surrounding the paddock where Twotone was and he took off like a rocket, covering the thirty or so metres of dirt in the blink of an eye. As his name suggests, he was dark brindle on one side of his coat and light on the other. If you squinted and took his head out of the equation, he looked like a sort of chimera – a cross between a cheetah and a wolf with a few other bits and pieces thrown in.

'He's an unknown quantity,' said Linda, watching Twotone keenly. 'He's a very young dog.'

'How old is he?'

'He's sixteen months old ... very well bred. He's by Mountleader Peer out of a bitch called Scotias Glen who's won several open races in Ireland.'

I nodded my head repeatedly in mock approval. I did not have the faintest idea about breeding dogs. It turned out that Mountleader Peer had been a runner-up in the 1996 Irish Greyhound Derby, which has a first prize of £100,000, making it the richest dog race in the world.

'He's a very nice dog but he's untried,' said Linda. 'We have to take him to Walthamstow for some qualifying trials. Now, I could take him to the track next week, and he doesn't chase; but on the other hand, I might take him to the track and he does a twenty-nine [seconds] dead, which would mean he'd be worth mega bucks to the owner.'

The 'owner' was an Irish outfit called 'The Dog Lovers Syndicate'. As their official agent, Linda would not give me any more details about them. 'They're very private,' she whispered, for dramatic effect. 'They like to keep themselves to themselves.'

Linda only sold dogs for 'trusted breeders' with whom she had a long-standing relationship. She said she was not in the business of selling dogs willy-nilly. Her reticence regarding the Dog Lovers fostered a belief in me that this syndicate was in fact a shadowy group of nameless, faceless men in suits, a spectral presence in the world of greyhound racing. Maybe they did not even exist. Maybe they were a front for Imperial Kennels?

'So what's your take then, Linda?' I inquired.

'I don't make a penny out of it, David,' she replied, looking me square in the eyes.

'C'mon. Ten, fifteen per cent . . .? You must get a drink out of it.'

'Not a penny.'

I didn't have a problem with her taking a cut from a sale. We all have to make a pound note somehow. I was just interested to know the *real* value of the animal, not the price I would have to pay as a sap.

'As you can see though he's an absolutely beautiful dog,' said Linda, still tracking Twotone's every move.

'Yeah, well, looks aren't everything, Linda. If they were, I'd be really successful.'

Linda laughed like a pantomime dame but the sound of yet another fighter plane overhead soon drowned out her cackling. There was a lot of activity in the gunmetal skies that morning. The word was Saddam Hussein was gonna get an ass kicking, so the military was busying itself, making sure Our Boys and the killing machines were well oiled and ready for action.

Back on the ground, Linda and I tiptoed towards the $64,000 question.

'Put it this way, if I take him to the track next week,' she said, 'and he doesn't run, the owners will more or less give him to ya. But if he goes and does twenty-nine seconds they'll want ten grand for him.'

'Ten grand?' I nearly swallowed my tongue. 'So what's the current asking price?'

'Four grand and he's yours now.' I checked my pockets. Nope, didn't think so, no four grand in there.

'Do you want to go in?' said Linda motioning towards the paddock gate.

'Sure, why not?'

I went into the paddock. Linda headed back to the kitchen, giving Twotone and me some quality time together. I went to stroke him, but he took off. A greyhound is officially a puppy until it's two years old, so I could forgive him the odd childish rebuke. 'Come on, boy. There's a good boy.' He sat at the end of the paddock, eyeing my every movement, waiting for me to move; then I as soon as I approached – whoosh – off he went again. 'Twoey, come on, boy. There's a good, good boy . . .' *Come on you little fucker*.

' 'Ere, try this,' said Linda strolling over with a handful of bone-shaped doggy biscuits. 'Twoey, *Twoey*,' I called out, intermittently whistling, but he would not take the biscuit. *Take the fucking biscuit*. After several attempts he sniffed my palm gingerly, looked up at me then bolted off to the other end of the paddock. Every time I went for him, he made a run for it. He even managed to scarper halfway through taking a shit before I could pet him.

I don't like rejection but I've learnt to live with it. However, if I were to buy this dog he would *have* to take the fucking biscuit. What was his problem? I had no idea what was going on in his head. He was nervy but Linda said he had the makings of a winner. Hmm . . . I respected his uncertainty, his caginess. He was a bit of a loner, a bit like me really. Did he know something I didn't? What utter nonsense. Humans are always projecting their bullshit ideas on to animals. You teach a dog to shake hands or roll over and all of a sudden he is qualified to be prime minister. Jesus. Any mutt with half a brain only does what you tell it to do because it's scared it'll get a kicking or, worse still, won't get fed.

Twenty minutes passed and Twotone stubbornly kept his distance. We were into a war of attrition. I liked his style: arrogant. If you want to make it in life you have to be an uncompromising sonofabitch. Maybe I was thinking all this because I was trying to convince myself that he was 'the one'. Self-delusion. I live for it.

'You been eating those biscuits?' said Linda, chuckling. 'It's all right, c'mon, boy.' Linda entered the paddock and Twotone went straight to her like a lapdog, no problem. Who was she, Dr Dolittle?

'David, good dogs are at a premium right now because the prize money's so good in Ireland,' said Linda. 'Trainers like Ian Greaves, the top man in Ireland, sell puppies for up to £6000 a time.'

Ninety per cent of all greyhounds racing in the UK are bred in Ireland. The wealth of available land for breeding, rearing and schooling, coupled with a long tradition of breeding dogs – and, of course, horses – and a greater cultural willingness to dispose of inferior litters, means that Ireland is indelibly linked with the best of the best. As an example of the Emerald Isle's dominance, the hundred fastest NGRC open race winners so far that year were all bred by Sean Dunphy at what the *Racing Post* called his 'greyhound empire' in Portlaw, County Waterford. As is the custom with many breeders, a Dunphy greyhound usually has a prefix to its name, as a mark of its bloodline. In his case, it is 'Droopys', as in Droopys Corleone, a contender for that year's Derby.

As with British cars, British engineering, British food and British weather, many experts see British greyhounds as duff. Along with most trainers in the UK, Linda does not have enough land for a track, so the majority of dogs she trains come from across the water pre-schooled. One punter at the Stow had told me that many dogs coming from Ireland were 'clued up' and suggested that they had already raced in unofficial meets as puppies before they got to the UK. Whatever happens in Ireland is anyone's guess; Imperial Kennels is more of a sort of prep school for greyhounds where the finer points of racing are honed.

Training a dog ain't rocket science: it is simply a matter of taking the athleticism that Mother Nature hath given the greyhound and programming it into a controlled activity. Pretty much as soon as a greyhound can walk, it is encouraged to chase squeaky toys and rags, which a trainer dangles provocatively in front of its nose, moving them backwards and forwards. Yes, this is a wind up for the dog and a crude one at that. The pup competes in these juvenile games with the rest of the litter and progresses to chasing a dummy lure in a gallop or paddock. Assuming it is not a runt, at around twelve to eighteen weeks old it heads off to a schooling track or racetrack where it is 'handslipped' i.e. released by hand behind a slow-moving lure, usually on a bend, to familiarise it with the sights, sounds and techniques of running round a track.

Once the trainer is satisfied the dog can or will chase the lure, the dog moves into the traps. Unfortunately, some dogs at this stage turn out to be either too smart or too stupid for their own good. If a pup susses out that the mechanical lure is a dummy, it can lose interest in the chase; and if it isn't interested in chasing . . . well, let's put it this way, it is in a puppy's *best* interest to chase the lure . . .

The next stage for our budding racer is to practise walking through the traps with the front and back gates open and a little gentle encouragement from its trainer. The claustrophobic atmosphere of the traps can freak a young greyhound easily, so this process continues until the greyhound is confident in the starting boxes and is able to exit the traps at speed and chase the lure.

After I'd moaned about Twotone's price Linda showed me what else was on offer. Like any salesperson, she had showed me the most expensive item first, clocked my reaction, and then set out an alternative stall.

'If you want something that's tried and tested I've got a couple of good racers for sale,' she said. Both were two-year-olds: a black and white dog called Ship of Dreams and a black bitch called Luck Sharp, both of whom were already running at the Stow. I wanted a dog with little or no form, something brand new and unspoilt that I could call my very own, so they were out of the frame.

Then there was a young bitch called Luscious and a couple of oldies in the twilight of their careers. For a moment, I contemplated the idea of buying an old dog as a charity case, to give it one last season around the track. What was I on? As for the bitch, Linda said that if I wanted to get the most out of a greyhound, a dog was a better proposition. Bitches tend to go off the boil when they are in season and are unable to race, which means they can't earn their keep. On the other hand, they often make better stayers than dogs – something to do with the female of the species being more dependable over the longer distance. That sounds familiar . . . However, the trouble with stayers is getting the starts: there simply are not enough races over 640 metres at the Stow compared to 475 metres, which is the most common distance run.

'A lot depends on what sort of greyhound you're looking for,' said Linda. 'If you want the maximum amount of races at the Stow you want a 475 [metre] dog . . . 435 dogs don't get much racing.'

Only heaven knew what I was looking for. Were big dogs better than small dogs, tall ones better than short? *Lonely Planet* didn't publish a guide to greyhounds so I had to have faith in Linda Jones and Dame Juliana Berners, prioress of Sopwell nunnery who, in 1418, became the first person to prescribe the 'points of a good greyhound'. In her *Booke of St Albans*, the great Dame wrote that a greyhound should have:

> A head lyke a snake,
> A neck lyke a drake,
> The feet of a cat
> A tail lyke a rat.
> A back lyke a beam,
> The sides of a bream.

Patience has never been a virtue of mine. I was getting dogged out. I had seen more tail than Bill Clinton. Despite the auctions, trailing through the greyhound press, making phone calls and mooching around the Stow, my total lack of knowledge on dog racing meant *any* purchase was going to be a gamble. Linda showed me round the rest of her pack of prospective mutts, bitches, stayers and sprinters. Nothing tickled my fancy. I was ready to call it a day, go home, and take up knitting or stamp collecting or something when a dog suddenly caught my eye. His name: 'Kevin'. Yes, Kevin. Well, that was his pet name. His race name was 'Zussies Boy'. He had a fawn-going-on-caramel coat and a savoury-sweet aroma, like freshly made scrambled eggs. His big, brown, soulful eyes melted when he looked at you. He also had what Linda called 'floaters', two extended ribs protruding from his coat like two chunks of Toblerone. Was this physical quirk an omen perhaps?

Kevin was a beautiful specimen, but he did strike me as a bit of a dumb blonde, in a manner of speaking. Yes, dogs can be dumb blondes too, you know. My folks once owned an Afghan hound, the most beautiful dog imaginable. He was sleek and gracious with long, flowing blonde locks. He was also as thick as two extremely short planks of wood.

Dog people put much stock on a dog's colour. For instance, blue dogs have a reputation for being suspect, perhaps only because they are rare and thus statistically amount to very little. Black dogs account for the largest distinct group and thus turn out many good runners. But there was such a kaleidoscope of markings amongst greyhounds I could not see how one colour trait was better than any other.

'Aw, everyone loves Kevin, don't they, sweetheart?' said Linda giving him a big hug. 'This one gets all the special treatment.'

Kevin was coy but not like Twoey. He shied away at first but it did not take much for me to bring him round. Like Twotone, the Dog Lovers Syndicate owned him too. Unlike Twotone, he did not have an attitude problem. He took biscuits, like a *proper dog*.

'So what's the score with Kevin then?' I asked.

'Well, he's out of Lakeshore Owney and Lakeshore Annie . . .'
Here we go again with that breeding stuff . . .

'Is he any good?'

'I'd say Twotone is the better of the two, but I'm putting my head on the chopping block here, cos I honestly don't know . . . I can't say for sure. Kevin could turn out to be the better dog. Who knows?'

Linda was hedging her bets. I told her I did not want to spend more than two grand on a greyhound; the asking price for Kevin was £2500. Buying a dog was now a matter of urgency for me, and she knew this, so she was bound to think I could be persuaded to find an extra £500 if need be. On the other hand, she knew that I knew that she knew that I knew deep down he was not in the same league as Twotone. Having spotted me coming up the M11 as a know-nothing, wet-behind-the-ears hack with more money than sense, natch, she would reason that, if I could find an extra £500 for one dog, why could I not find an extra £2000 for the other? If there's one born every minute, I had stumbled into Imperial Kennels on the stroke of sixty seconds. *Fuck it: you only live once.* I told Linda to inform the Dog Lovers Syndicate that I was interested in Kevin and Twotone, but they had to be flexible on price. 'I can't promise anything,' she said. Whatever. Linda, me, the Dog Lovers, Kevin and Twotone were now inexorably joined in a two-horse dog race. Let the games begin.

chapter 7

The going for the trial was −10, which meant that the track was running 10 hundredths of a second slower than normal. The going could run anywhere from −60 to +30 so it was an important factor when considering a dog's real times, particularly as around a quarter of a second generally separates the fastest dog from the slowest in the race and no more than a couple of a seconds separates a £40,000 Derby winner from a £200 scrubber.

Trials are held every Wednesday, from 10a.m. to just after lunchtime. Linda told me to see her in the paddock, so I walked the length of the home straight, through the empty betting ring to the far end of the stadium, stopping briefly to see what the competition had to offer. There was a small number of people dotted around the stands − their grey faces a counterpart to the overcast sky. Trials are a purely technical exercise, no-thrills racing. There aren't the distractions of a race meet. There was idle talk but on the whole the punters or aficionados kept one eye buried in their trial programmes (A4 sheets of photocopied paper with basic information about the day's 47 trials, a sort of simplified race card), the other on the track.

Twotone and Kevin were down to run against each other and a dog called Kinda Funny in trial number 39, over 435 metres, in traps three, five and one respectively. Recently Twotone and Kevin had both started their training off with a couple of 235-metre warm-up trials, before moving up to 435.

There were plenty of single guys sitting around, making notes and scratching their heads as the dogs came out in quick succession, some in single trials, others in twos and threes. One middle-aged couple filmed each trial with a camcorder; an old boy had a pair of binoculars; several people were scribbling notes on scraps of paper or the *Racing Post*. Something told me I should have brought my anorak.

The trials were a mixed bag: Doubting Thomas in the twenty-second trial bolted out of trap three, buckled and then head-butted the ground and rolled over, while his two competitors sailed by; two trials on, She's A Fantasy pulled up lame just before the third bend, yelping in agony; Balleric Sunrise decided to go walkabout after his trial, as did Blue Lad, who had the good grace to finish before leading his kennel hand on a Benny Hill-style chase across the track's central reservation. 'He's trying to get on the winners' rostrum,' joked one of the spectators. No one responded.

It was nearing Twotone and Kevin's trial, so like a child of Hamelin I followed the sweet sound of greyhounds yelping into the paddock, ignoring the clearly visible 'No Entry' sign. An embittered-looking fat bloke dressed in a white polo shirt emblazoned with a Cross of St George and blue track pants and trainers approached and confronted me immediately. By the state of him I guessed he'd never walked past a gym, let alone inside one.

'Have you got a licence, mate?' he asked.

'I'm here to see Linda . . .'

Before I could say Jones he said, 'Linda who?'

'Linda Jones,' I said.

'She ain't here, mate.'

'Well, I've been told she is.'

'Wait outside by the wall, mate, and she'll come out to see you.' So she *was* there, stoopid. Was I becoming a misanthrope or was the world populated by unhelpful pricks? That's unfair. The guy was only doing his job. To get into the paddock you have to be a licence holder, which means you have to be a trainer, kennel hand, vet or track official, or have friends in high places. This is to stop unscrupulous characters from nobbling the dogs. A dog can be in the kennels or the paddock for anything up to four hours during a race meet, depending on the time it arrives and when it races.

Linda had twelve dogs on trial so she had her work cut out. We didn't chitchat for too long. 'Are they well?' I asked, which is dog people talk for, 'Has he got the shits/a club foot/eight Mars bars in his gut?' Linda said the pair were OK and scurried back into the yapping, yelping paddock in the kennelling area.

I took a seat in the stands and watched as Twotone trounced Kevin by four lengths, recording a time of 27.60 compared to 27.82. Given the difference in their prices every spot between the two dogs cost around £68, or £1500 to buy not even a quarter of a second's difference in speed. At the time the track record at the Stow over 435 metres was 25.71.

Even a novice like me could see that a novice like Twotone was patently better than a Kevin but at £4000 he was double my budget. Besides, he had a stinking personality, not taking that biscuit and all. Twotone cost £4000 and he couldn't even take a poxy dog biscuit from me. For four grand, he ought to dance for it. At least Kevin and I could get along. If I was going to pay four figures for a dog, he had to take the biscuit. Also Kevin was a truly beautiful animal. He was very docile, but fast enough to make the grade – just not as fast as Twotone.

The race manager grades the dogs initially on their performance during a trial, which presents a trainer with an opportunity to pull a fast one. Based on time the race manager will grade the dogs according to their relative speed. Slowing a dog down, or 'time finding' as it's known, is the best way to ensure a dog has an advantage when it eventually races for real. Time finding, while not punishable by death, is prohibited and could result in a fine or a trainer being suspended or banned from a track.

Before a trial or a race, each dog is weighed and has its particulars recorded in an individual identity book. As soon as they are processed, the dogs are kept in a kennel until their trial. Twotone had weighed in that morning at 35.5 kilos which was 1.5 kilos heavier than Kevin. If a dog lost or gained more than a kilo between races the alarm bells went off and the race manager would automatically disqualify the dog and question the trainer.

That night I called Linda to haggle.

'You sure you can't take two grand, Linda?' I said, pleading down the phone.

'No, sorry, David. I've had a word with 'em and they're not moving.'

'I'll make 'em famous.'

'They don't want to be famous, they're publicity shy.'

'All right, I'll make you famous then.'

'I'm famous already! Ha ha ha!'

I told Linda I'd have to think about it. I'd seen *Glengarry Glen Ross*. I knew how to close a deal. Yeah. The tables had turned. Now that she knew I was seriously keen she'd tell the Dog Lovers I was game and those little euro note signs would start rolling around their eyes. I cracked open a beer, kicked back and waited for the phone to ring.

Linda had me in her sights. If I wanted a dog that had more than three legs and wasn't called Satan and chained to a scrapyard fence in Bermondsey I'd have to fork out at least two-and-a-half grand, but my silent partner (i.e. my publisher) would only stump up £2000. I wanted Twotone but The Dog Lovers Syndicate would not budge on price. Despite my best efforts at begging, borrowing, stealing and blackmail the only way I could raise the extra £2000 was from my own coffers. If two-and-a-half 'large' seemed steep for Kevin, £4000 for Twotone was vertiginous. I could speculate to accumulate but this was business, baby. If I had learnt one thing during those tedious economics lectures at university, it was always get some other mug to invest in your daft enterprises. I did not have time to go traipsing around looking for more investors or another trainer and other dogs. I was down to a shortlist of one: Kevin. Nevertheless, I was still a monkey short of the asking price.

For some reason Margot had come round to the idea of me owning a greyhound. In fact, she even went so far as to throw her hat in the ring and offer to stump up the extra lolly. She said she simply wanted to 'help', which smelt fishy.

Anyway, I was all set to relieve her of the dough when we headed to the Glastonbury festival and a bunch of meddling hippies screwed things up. Margot and I were trudging around in the mud pretending to be on acid and talking about what fun she'd have as a fully paid-up member of the syndicate when out of the mud and marijuana haze appeared a shabby stall run by an outfit called Greyhound Action. A couple of do-gooders were handing out leaflets featuring the slogan 'You bet ... they die' and a picture of a skeletal greyhound that had been 'tied to a lump of concrete and drowned'. Like most animal rights organisations, Greyhound Action was low on subtlety and high on impact. Somehow I don't think Saatchi & Saatchi was running their ad campaign.

'Jesus fucking Christ,' I muttered under my breath.

'What was that?' said Margot as I tried to steer her away from the stall towards a mung bean burger bar.

'Support Greyhound Action!' came the cry. 'Thousands of innocent greyhounds killed every year!'

A jobless crusty wearing a t-shirt that looked like a used sanitary towel was working the crowd. I bet he lived in a converted Bedford van and had toenails like talons. The bloody soap dodger caught Margot's attention.

'Oh look, there's something about greyhounds over there.' Margot ambled over to the stall.

'Would you like to sign our petition?' asked Crusty.

'That's all I need,' I mumbled again. 'Fucking hippy wankers.'

'What was that?' said Margot.

'Nothing, sweetheart. I'm starving. Shall we get something to eat?'

Crusty butted in. 'Would *you* like to sign our petition?'

'Er, no thanks. I can't read.'

'Sorry?'

'So what's this all about then?' I feigned interest, hoping perhaps I could embarrass the poor fool behind the counter. Subterfuge and diversionary tactics had not worked. In fact, not only had they not worked, Margot was signing Crusty the Clown's petition! Traitor! Consorting with the enemy!

'Why the hell did you do that?' I scowled as we walked away.

'Aw, I felt sorry for him sitting there behind his little stand. No one was paying any interest.'

Let he who is without sirloin cast the first stone-baked vegetarian pizza. How dare they steal my thunder with their animal rights crap? And to think I was missing the 2002 FIFA World Cup third-place play-off between South Korea and Turkey for this nonsense. Margot was on the verge of giving me the money then this happens. Fucking hippies.

Greyhound Action claims that at least 40,000 greyhounds are bred every year in Britain and Ireland, with a similar number 'disposed of'. The consensus both inside and outside the industry is that at least 10,000 greyhounds retire from racing in the UK every year. According to the British Greyhound Racing Board, the sport's marketing arm, up to 2000 of these dogs find good homes, either with their owners or other individuals. For the other 8000 their fate is less clear. Refuges and charities save many but admittedly others are abandoned or put down by their owners, used for laboratory experiments or shipped to Spain and used as *galgos* or coursing dogs. This dark side of the sport means that Greyhound Action, along with several other animal rights organisations, including the League Against Cruel Sports, want to ban greyhound racing on the grounds that it is cruel. In a liberal democracy such a demand is fine. But if cruelty is the only criteria for banning stuff then let's ban Christmas. I'm still in therapy over December 25th 1974. I asked Santa for an Action

Man with gripping hands and got a box of fucking Quality Street instead.

I had always been too busy being an oppressed minority to bother with little things like animal rights, so I never really questioned the moral implications of racing dogs or keeping animals in kennels, cages, aquariums or little jars with a spicy marinade. Now the animal rights lobby was slowly crawling out from under its collective rock, getting on my case, getting in my face. Even my editor at the *Evening Standard* started getting heavy with me.

'If you buy a greyhound you'll never work for this paper again,' she said, with only a hint of irony.

'C'mon, Liz, that's a bit strong.'

'They do wicked things to greyhounds you know.'

'That's, er, a fallacy,' I replied, limply.

'What about what they do to them in Spain, eh? It's barbaric.'

'Tsch.'

To ram home the point Liz sent me some information about the poor state of the Spanish *galgos*, many of which are hanged from trees, stoned, thrown into wells and set on fire at the end of the coursing season every spring by their owners or *galgueros*.

I love animals, I really do. I especially love to eat them. Two-legged, four-legged, one-legged on a frigging pogo stick, I don't care. If it has a pulse and a three-second memory, I'll eat it. And if an animal exists that has a conscience or a soul, even better, I'll eat that too.

But something did disgust me when I saw those *galgos* hanging from trees like cured meat in a butcher's shop; and it wasn't the obvious graphic shock horror. Maybe I'm anthropomorphising dangerously here but the images were reminiscent of old photographs I'd seen of black people lynched in the Deep South, surrounded by proud grinning Klansmen: judges, policemen, farmers and other pillars of the community.

Still, I couldn't change the plight of the *galgos*, let alone the course of human history. Maybe I'd look into it when I went to

Spain in a couple of weeks. Yes, I had become a journalist because of a genuine desire to right wrongs, redress the balance and expose 'the truth'. And I tried, without preaching, to impart these same noble ideals to my bright-eyed and bushy-tailed students at the university where I moonlighted. But I had bills to pay, and the *galgos* and the truth and all that other stuff right now was just another awkward obstacle to overcome, a temporary setback, and an irritant that simply got in the way of me going about my bees' wax.

chapter 8

I shared a flat with a Jewish doctor named Paul. A friend had once described our place as 'very *Withnail and I*'. We lived like a pair of bums in that grotty little flat but our cohabitation did provide me with one essential luxury: a fat ride. Dr Paul had a metallic blue Mercedes E Class, or 'Jew canoe' as he liked to call it, fully loaded, with air con, heated seats, cruise control, the works. I was going to drive the canoe out to Imperial Kennels to close the deal, having talked my agent Julian into investing the extra £500 needed for Kevin's purchase. 'I don't know how I'm going to explain this to the accountant,' he had said. 'I don't think a greyhound is tax deductible.'

Tax, bills, commitments, responsibilities ... I had to start cleaning up my act. I was thirty-six years old and still hustling. Clothes maketh the man, so from now on jeans and trainers were out; it was time to whistle up, don the camel-hair coat, the brogues and the Gucci watch. I hung out on the Portobello Road too much and the 'hood rat' look had rubbed off on me. Anyway, like most of my friends, Dr Paul thought my dog-racing idea was bullshit. When I told him I was about to buy a greyhound for £2500, he nearly fainted.

'If I told my old man I'd just spent two-and-a-half grand on a dog he'd say I was fucking mad!' he said.

❉   ❉   ❉

I collected the money in used £50 notes from the bank. I did my best to look 'respectable' but still encountered the usual pettifogging security checks. The bank teller pulled a wad of cash sealed in pink cellophane from a drawer and placed it in front of her VDU. 'Would you like it like this or would you prefer me to count it out for you?' she said, peering up at me. 'Let's count it, shall we? Just to be on the safe side.' The teller took umbrage and hastily counted the money. I lost track of the tally at £750. Whatever happened to the customer always being right?

As I left the bank a fat bloke in an Arsenal shirt bumped me. 'Easy,' I said, sneering. I felt empowered. I was the big man, in the big car with big cash in his pocket. I walked round the corner to McDonald's and got myself a Filet-O-Fish and a Coke and then crossed the Holloway Road, bouncing through the crowds of commuters and early risers. Sitting outside Barclays was a tramp, begging. I thought about the two-and-a-half grand in my pocket and how sacrificing a pound for this poor soul would make little impact on my bank balance but bring a whole lot of love to his heroin addiction. There are now more beggars on the streets of London than there are stray dogs. I walked on. I got in the car, pressed the central locking button and headed for Lakenheath.

I cruised down the lane towards the kennels. A voice on the car radio said the ban on hunting with dogs in Scotland would come into force that day. An old nag stood in a field, posing as though waiting for the sun to break through and the picture-postcard moment to arrive. The birds sang, frogs croaked, manure stank. God, I hate the countryside.

I reached the iron gates of hell, I mean Imperial Kennels, and steeled myself. Just as Paul Kenyon had infiltrated the world of greyhound racing posing as an owner, I too had infiltrated this murky subculture: posing as a complete idiot. This was not a hard act to pull off. Until I started swotting up on greyhounds my ignorance of the breed and dogs in general was blissfully mind-blowing. I thought a lurcher was a dog that leant to one side when it ran and that a whippet was a small breed of half-dog, half-ferret indigenous only to the north of England. I crossed myself – like I believe in that shit – picked up the brown envelope, put it inside my jacket and made my move.

'I think our path is mapped out for us the moment we're born, David,' said Linda as we strolled around the kennels, looking up towards the heavens as another jet streaked by. Greyhound racing *and* philosophy: an interesting combination. I was getting concerned about the noise from Lakenheath. Didn't it freak the dogs out?

'They don't pay it no mind,' said Linda.

I was really clutching at straws, setting up the fallout position, with that jet fighter thing: if Kevin proved to be a lemon I could blame it on the US military. We headed back to the kitchen for a cuppa and the last rites. I still had an opportunity to bail out. If I made a run for it I could be over the back fence, sneak round the side of the kennels, slip into the Merc and take off without anyone noticing. No, that isn't my style. My problem is I did not know how *or* when to give up.

The phone rang and Linda answered it, wheeling and dealing down the blower while her daughter Sarah, Mark, Kelly and a Belgian named Patrick (who had recently joined the kennels after working in Ireland) stopped carting around dog leads, bales of straw, bowls of water and food, buckets and spades, to join us for a celebratory cup of cha.

'He should've won,' said Patrick, referring to Kevin's last race, which I had missed. I was never big on homework. 'But at the third bend he was in second place and they tipped him out from behind. Somebody ran into his hind legs.'

Kevin wound up finishing third. Sarah jumped to his defence.

'They can be a bit green at first,' she said. 'But the more they run, the more they get used to what they're doing and then improve.'

'Twotone got off to a flyer, didn't he?' I said, still thinking about that arrogant little fucker and what could have been.

'Yeah, he won his first one,' said Sarah with a cheeky little giggle.

'But he's had a cut on his foot since,' said Linda, interjecting, 'so we've laid him off. He's had to have antibiotics, but he looks all right. You ain't changed your mind have ya?'

'No, no, no,' I said, unconvincingly. 'Unless you wanna change your mind and knock off that fifteen hundred quid.'

The small talk got smaller and smaller, moving from sexual innuendo, to the World Cup and on to food and holidays. Linda said she wasn't the holidaying type as she had 'too much work to do'. One of her owners however had recently treated her to a Caribbean cruise. 'I do like a man with a few quid in his pocket,' she joked. Jesus, there was nothing in the budget for *that* level of hospitality. The only Caribbean cruise Linda would get from me was a lift to the shops on Eriswell High Street.

' 'Ere, you've been on holiday, haven't you, David?' said Sarah.

'That's right. I've just come back from Ibiza. Can you tell by the tan?'

'I was just going to say, you've got a *bloody* good tan,' joked Linda.

Oh how we laughed.

'We've got one in the final tomorrow night at Hove and one in the final on Saturday night at the Stow,' said Linda, doling out lumps of meat and pouring vitamin B into dishes, 'so we're pretty busy at the moment. Actually, I've got a little job for ya.'

Linda passed me a container of potassium tablets and had me crush them, then sprinkle tiny measurements into the dogs' dinners. The greyhounds at Imperial get more nutrients in their three squares than probably 70 per cent of the world's population get on a daily basis. Apart from the moody types who give their dogs contraband, some trainers give their dogs an extra boost with perfectly legal supplements like creatine, a muscle-building metabolite. I had tried it myself many years ago but quit after reading stories about athletes dying on it. Vitamins, minerals and good food aside, Linda uses nothing suspect on her dogs. She does, however, have one 'secret ingredient'.

'People are always wondering why my dogs do so well,' she told me, 'so you always get one or two who think you're giving the dogs something dodgy to boost 'em up. I had a trainer approach me once at the track saying, " 'Ere Linda, what d'you use on your dogs, you know, to get 'em going?" ' Linda starts hamming up the 'wanna buy a watch?' routine. 'I said to him, "Come over 'ere and I'll tell ya." He thought he was on to something . . . grinning his face off he was. I pulled him to one side and said "I've got this secret ingredient that I use." "Really, really, what is it?" he says, "It's called TLC." "What's that?" he says, thinking it's some new drug. "TENDER LOVING CARE, mate, now sling your hook!" '

The phone rings *again*, and Linda's back on the case. I chat to Sarah who tells me she couldn't imagine doing another job. 'The dogs are brilliant, they're lovely, they're happy. It's great to work with the dogs but it's also great to be outside. You've got no one breathing down your neck, saying "do this, do that". Everyone knows what they've got to do here. We all get on with it . . .' Sarah then whispers, 'When *she's* not cracking the whip.'

' 'Ere, you talking about me you little bitch?' jokes Linda. 'She's a little bitch, 'er.'

'I was just saying you like cracking the whip, Mum.'

'You're giving me a bad name,' says Linda. 'If he puts all that in the book you're sacked.'

We get through feeding and then knuckle down to business.

'I'm trusting that you're not going to shaft me, Linda,' I said, swatting flies.

'I think you're quite safe there.'

I reached inside my jacket and pulled out the brown envelope with the two-and-half gees. 'You drive a hard bargain, Linda.' Somehow it felt unreal, parting with £2500 for a dog.

'Aren't you gonna count it?'

'Why, shouldn't I trust you?' asked Linda.

'Well, yeah, you should, I guess.'

'Well I don't need to check it then, do I, David?'

'I guess not.' Linda put the envelope in her pocket.

'What about a receipt?'

'Do you want one?'

'Well, yeah. You know, tax and all that. Not that I ever pay any.'

Linda scanned the kitchen. I expected her to produce one of those WH Smiths receipt books but she started rummaging round for some paper. Then I noticed something strange on the shelf above her head.

'What's that?' I asked as she tore a piece of scrap paper in half and scribbled away.

'Oh that,' she said, looking at the stuffed hare mounted in a trophy cabinet set against a crudely painted rural scene. 'The staff at Romford presented him to me a few years ago when they stopped using real hares.' There was something spooky about that hare. He made my skin crawl.

'Lovely, ain't he?' said Linda wistfully.

'Charming,' I said.

Linda handed me the receipt:

Received on behalf of the Dog Lovers Syndicate, the sum of £2,500.00p in payment of a fawn greyhound named Zussies Boy.

L. E. Jones 31/7/02

IMPERIAL KENNELS
UNDLEY COMMON
LAKENHEATH, SUFFOLK
IP27 9BY

Deal done.

'What about insurance?' I asked.

'What about it?' she replied nonchalantly.

'Well, should I . . . I mean, can I insure him?'

'To be honest with you, David, no one bothers. It's very difficult to get insurance for a greyhound and the companies that do it charge astronomical premiums. Hopefully Kevin won't get injured. It's just one of the risks you have to take in this game.'

Linda told me a story about someone who had bought a greyhound that had made it to the quarter-finals of the Derby for something in the region of £18,000. It was out in the paddock early one morning, roaming around as happy as Larry. When feeding time came, one of the kennel hands went out to fetch the dog and noticed he was lying under a tree.

The kennel hand called out to him but the dog didn't respond. When he got to the dog he discovered it was stone dead. Apparently it had died of an aneurysm to the heart. I hoped Kevin was made of sterner stuff. I told Linda to make sure he lay off the booze, fags and fry-ups.

So now I owned a racing greyhound, a running machine. The training fees worked out at £7+VAT per day, a couple of quid dearer than I had bargained for. Then there were occasional vet's bills, de-worming, de-fleaing treatments and a physiotherapy service run by a former trainer called Ron Mills, which he did for Linda and only one other kennel.

Ron, who preferred the term 'sports massage therapist' to physio, visited the kennels once or twice a week and worked the dogs with massage and ultrasound in a little room next to the kitchen. He was in the process of completing on an apartment in Marbella. I was pleased that some of my kennel bills were going to an even better cause than Kevin. Ron had trained on humans and gave Linda a going over sometimes.

'Muscles are muscles however they're packaged,' said Ron, gliding his hands over his first patient, while Peter the kennel hand held the agitated mutt down. 'The drugs are the same as those given to humans, they're only marketed under a different name.

'This one's running on Saturday and he's got symptoms of a pulled hamstring.' Ron starts working the dog's hindquarter. It yelps and screams, whistling like a kettle on the boil. 'If you put pressure on the calf here, he comes up on it. I usually find these problems by touch. I start an examination with some basic stretching . . .' Ron trails off for a moment . . . '. . . He's got a bloody flea there. Dead though. That's the first one . . .' Then returns to the examination proper. 'Then I go over the body, checking the muscles. What we're dealing with is a tight muscle, so I'm going to massage it out.' The dog screams pitifully. 'No pain, no gain,' says Ron. 'I try and be as gentle as I can with 'em. They don't hold it against me.'

Within minutes Ron had broken down the adhesion in the dog's muscle, turning him to jelly. His tongue was hanging out and his eyes were glowing with almost post-coital satisfaction. 'There you go,' said Ron squeezing the muscle, 'gradually the pain goes . . .' The dog lay there, gaga. You could've picked him up and used him as a stole he was now that supple.

Kevin was certainly in the right place for five-star treatment: and at an average monthly cost of £250, boy, he'd better appreciate it. I've stayed in hotels that didn't offer the level of service Linda did. Kevin's prize money would go immediately to Imperial Kennels and I'd have the balance to pay. Linda wasn't cheap. Good women never are. In fact, she was probably the most expensive trainer in the country. But you can't put a price on quality. She wasn't the reigning champion trainer for nothing. Besides, providing he didn't turn out a lemon, Kevin's winnings would cover the bulk of his upkeep. And if he made it as an open racer, if he had a decent strike rate of, say, one-in-four wins, I'd be able to have a tasty little flutter on him from time to time.

'Have I got a decent dog then, Linda?'

'You think you're lucky, don't you? You said you think you are a lucky person, that you had a tough upbringing and all that.'

'Yeah, that's true. I'm lucky that I'm not six feet under or in jail, I guess.'

'Well then. If you're lucky, you'll be all right. Because it's luck more than anything else you need in this game.'

I was now officially 'dog people', although I didn't feel like it. Jesus. I owned a bloody greyhound. Well, half of one. No actually, a quarter to be precise. Whatever. Morally, if not technically, Kevin was mine, all mine. Maybe he could be the son I never had. And I could be the father I never had. And my father could be the grandfather he never had which would make me the illegitimate brother Kevin never had, which would be physically impossible because he's a dog and I'm a human and . . .

chapter 9

To celebrate my new acquisition I treated myself to a bottle of Moet, a video and a lobotomy. I could not find anything along the lines of 'How to Own a Greyhound III' at Blockbuster so I bought a copy of *Steptoe and Son Ride Again* – not a particularly educational film but hilarious to say the least. Just to refresh your memory, it's the one in which Harold, using the proceeds from the sale of the family nag, buys a greyhound from some dodgy geezer and lives to regret it.

'Fear not, Dad, the family fortune is intact,' smirks a drunken Harold, staggering into chez Steptoe. 'Meet Hercules the Second!' Cue: mangy-looking dog.

'What's that . . . a greyhound? Oh my gawd!' The 'dirty old man' could hardly believe it. 'A greyhound, a bleeding greyhound. You want your head examined!'

Maybe I needed my head examined too. What had I done? I had just bought a dog for two-and-a-half thousand bloody pounds. Life had imitated art: I had become the dumber half of Steptoe and Son. The following day, having just managed to prise my head from my hands, I set off for the Stow to do the paperwork on Kevin.

'Are you waiting to be seen?' said a buxom young sister from behind the counter in the racing office. From her accent, I guessed she was Bajan. Her name was Alfie. 'Uh?' I replied. I was temporarily hypnotised by her heaving breasts. I had not seen tits like that since I was eighteen months old. Four greying men draped in a variety of polyfibrous garments were standing around in the corridor. One had a hearing aid. The other was called Ron.

The sum of their ages would have taken you back to Moses and the Ten Commandments. My mobile rang.

'Sorry,' I said, giving Alfie an apologetic smile. 'I have to take this call.'

I noticed the codgers eyeing me as I yapped on my mobile. Ron had thick bifocal lenses in his glasses and a silly tartan hat. He looked like he fancied his chances: *in your acrylic dreams, old man*.

' 'Ere you are,' said Alfie to one of the codgers. 'Did you get a wage sheet?' Octogenarian bastards: why were they staring at me? I'm an owner. Respect is due. The old men shuffled off and I got down to business. Firstly, I had to re-register Kevin under my name. That cost £30. Then I had to transfer his paperwork from his previous owners to me. That cost £25. Then if I wanted to change his name from Zussies Boy to something, well, more interesting, that was £25 to the NGRC and £25 to the Irish Coursing Club (ICC), the official body for registering greyhounds bred in Ireland.

Linda had warned me that 'anything to do with the NGRC costs money'. *Hello?* It only cost £15 to change a human being's name by deed poll. I was already £2500 down and the till was still ringing. I decided not to change Kevin's name. Everyone was getting in on the act now. It was like I had a sign saying 'Insert Here' riveted to my arsehole.

The NGRC heads a tripartite group of private organisations that runs licensed greyhound racing in the UK. But the industry is ostensibly split into two groups: the tracks that are licensed by the NGRC are the major players, attracting off-course betting, and some of these are owned by the Big Three bookmakers – Ladbrokes, William Hill and Corals.

Private companies, leisure consortiums or family businesses however own the majority. On the other side of the industry, what you might call 'the dark side', are an estimated 27 independent or 'flapping' tracks which do not have off-course betting because the provenance and form of the dogs are uncertain.

Of the three organisations that run licensed greyhound racing, the NGRC regulates racing to control the integrity of betting. The British Greyhound Racing Board (BGRB) comprises primarily race promoters and bookmakers who 'promote the best interest of greyhound racing' in the UK. Finally, the British Greyhound Racing Fund (BGRF), also composed of promoters and bookmakers, collects a voluntary levy[3] from bookmakers of up to £4 million a year, which, unsurprisingly, many do not pay. The levy is spent largely on infrastructure and capital projects at tracks, such as restaurants and bars.

Under NGRC rules, an owner can change a greyhound's race name twice; were it not for the extra charge 'Zussies Boy' would have been history. I mean who or what the fuck is called Zussie? Moreover, surely Zussies Boy should have an apostrophe, as in 'Zussie's Boy'. For some reason race names do not have apostrophes. While I am at it, I may as well bitch about people always getting the bloody name wrong. I am sick of hearing 'Zessies Boy', 'Zassies Boy', 'Susies Boy' and 'Zossies Boy'. At least it wasn't the worst moniker around. There are animals on the circuit with all manner of crazy names. How some owners have the front to call their dogs Big Pockets, Potato Blight, Horseshoe Paddy, Vigilante, Jo King Only and Climb Max, I'll never know.

For a brief moment, standing in the racing office, I regained my social conscience and liberal sensibilities and thought about renaming Kevin, 'McDonalds Suck', 'Where's Osama' or 'You Sank My Battleship'. Stupid names are all part of this crrrrrrraaaaaaaaaazzzzzzzzzy game. There is such a high premium on good names, creating something decent that hasn't been used already is beyond the imagination of most owners.

---

[3] In horseracing, the levy is mandatory.

Dog people usually lump any old shit together with a family member's name or breeder's prefix. It is also voguish to name dogs after minor celebrities and sportsmen, which has given rise to the likes of Fat Boy Slim, Louis Saha and Bomber Graham. Maybe one day, when I 'made it' someone might name a greyhound after me. I can see it now in the 19.30 at the Stow, trap one: 'Matthews' Turkey'.

I filled out a couple of forms and received a photocopy of Kevin's identity and race record book, containing details of the identification markings on his ears, his whelping date, sire and dam, anatomical marks (literally from his head down to his toenails), vaccination records and details of his trials and races to date. A few days later an envelope came in the post with four owners' passes providing free entry to the Stow and four half-yearly parking passes for the stadium car park. I had arrived.

Between Kevins first trial on June 12th and the beginning of August, he had had his first three professional races, coming fourth twice and third once over 435 metres. I had not seen any of these races as I had spent the better part of the month on holiday, raving in Ibiza and mainland Spain and indulging in other quaint 'sports'. At this point, it is worth using a little suspension of disbelief, while we go back three weeks, back back back in time to July 7th 2002 . . .

chapter 10

The early morning dew lay on the cobbled streets like gossamer. I'd been up since 5a.m. and was still feeling the effects of the previous night's bacchanal. It was now 7.30a.m.

'Here, get your laughing gear round this.' Scott lifted the goatskin, aimed it at my face and squeezed. Duck, dodge or drink? I opened my mouth and felt a jet stream of warm acrid wine hit the back of my throat. 'That'll sort ya,' said Afroman. I shook my head and grimaced as the wine kicked my palate. Men dressed in the traditional red and white outfit were jumping around necking bottles of cheap sangria and beers. The thought of alcohol at that time of the morning even rankled *my* thick skin.

Scott and Afroman (named so on account of his massive ginger hairdo) were a couple of Aussies I'd met on the way over from London. I had gone to Pamplona with my friend Owen for the *Fiesta de San Fermin* and the notorious *encierro* or 'running of the bulls', a tradition in these parts since 1591. After a twenty-four-hour red-eye drunken convoy of fifteen coaches, packed mainly with beer-swilling antipodeans, another twenty-four hours of partying in the city, and a couple of hours' sleep somewhere in between, I was ready for it. Owen came down to the City Square but bailed out of the *encierro* at the last minute. 'You know what? I think I'm gonna take a raincheck on it,' he said. At 6ft 6in he was worried that his height would make him vulnerable in the crowd. Owen had eaten snake in Cambodia and rat in Vietnam so I thought he'd have the stomach for the bull run. But I think his arsehole went at the last minute. Then again, if I had a brain I'd let my sphincter do the talking too.

Scott, Afroman, a bunch of other nuts and me followed the Big Man – an XXXL-sized Aussie tour leader – along the cobbled streets into the old city. Everyone was trying to laugh off the nerves and tension. As we walked through the crumbling citadel we passed the same stalls I'd revelled around the night before, bulging with calamari, *bacalao, paella* and *pollo y patatas*, a.k.a. chicken and chips. The Big Man gave us some rudimentary 'advice' on what to do in the race. He'd done the run once before. Once was enough for anyone he said. 'It's every man for himself out there boys,' said the Big Man. 'As soon as you see the bulls, run. Don't hang about. Don't wait for your mates. When it comes to the run you're on your own.' On the coach coming over from London they had shown a video of the previous year's run, but I had been too drunk to pay attention. I didn't have a clue what to do other than run, pray and keep my powder dry.

'We shouldn't run until we see the whites of their eyes,' said Afroman, grinning maniacally, as we reached the *Plaza Consistorial*, the City Hall Square. This was our starting point: 280 metres from the Santo Domingo corral where the six fighting bulls and two herds of steers were kept. The total length of the run from Santo Domingo to the bullring was 825 metres. I used to do a seven-minute-mile jog on a daily basis. I could run. I figured I could cover the 825 metres in four minutes without obstruction. A greyhound could do it in under 60 seconds. But I was no grader. A bull could cover the distance in around two minutes, which made me second favourite.

'Those who are about to die salute you,' I said punching the air. What a clown. I looked up at the City Hall clock. It was nearly eight. Large sections of the crowd started singing mournfully in Spanish. I think it was some sort of prayer.

I noticed a groundswell of bodies moving rapidly in my direction, up the inclined street and away from the corral. The first rocket or *cohete* went off dead on eight o'clock. This meant the corral gates were open. Half the crowd of two thousand or so runners, or *correadores*, took off instantly. 'Wait, wait,' I shouted. *You're not supposed to run until the second rocket. Uh?* I looked round and Scott had bolted. Afroman looked at me and smiled ruefully. The second rocket went off. This indicated that the bulls had now left the corral. I looked down the street towards the corral and saw a sea of freaks headed my way up the steep narrow street. As soon as I saw the bulls, I split. Fuck they were faaaaaaaaaaaaaass ssssssssssssssst!!!!!!!! I'm running, I'm running, I'm running. Either I'll be gored to death by a ton of raging meat or crushed under the stampeding crowd. I'm running, oh Jesus I'm running. What was I doing here? This had *nothing* to do with greyhound racing. Shhhhhhhhhhhhiiiiiiiiiiiiitttttttttt!!!!!!!!!!!!!!!!!!!!!!!!!!!!

I'm running for dear life through the *Plaza Consistorial* and into the *Calle Mercaderes*, the only part of the course drenched in sunlight, as tall buildings overshadow most of the route. The bulls remain tightly bunched, steamrollering forward through the crowd. I reach the notorious *Calle Estafeta*, where there's a sharp right turn. Eight tons of muscle speeds down the cobbled street like a bovine tsunami. As the bulls hurtle past me in a cloud of dust I'm mesmerised, transfixed by the sight of such large animals moving effortlessly with force and grace.

I gather my senses and get going again, turning into the bend ahead of the last bull, which rounds the corner, skids on the wet cobblestones and careers into a wall, buckling under his own weight. There's a pregnant pause. For a moment he lays still, dazed and confused. As a herd animal a bull is most dangerous when separated from his *compadres*. Half of the remaining five hundred-strong crowd freezes, watching his every move; the other half pursues the herd into the distance. The bull rises, looks one way then the other. A Japanese photographer in full Nikon splendour, grappling with what looks like a mini tripod leaps out of the crowd and sets himself on the cobbled street for that Pulitzer Prize-winning shot. The bull rushes him, head down, like a 515 lb Jonah Lomu, and hits him full on in the solar plexus – BOOM!

– snapping his head back so that the terrified man cartwheels six feet into the air.

A roar goes up from the spectators as the photographer spins through the air, arms and legs wheeling like clothes in a tumble drier, and hits the ground. After a while, he springs to his feet and in that moment he and the bull share a common animal instinct: survival. The man clambers into the relative safety of the crowd, legs and arms flailing, and disappears with his pride bruised but his dinner party anecdote intact.

I'm frozen, gripped by the unfolding drama. I focus on the bull, awaiting his next gambit. A bull's balls are bigger than its brain so little wonder where most of its thinking comes from. I look to the side: no one is moving. The bull swings his powerful meaty head around again, searching for the next target. A bull has no concept of colour and very poor depth of perception. It goes for the biggest moving object it can identify. The average Spaniard is a 5ft 9in scrawny motherfucker. I'm 6ft 2in and not far off 200 lbs. I am the only black man in sight out of a crowd of several hundred runners. He can't see colour, right? Whether I'm the intended target or not, he heads in my direction.

I turn on a sixpence and make for the barriers around ten feet away, a distance I must've covered in two strides. Even with this generous head start the bull quickly narrows the gap with a chilling desire to maim or kill. Faced with, or more correctly, running away from, a creature that is equal in size and weight to a Ford Fiesta, and has a break horsepower to match, I make for the barricades but find every conceivable way is blocked by the frenzied crowd. I fall. I had been warned about this. Now I remember. The Spanish in their lust for blood and gore will do their level best to keep you in the game, even if it means you being gored in the process. It's nothing personal. If you've chosen to run with Pamplona's finest you stay in the race, *you little chicken-shit thrillseeker you.*

Jesus fucking Christ Almighty. I clamber to my feet, battling through the mass of spectators, my legs collapsing beneath me. I punch and kick my way along through the crowd, fighting desperately for a way out of danger. The only thing between the bull and me is tumbling bodies. The first person blocking my path I grab instinctively by the scruff of the neck and fling to the ground. I punch another in the kidneys, sending him careening away from the barrier. More space. I feel an elbow in my jaw. 'Motherfucker,' I yell and lash out. I feel the weight of the crowd behind me intensifying. I feel the bull's presence. No time to look back. *It ain't gonna be me*. Someone falls in front of me, screaming. I stumble again, caught in a human domino effect. I leap up, stick my right leg out and impale it in a runner's back, then bunk myself up with my left leg on his neck, crushing him underfoot, giving me the necessary leverage to leapfrog over a few more bodies. I trample one, two, three more runners in front and feel someone's spine crack, like treading on a massive cockroach. This is dog eat dog, man eat man. The most dangerous single exercise I have ever encountered. Never again. This makes professional boxing look like a tea dance. There is no time for the milk of human kindness. It's every mad fuck for himself.

I find myself in an orgy of screaming bodies but with just enough time and energy left to shimmy my way through a gap in the barricades. I dive in, meet resistance again from legs hard pressed against the wood, determined to keep the runners out. I have half my body through and can feel the weight of the spectators pushing me back, and the collapsing crowd of runners pushing me forwards. The bastards. Both sides are playing me like a fucking accordion. I continue to force my way through, kicking out behind me and punching out in front. I let rip a right hook into a standing spectator's crotch and hear him wince. He buckles long enough to fall off the barricade, creating a body-sized hole for me to smash through. I clamber to my feet, turn and hear a thud followed by a high-pitched 'zing' as the barricade vibrates under the bull's force. I have made it with inches to spare. The bull gives a contemptuous snort. Pandemonium. Perhaps it was an over-active imagination, the previous night's sangria or simply fear but I swear I saw smoke billow from his flared nostrils.

A sea of red and white sways in front of me, and a thick blue line of cops baton-charge. A small squat cop catches me on the shoulder with his truncheon. 'Fucking bitch,' I yell. I want back in the race. The police are trying to stop any spectators or surviving runners from crossing the barriers back on to the cobbled streets. The cops baton-charge again. The crowd reels backwards. I spot another gap in the barriers and make my escape as the bull tears off thirty feet ahead of me.

I make my way up the narrow, crowded *Calle Bajada de Javier* behind the bull. Spectators pack the balconies on either side. Still enraged and freaked by the crowd he indiscriminately attacks. I get complacent and slow down. The bull turns, heading in my direction once again. I do a 180 as the crowd dissipates to find huge barricades blocking my escape route back into *Calle Estafeta*. Shit. From where in God's name did they come? Sick Pamplonan motherfuckers! Did they erect the barrier to keep the bulls out or the runners in? This devious twist in the race sends the crowd fleeing; people try desperately to scurry up door shutters or clamber on to a balcony for sanctuary.

Corredores from the corral with long sticks and men with rolled-up newspapers try to beat the bull back on to the path to the bullring. The bull butts a cumbersome runner and takes off back up the street. Absolute mayhem. It's hard to say at this pace which presents the greater risk: the runners or the bulls. I pass through the *Teléfonica*, a causeway leading to a narrow channel of wooden fences that funnels straight into the bullring.

I reach the gates of the bullring panting and sweating. There's a backlog of people fighting to get to the bullring and their moment of glory. After storming the barricades with scores of runners, chanting 'Toro, toro', I come running out into the centre of a gladiatorial masterpiece: a two-tiered amphitheatre the size of a football stadium. People are going nuts, giving each other high-fives, hugging, crying, laughing, screaming. I spot two brothers and we connect instantly with an eerie sort of recognition. We indulge ourselves with a handshake. What a buzz.

The endorphins are starting to work their magic, but the Basques have one more trick up their sleeves. A final rocket goes off indicating that the last bull has entered the ring and the race is officially over, then, one by one, steers are released into the bullring for a five-minute workout with the few hundred remaining wannabe matadors. It's bad form to hit the bulls with anything other than a newspaper. Despite the debatable merits of the bull run, it is seen as disrespectful to touch or harm the bulls. A man wearing a cowboy hat puts this coda to the test by trying to rodeo ride one bull. He is quickly grabbed by a baying mob of Spaniards and punched to the ground. Another foreigner, dressed as a pantomime cow, narrowly escapes an impromptu mating with a steer, providing the morning's biggest belly laugh.

Dust and sand flies, vicars, nuns and assorted fancy-dress freaks run around making like El Cordobes and I get out of the ring as the third bull enters. My adrenaline is spent. A series of rockets go off, indicating the end of the event. At just over seven minutes, the first run of the *Fiesta de San Fermin* was nearly double the average duration. The longest ever bull run was on July 11th 1959, lasting thirty minutes when one of the bulls fell behind. Eventually a dog was used to bite the bull and drive it to the bullpen.

'You ought to be ashamed of yourself,' Linda had said, tut-tutting, when I told her of my 'holiday' plans just before I left for Spain. 'I hope those bulls give you what for up the you know what.'

Animal cruelty is a subjective business. One man's meat and all that. While Linda abhorred bullfighting, she wasn't averse to the odd spot of hare coursing in Ireland. 'But I'm not a fan of it,' she insisted. And despite my interest in Latino bullshit, I found more domestic activities like badger baiting, cockfighting, playing chicken and dogging pretty disgusting. Yes . . . one man's meat. I bet a few vegans would be happy to see the likes of Linda and me leathered. And given half a chance the anti-vivisectionists would have a piece of us too. Where did the buck stop? What about pet owners? Somewhere, a mob lay in wait for the owners of Polly and Fido. And what about insects? There are hardcore Jains whose religion requires total respect for any living, breathing organism and who wear facemasks to stop themselves from even breathing in bacteria, which they consider their spiritual equals.

Pamplona had given me an entrée into what it was like to be the hunted rather than the hunter. I'd given those bulls a chance to take a chunk out of me, which is more than can be said for your average fisherman, foxhunter or pheasant shooter, so I was square with the animal kingdom. In the local papers the following day the Spanish press was full of reportage and gory pictures of the bull run and the gored victims, many of whom were dumb foreign tourists seduced by *The Sun Also Rises*, the book that put Pamplona and Ernest Hemingway on the map.

Aw, I know all that Pamplona stuff was bullshit. Goddamn macho Hemingway crap even got me talking and writing like a Goddamn Yank, already. The good citizens of Pamplona erected a bronze statue in the old man's honour, right outside the bullring. For all that hard-drinking, beardy, bullfight stuff he never actually ran the *encierro* himself. Blew his fucking brains out cos he couldn't deal with being a fag though. I guess that's pretty macho. Well, goodbye Papa . . . and goodbye Pamplona. I had more important races to run, more pressing obstacles to overcome. The moment of truth had arrived. Er, almost.

chapter II

'Your balls have got bigger,' said Margot when I got back from Pamplona. And so they had. I didn't put a ruler or a pair of callipers to them but with the strategic use of a shaving mirror I guessed that they'd grown by around 10–15 per cent. So with my new and improved, bigger, better balls I was ready to hit the track for the first time as a hotshot dog owner.

Tonight was the big night. Now I was finally going to see Kevin in action. I was sweating over a contentious piece about infidelity which I had just filed for the *Evening Standard* and was racing to meet another deadline. I had planned to go suited and booted to the track, maybe even wear a *boutonnière* to mark the occasion but I was pushed for time. I jumped into the Jew canoe and toed it across London, as Kevin was down to run in the second race of the night, a P8 scrubber's affair at 19.43.

I decided to make the trip on my own. This was my moment and I wanted it to be private. But more importantly, I didn't want to 'big up' the affair only to see him come last in front of all my friends. I'm sensitive like that.

I got to the track with about ten minutes to spare before the race. I had the runs, so I rushed to the toilets, clenching my butt cheeks like I was trying to crack a walnut. I managed to get inside the cubicle and pull my pants down moments before pebble-dashing the WC. Ah, Bisto . . .

There were a few minutes before the off. I turned to the side to reach for some toilet paper and . . . no toilet paper. Jesus. I was in such a hurry to get to the toilet I had left my bits and pieces – mobile, notebook and so forth – in the car so I had nothing to wipe my arse with. Not that I'd use a mobile phone for such a delicate exercise, mind you.

The only paper I had on me was the receipt for Kevin and a hundred quid in used notes. Wiping my backside with the receipt would have been a tacit admission that Kevin was shite and owning him wasn't worth the paper the receipt was written on. That left the money. I took a fiver out of my wallet. I heard the announcer say, 'There are three minutes before the off.' I stared at the fiver. What to do? I looked at my watch. I opened the cubicle door tentatively and noticed a group of lads chatting and rolling up a joint. In the cubicle next door, I could hear what sounded like an old boy honking up and letting a good one rip. Two minutes to go. I couldn't leave the cubicle like this, cack pouring out of my backside like a chocolate waterfall. I looked at the fiver again and turned it over. Elizabeth Regina. There goes the knighthood. I wiped my arse and threw the fiver into the WC. That would give the next patron something to think about. *Welcome to the high-rolling world of greyhound ownership.*

I got out and down to the heaving jungle that is the betting ring with just under a minute to spare.

The betting ring was the usual bear pit of machismo. The crowd was milling around to the strains of 'Golden Years' by David Bowie which was playing on the stadium's PA. I was woefully ill prepared for the event. I was dressed like a bum: crummy old running shoes, dirty jeans, baseball cap and a hooded sweatshirt with the logo 'CRIMINAL' emblazoned across the chest. This look *had* to go. I resolved to return wearing more suitable attire for a man of my new-found status. I also made a note to carry my own toilet paper in future.

Kevin left the kennels with his five fellow competitors, paraded fifty or so metres from the kennels to the betting ring and then went to the traps. The punters eyed the dogs as they pissed and shat themselves – the dogs that is, not the punters. I was mindful of a dog that relieved itself before a race, taking that as a sign they may well have been 'bunged up' with a Mars bar, porridge, a pint of lager, or what have you.

I craned my neck towards the traps to make sure everything was OK, no mustard jars around. The kennel hands then paraded the dogs back towards the boxes and started loading them up for the race. Kevin was in trap three, but it was too early in his career to say if this was a natural position for him. Nevertheless, for him to make it in a coffin box he had to show early pace and get to that first bend in front to stand a real chance of winning.

Kevin was up against Chrissys Charm in trap one; Baltovin Maid in trap two; his kennel mate Twotone in trap four; Bush Bill in trap five; and Miss Spartacus in trap six. 'Go on the three dog,' I cry, crunching the words out through tightened jaws. A couple of punters frown at me. 'The three dog . . . Zussies Boy . . . he's mine. I mean I own him.' The punters look at each other and go back to looking at the bookmakers' odds as the market starts buzzing.

'Seven a four the field.'
'Two elephant.'
'Two carpet.'
'Seven a four.'
'Shoulder the favourite.'
'Three bar one.'
'Top ching.'
'Three dog here.'
'Three to one bar one.'
'Three and a half, tenners.'

I look at my race card. I have thirty seconds to place a bet. The bookies are laying Kevin at 4–1 and Twotone at 7–1. Hmm. . . Perhaps the bookies knew something I didn't. Twotone had won his first race, a P8, on his maiden outing on Thursday July 4th 2002 at 8–1, beating the 4–7 favourite Knockard Terri to a pulp. I count out £50 in tens. And take a step forward. Hang on. I look at my race card again and look up at the bookies' prices. Twotone, 7–1? On current form, Twotone had the slowest times. All the so-called 'smart money' was going on Baltovin Maid. And the *Racing Post* had picked the trap one dog.

A little voice said, '*Put the fifty on Twotone. You know it makes sense.*' Nah, I can't bet against my own dog in my first race! '*But look at the INFORMATION.*' I recheck my race card. The Dog Lovers are still down as Kevin's owners. It'll be another week before the name's changed. *Steady on* . . . Suddenly there's a rush. I'm crowded from all sides. I lose my bearings for a second. I feel like a tourist on the Tokyo subway. I'm an owner, for Christ's sake, you can't manhandle me! I bowl over to the first bookie I see. 'Gimme a tenner on the three dog mate.' He snatches the money and hands me a ticket. The race steward in his tight black jodhpurs and bowler waves his magic flag. A bell rings, the lights dim. 'Hare's approaching . . .'

I hear the click and whir of the mechanical hare as it makes its way round the track like a miniature funfair ride, jolting and jerking as it hits each bend nearing the boxes. I can see Kevin's little face behind the bars. Aw . . . BANG! They're off!

Kevin's bumped at the off by the one dog and is last at the first bend. 'Oh you fucking Muppet.' They take the corner and he closes the gap going into fourth place at the second bend. 'Go on four, kick arse,' someone cries. *Fuck off four.* 'Go on Zussie . . . go on. Go on, boy.' Down the back straight he charges past Bush Bill, Chrissys Whatever and Miss Thing into second place. Nice. He's now up on Twotone's backside. 'Go on Kev, go on, my son!' I cry, stabbing a clenched fist at the air.

At the third turn he's still up on Twotone. 'Go on, boy, go on!' I'm throwing left and right hooks, shadowboxing, as Twotone and Kevin hit the fourth and final bend. 'Come on, come on, come on, keep coming, keep coming, keep coming keep . . .' And the winner is: Twotone, by 2¼ lengths. Shit. Fuck. Piss. 'Fucked up at that bend,' one of the bookies says to me. 'Yeah,' I say. I rip up my betting slip and head towards the kennels to congratulate my £2500 dog on bagging the £28 second prize. Ne'er mind. At least he'd set a personal best of 29.96 over 475 metres, which was, er, the first time he'd actually run *competitively* at that distance, so that was no mean feat.

'*Dividends for race two,*' says the announcer over the PA, '*win four, 22 pence; place four, 21 pence; place three, 24 pence. Forecast four and three pays 2 pounds and 75 pence. Trifecta four, three, one, pays 6 pounds and 67 pence.*'

The *Racing Post* had accurately picked Kevin for second place but curiously didn't rate Twotone to finish anywhere in the first three. I'd already figured out that the best average any newspaper tipster could hit on a card was one in three wins. Occasionally they did better, but more often than not they faired far worse. The moral of this: don't listen to tipsters. Dogs, horses, stocks and shares . . . Look, if these characters are so good at picking the next big thing they'd be making a tasty income from a beachside villa in the Caribbean, instead of eking out a living at a crummy desk.

Now, I could have had a forecast on Twotone to win and Kevin to place. Did I take the bet? No. More significantly, there were certain 'factors' I should have taken into consideration. But did I pay attention to these factors? Did I bollocks. In the end, I put a tenner on Kevin to win, purely out of loyalty. I could not bet against my own dog now, could I? Loyalty however means jack at the track. Such sentimentality is best left at the gates. To be a gambler, as opposed to being a mug punter, you have to be dispassionate about luck, coat colour, funny names, big cuddles and all that puppy-dog crap.

So Kevin was beaten into second place: story of my fucking life. He tried his best but his best wasn't good enough: the sequel to the story of my fucking life.

I went up into the bar and got myself a Jack D and Coke. It cost £2.55. Cheery ads appeared on the Tote screens in between the forecast and trifecta information. 'Happy twenty-first, Julie. Love from all of us.' Screw Julie. 'Goodbye Tom, good luck in

Leeds.' *Who cares?* 'This next one's 5–2–3,' says a punter at the table next to me. 'Nah, you want six in there,' says his mate. Everyone had moved on. Time waits for no man at the dogs. 'Sonofabitch,' I mumbled over the Jack D. I laid the race card out in front of me, smoothing the creases, and went over Kevin's form again, trying to make sense of a senseless enterprise. 'Sonofabitch.' There was no point trying to rationalise the race. Whatever way I looked at it, he hadn't won. Get over it. But he'd come so close; and his nemesis once again was Twotone, the Cain to his Abel. Seven-to-one he romped home at. I was starting to develop a grudge against that meddling dog. Kevin had now had four losses on the bounce compared with Twotone, the glory boy, who in the same period had won three out of five races. Something told me that the £1500 difference between them was going to prove very costly in the end.

chapter 12

The greyhound breed, including Salukis, Borzois and Afghans, is around eight thousand years old. Ancient Egyptians prized them for their speed, agility and hunting skills and kept them as pets. Although their exact origin is unknown, illustrations on Egyptian engravings and pottery dating back several thousands of years prove that greyhound-type dogs most certainly came from the Middle East. The Pharaohs used to bury themselves with their greyhounds, along with their wives, servants, liquid assets, tellies, videos, dishwashers etc.

In 800 BC, Homer became the first author to write about greyhounds in literature. Alexander the Great's and General George Custer's favourite dogs were greyhounds. In fact, Custer coursed his fourteen greyhounds the night before the Battle of Little Big Horn, although it did him little good the following day when Sitting Bull, Crazy Horse and the gang kicked his ass.

Britain and Ireland have the Romans to thank for the introduction of the greyhound, along with the hares that they coursed. Greyhounds have long been associated with hunting and nobility. For hundreds of years, right up until the nineteenth century, it was a crime in Britain for peasants to own a greyhound; such an animal was solely the property of royalty and lords and ladies of the realm. I could go on. To cap it all, the greyhound is the only dog referred to by breed in the King James Version of the Bible. In Proverbs 30, verses 29–31 Solomon says:

There be three things which go well, yea
Which are comely in going:
A lion, which is strongest among beasts and
turneth not away from any;
A Greyhound; A he-goat also.

A common misconception about greyhounds is that their name has something to do with colour. In fact, grey greyhounds are quite rare. There are as many theories on the etymology of the word 'greyhound' as there are markings of the breed itself; the most popular notion is that the word greyhound comes from the Saxon 'grei' which means beautiful. Chaucer is the first writer recognised to have use the word 'greihound' in English literature. In *The Canterbury Tales* he writes, 'Greihounds he had as swift as fowl of flight.'

The first record of a greyhound race meeting in Britain dates back to 1876 in a field near the Welsh Harp, Hendon Way, in north London, when dogs chased a 'hare' dragged along by a hand-operated windlass. Nevertheless, the invention of a revolutionary mechanical dummy hare in 1912 by an American engineer named Owen Patrick Smith was the real genesis of modern greyhound racing. It would take another seven years before Smith's invention took off in America, while the British were reluctant at first to adopt the novel sport; most aficionados, rooted in romantic notions of tradition, the landed nobility, still viewed greyhounds as purely coursing animals.

Then in 1926 an American named Charles Munn, a retired chief constable called Sir William Gentle and a Canadian ex-pat, Brigadier-General A.C. 'Critch' Critchley, formed the Greyhound Racing Association (GRA) and invested £22,000 in Britain's first greyhound track at Belle Vue in Manchester. On July 24th of that year a dog with half a tail called Mistley flew out of trap two, to the delight of 1700 screaming spectators (half of them received free admission). Twenty-five seconds later, Mistley became the first winner of a greyhound contest run on a circular track over

440 yards in the UK, winning the race by eight lengths. Britain had finally gone to the dogs.

To get the ball rolling in those primitive days of racing, greyhounds were recruited from the world of hare coursing and trained to chase the dummy hare, which in the pre-animal rights days (and until relatively recently at many tracks) was a stuffed hare. In total, there were six races: one over 440-yard hurdles, two over 500 yards, and three over 440 yards. In the early days, eight dogs competed in each race; limiting races to a maximum of six greyhounds, which is unique to Britain, was not introduced until 1927.

The promoters of that first meet had captured the zeitgeist. By the third day of racing at Belle Vue 16,000 paying customers went through the turnstiles. The following year the GRA moved its headquarters to White City and attendance figures for greyhound racing in Britain reached 5.5 million. In 1930 this had risen to a phenomenal 13 million. The number of tracks in Britain would soon mushroom to 220, a number that exceeded professional Football League grounds by three-to-one. In 1936 the GRA floated on the stock exchange at a time when record numbers of 70,000 to 80,000 punters would flock to the Derby at White City, the epicentre of British greyhound racing.

Greyhound racing continued to thrive with little or no change. Apart from the odd technical innovation, such as new mechanical lure designs and faster traps, it remained true to its roots. There were one or two exceptions however.

In 1937, for instance, an old Harrovian and adventurer called Kenneth Gandar Dower introduced cheetah racing to Britain as an alternative to greyhound racing after importing eight big cats from Africa and promoting highly publicised races at Harringay and Romford stadiums. The cheetahs, however, showed little interest in racing each other and even less for the dummy lure. Their lack of competitive spirit meant that Dower's unique sport was soon consigned to history. Fortunately no spectators were eaten either.

In the early 1930s in America another bizarre variation of dog racing was launched. Trained as jockeys and dressed in silks, monkeys were made to ride on the backs of greyhounds. 'They are displaying exceptional skill,' the *New York Evening Journal* reported in 1933. 'You get a run for your money with these critters – and that's a lot more than you can say for bettors at the horse tracks.' The practice carried on into the 1950s at some tracks in the US. Once again, the British public was too discerning for the 'sport' to take hold in the UK.

By the 1950s and 1960s the dogs was the place to be and tracks continued to spring up across the country. Greyhound racing was now a sport in its own right. It was no longer an adjunct of hare coursing or 'the poor man's horseracing'. The dogs had become popular not only with the hoi poloi; the bug had bitten royalty, aristocrats, high rollers and movie stars too.

When the Stow opened in 1933, pioneer airwoman Amy Johnson was guest of honour. Hollywood greats like George Raft and Lana Turner were faces in the crowd long before Vinnie, Brad, Madonna, Guy and that bloke from *The Bill* got in on the act. Nowadays football has the upper hand on celebrity patronage. The tables have turned. Unlike greyhound racing, the nineteenth-century origins of football have no noble pretensions. Football was a resolutely working-man's game for over a century until courtship by the middle classes, pop stars and cynical politicians in the mid-1990s suddenly gave it bourgeois cred.

In the early days the dogs, like horseracing, the movies and radio, was a simple form of escapism. The public went for a night out, the excitement and the atmosphere, all of which was enhanced by the very presence of large numbers of people. But when in 1963 legislation was passed allowing bookmakers to ply their trade on the high street, suddenly punters didn't need to visit the track to make a bet. That's when the rot set in. The Stow had largely managed to buck the downward trend and escape the clutches of the developer's bulldozer, mainly by marketing itself more towards the 'six-pack' crowd, although like other tracks it had seen a disturbing fall in attendance. I decided it was time to ingratiate myself with the management at the track. 'Would you like a cup of tea?' said Ann. 'Oh yes, please.'

Ann Aslett is the marketing director at Walthamstow Stadium and, like most of the inner circle, a descendant of William Chandler, founder of the Stow. We first met in her little office, crammed with trophies and old photos, where she gave me a grilling about my journalistic exploits. 'I'm not doing a Kenyon,' I said, which seemed to satisfy her curiosity. However, it wouldn't be the last time she'd show concern about how dog racing, the Stow and, more importantly, the Chandlers, who owned the stadium, would be portrayed by me.

'Greyhound racing is great entertainment,' said Ann, offering me a biscuit. I took a Bourbon and a custard cream. 'It's a little bit different from the cinema or a club but I think that's why people enjoy it. It something *different*, isn't it?'

'Yes, very different,' I said.

Ann is a classy sort of broad, cultured, in her late forties or early fifties, I think. Her husband is a writer too. He has a yacht. He obviously knows something I don't. Ann gave me the deal about the Stow, but not in an oily, used-car salesman sort of way, which is what I expected from anyone connected to a dog track. As a director of the company she is forbidden from betting at the track, as is her right-hand woman Tracy Cooper, who is what a tabloid newspaper would call 'a pretty young blonde'. She's no dummy though. While it is Ann and Tracy's job to sell the merits of the Stow to anyone who'll listen, Tracy is as much an anorak as a PR. She knows her dogs and even has a tipster column in the local rag, imaginatively called 'Down the Dogs'. Ann is people people but Tracy is dog people.

'You've got your "dodge pot", that's a dog that doesn't know where it is on the track and runs all over the place,' said Tracy, 'or a "screw" which is one that lifts its tail in the air when it hits the bend, thinks "fuck that" and baulks. Or there are some trainers here,' she continued in a whisper, 'and I can't name names . . .

who put their dogs out then say "it's a fucking cripple" because they know it's carrying an injury. The trainers know the dog is good enough to run, so they won't pull it out, but they know it can't win.'

To be a tipster or to make a living out of gambling you have to know what's going on off the track as much as on it. Inside information is a very useful tool. 'If you're just a straight owner and pay your dough and go, you don't get a lot of info,' said Gillian, the Stow's resident photographer, who had just strolled into the office.

'I don't want to put a downer on things,' I said, changing the subject, 'but don't you ever wonder about the, you know, animal rights issue? I heard you've had a few demos down here.'

'They're entitled to protest,' said Ann. 'I don't have a problem with that. But we're *very* keen on the dogs' welfare. For instance, we work with the Walthamstow Greyhound Owners Association to make sure all dogs are re-homed. None of them are put down.'

To help fund the Stow's Retired Greyhound Fund their Directors matched every penny raised during their annual charity night 'pound for pound' which, according to Ann, was rapidly approaching £40,000.

Ann is an animal lover. Just like me. But we both share the same common duplicity when it comes to animal rights.

'Do you eat meat?'

'Yes, I do. Why do you ask?' said Ann, concerned.

'I'm just curious . . . you know . . . about our relationship with animals.'

'I'm sure that my dog has got a soul but I still eat steak for lunch. And if a dog has a soul then surely so does a cow. How do you explain that?'

'Hmm . . . I can't.'

'Biscuit?'

'Oh, thanks. So tell me about the Chandlers . . .'

Established in 1933 by the bookmaker William Chandler, and

still owned to this day by eight of his descendants, the history of the Stow is part of London's lesser-known urban folklore.

Bill Chandler, as the mercantile name suggests, was born into a poor working-class family in the East End of London in 1890. After starting out as an illegal bookmaker, with runners on street corners in and around his neighbourhood, Chandler quickly moved up in the world, went legit and became a bookmaker at horseracing tracks throughout the south of England. After a few years the pauper from Hoxton had done good, securing the No. 1 pitch at every racecourse in the South.

The next move was to become a rails bookmaker – a bookie operating in the Members Enclosure – alongside William Hill, Joe Coral and Max Parker, the founder of Ladbrokes. Chandler built a bookmaking empire and a reputation based on extravagant wagers and daring business ventures. As early as the 1920s he was known to take bets of £500, £800 or £1000 in his stride and barely a dog race went by at White City in which his book averaged less than five grand. On an eight-race card he would handle between £40,000 and £50,000 on a Saturday afternoon on top of income from his office and his own track. One evening at White City, he lost a reputed £120,000 on one race when a dog called Ribbon was beaten in the St Leger. Chandler's response was to casually turn to his clerk, open his book and start taking bets for the next race. Tall, dapper and charismatic, he was the archetypal old school bookie. One reporter once described him as, 'Loud-mouthed and loud-suited, cigar in mouth and two bottles on the bar, he exists now only in the imagination of the cartoonist.'

Chandler's interest in greyhound racing had started at White City. Aside from his bookmaking activity he owned a number of prize greyhounds including Peerless Call who beat the legendary double-Derby winner Mick the Miller in the London Cup in 1927.

When Chandler stopped betting at White City in 1931, he was approached by a wealthy dog owner called Gilbert, who had built the Regal Cinema in Marble Arch, about a piece of land in

Hackney. Chandler took one look at the land and bought it straight away. Chandler, Gilbert and another man named Wrightson invested £20,000 together and Hackney Wick Stadium was born. But within a couple of years Chandler had sold his £5000 worth of shares for a mere £500. Hackney Wick became one of east London's prosperous tracks and those same shares would've soon been worth £20,000. Despite the apparent gaffe Chandler described it as, 'Still the best day's work I ever did', for three weeks after selling his shares he had bought the Crooked Billet ground at Walthamstow, a small whippet racing and 'flapping' (unlicensed) greyhound track. A journalist at the time described the deal:

> He [Chandler] got out of his car, saw the owner standing on the track, asked him his price, agreed it, went around to the man's solicitors, and paid out the purchase price in cash on the spot.

When Bill Chandler died in 1946 aged just fifty-six, the dog man *par excellence* left a legacy with a long tail. Three grandsons, Charles, Jack and William, are respectively the Stow's chairman, managing director and secretary while a fourth, Victor, became one of the pioneers of offshore internet betting and a key figure in the introduction of tax-free gambling to the UK. Victor also lends his name and £15,660 in cash to the Victor Chandler Grand Prix competition every September and October, which along with the exotically named UK Packaging Arc in February and March are the Stow's biggest races. However, I had no chance of getting my hands on any of that Grand Prix lolly.

chapter 13

Twelve days after my debut at the track as an owner, Kevin was up against two of his old adversaries: Chrissys Charm and Baltovin Maid. This time he was evens favourite at the off. He trapped well but so did Baltovin Maid, who edged him to the first bend and maintained the lead. From then on in it was the same story as before: Kevin playing catch up right to the wire, beaten into second place by 2¼ lengths.

Perhaps it was a little late to start looking at bloodlines. But I thought I'd better pay closer attention to my 'investment' and look deeper into what I'd bought. Belgian Patrick knew a guy who ran a website (www.greyhound-data.com) listing all the details of every racing greyhound bred over the last four centuries.

Using this intriguing site, which listed the details of 873,640 greyhounds and nearly a million races from four continents, spanning four centuries, I traced Kevin's bloodline right back to Claret and Snowball the two nineteenth-century coursing dogs from which all modern greyhounds are descended.

Kevin's paternal great-great-grandfather was I'm Slippy, winner of the 1983 Derby. That was promising. Old Slippy sired at least 2623 offspring from a canine harem numbering scores of bitches, including Bangor Exchange, who begat Bangor Return, who in turn begat Bangor Jane, who in turn gave birth to Lakeshore Owney, Kevin's old man. In the line were Meadow Fescue, Miss Cinderella, Harmonicon, Husky Whisper II and

Brown Eyes III. I could name every one of Kevin's ancestors right back to the early nineteenth century yet I didn't even know my great-great-grandmother's name.

If only he had had that wonder dog Scurlogue Champ in his family tree, he may have inherited some balls. Scurlogue Champ was the Muhammad Ali of greyhound racing. A guy from the Fens called Ken Peckham, a double of Benny from *Crossroads*, had owned and trained him throughout a remarkable career. Between July 1984 and August 1986, he won a phenomenal 51 races from 63 starts, most of them marathons. His modus operandi would be to meander out of the traps and tail off for a circuit, giving the opposition a clear 15- to 20-metre head start before reaching remarkable speeds in the latter stages of a race, when he'd cut through the field like a hot knife through butter. He broke 20 records at the 23 different tracks and at one stage won 16 races on the bounce. He'd regularly run in front of ten to fifteen thousand screaming punters and won the big classic, the Cesarewitch, when it was staged at Belle Vue. He could cream a race by up to fifteen lengths. Bookies would not take bets on him. Managers and agents, in pursuit of some action, courted him like a pop star or Premiership footballer.

Peckham was offered up to £75,000 for the dog but he would not sell. Why should he? A dog with an 80 per cent strike rate was a walking, barking cash machine. The Champ was on course to beat the record for the most consecutive wins set by Westpark Mustard, Peruvian and Mick the Miller, when he stumbled on a stone on the track at Peterborough in an apparent betting coup (there'd been big money on the trap four dog, Sneaky Liberty). A punter then ran on to the track, right by the finish line, in an attempt to stop the race, and that was the end of that. He never amounted to anything at stud either.

A significant feature of Scurlogue Champ was his size: he was around 38 or 39 kilos, a good 10 to 15 per cent bigger than most dogs. Peckham had admittedly bulked him up, but as my flatmate Dr Paul noted when I showed him the video, 'That dog's moody.

If he were an athlete, he'd be drug tested every time. He's like Ben Johnson.'

Maybe they just don't make 'em like they used to.

Another dog I remember from blurred images on a TV screen was Ballyregan Bob. He too raced between 1984 and 1986 and became a racing legend, achieving a remarkable 32 successive wins over 695 metres, a world record that stood for Bob's overall record of 42 wins from 48 races, giving him an incredible 87.5 per cent strike rate. Remarkably, he never won a classic; never won the big one, the Derby.

But the granddaddy of them all, of course, was Mick the Miller. Mick raced between April 1928 and October 1931 and secured 15 victories from 20 races in his native Ireland before achieving another 46 wins from 61 races in England and Wales. He had a lower strike rate than his two modern rivals but, significantly, he won the Derby twice, in 1929 and 1930, plus a St Leger, a Cesarewitch and a Welsh Derby. He also broke five track records and notched up a British record of 19 consecutive wins. He was such a public icon that after his death he was stuffed and put on display in a glass cabinet at the Natural History Museum. I doubt David Beckham will ever get such star treatment.

On the face of it, any greyhound's historical breeding record can look rather impressive. However, this is often no more than smoke and mirrors, or at least a case of six degrees of separation. With a big enough laptop and a firm grasp of ancient language, I could probably trace my roots back to Shaka Zulu, Alexander the Great and Jesus. We all have to come from somewhere after all.

History, genealogy and all that is fine and dandy, but it doesn't pay the rent. I was in this business to make some moolah. According to the BGRB, British greyhound owners had won an estimated £11 million in prize money the previous year. So far, I had 'made' £56 from Kevin, but I had not even received my first kennel bill yet. That was bound to be £250. I had a long way to go to make a dent in the 2002 BGRB tally.

Kevin had had five races, including two under my ownership, now known as the 'Headline Syndicate', but was yet to win one. All of his races had been either P8 or A8 grade races, the lowest at the Stow. I was starting to get anxious.

'He's still a pup,' Linda kept saying. 'He's still learning, give him time.'

He had a lot to learn all right. Admittedly, he was still only seventeen months old. I was too impatient. Greyhounds hit their peak between two and three-and-a-half years old. No, what was I saying? He had to get a move on. At his level, a £68 first prize was chicken feed; after that, the money was derisory: £28 for second place and £25 for all other placings. I could not gamble on him to make up the shortfall in his kennel bills if he kept losing.

The boy had to toughen up his act. I would tell him as much after a race and then give the big lug a big hug. He had to stop being bullied out of the running. He was such a soft touch. If another dog so much as looked at him, he'd drop off the pace. Repeatedly he was bumped by more experienced opposition, usually at the first bend. He just did not seem to want to get on the bunny. His trapping skills were suspect too. Half the time he seemed to be asleep in the traps. What was he waiting for, Crufts? I guess, like his owner, he was simply a late starter.

Fortunately, he was still racing in the evenings. But if his performances didn't improve the race manager would soon stick him on the BAGS circuit – the 'Bookmakers Afternoon Greyhound Service', which pipes daytime races into the high-street betting shops via the Satellite Information Services (SIS) system.

BAGS started in the 1960s when the bookmaking industry negotiated contracts with track promoters to provide greyhound racing during betting shop hours. This novel idea was a ruse to keep punters spending whenever horseracing was cancelled due to bad weather. Greyhounds ran whatever the weather and the standard of BAGS dogs was ropey so nobody gave a shit if the odd dog was busted up due to bad track conditions. Add pitiful prize money to the equation and BAGS racing soon proved a cheap and convenient alternative to the gee-gees. All this is good news for the bookmakers, promoters and compulsive gamblers but bad news for small-time owners like me. If your dog winds up being a regular on the BAGS the chances are that is where it will stay. Consigning a dog to BAGS racing is like contracting herpes: you keep that shit like luggage. And if that happened, Kevin and I were both doomed.

chapter 14

The following Sunday I was heading for the kennels when I saw dark clouds looming overhead. In another half an hour or so it would be pouring with rain and the clouds went on and on and on. I'd just hit the M11 and could see that by the time I got to Lakenheath the kennels would be a mudbath, so I decided to do a U-turn and head for home.

On my way back into London I drove through Hackney Wick, dodging hordes of greedy shoppers, traffic and double-parked cars. People were scuttling around with bedding, tellies and videos, carpets, food processors and a variety of consumer goods. It was like the LA Riots all over again. Hackney Wick car boot sale was in town.

Hackney Wick Stadium had been host to one of the country's biggest car boot sales on the site long before the dogs had stopped running. In fact, an old acquaintance of mine used to manage it; his brother had done a deal with the owner and old family friend, George Walker, and had started using the site as a market in the early nineties. The stadium had been redeveloped in 1995 at a cost of £18 million but Walker's company had slipped into receivership while the party celebrating its opening was still echoing round the stadium.

Since the dog track ceased operating the stadium had provided the great unwashed of the East End with countless tacky, cheap and often dubious goods. The site was bought in early 2003 by the London Development Agency and the word was they would use it as the platform to mount a bid for the 2012 Olympics. Perhaps if the Olympics introduced greyhound racing, darts, snooker, bowls and shove ha'penny – you know, sports the British are actually good at – then maybe we'd win some medals.

I pulled up and found a parking space by the side of Hackney Marshes, a good quarter of a mile from the action. A gang of police officers and parking attendants were busying themselves, issuing tickets with the usual contempt. Drivers were remonstrating with them, failing to see the problem in parking on the kerb on a double yellow line with an out-of-date tax disc.

I hadn't been to the market in years. When I rounded the bend into Waterden Road, where what was left of the old dog track stood, I hit a gauntlet of street peddlers and hustlers: Romanians, Somalians, Turks, pikeys, beggars, fakers, fakirs, fences, muggers and thieves – the market offered a snapshot of neo-Dickensian Third World London.

I wheeled my way through the crowd, surfing the waves of half-cooked jerk chicken vendors, takeaway outlets of questionable provenance, bootleg CDs, asylum-seekers, pickpockets and assorted electrical goods, until I was inside the track. I contemplated one man's offer of a snide Rolex watch. 'Twenty-five pounds, you have.' 'Thanks but no thanks,' I said and moved on.

A couple of weeks earlier the British anti-piracy organisation Federation Against Copyright Theft (FACT) and the police had raided the market, making seven arrests and seizing a 'large quantity' of bootleg CDs, videos and PC software.

An impressive grandstand, which had apparently been built at huge expense without planning permission, lines one side of the track. By the time it had gone up the company running the show, Brent Walker Entertainment, had gone down and it was never used. The iron rails on which the hare once ran are still visible in sections of the stadium. I could see the ghosts of the dogs, the punters, and the bookies weaving their way through this colourful sea of faces, strangers to what had once been.

'You from the council, mate?' A tall likely lad in his forties approached me as I slipped out of a doorway that led to the track's scoreboard. 'No, I'm just taking a trip down memory lane,' I said. 'But it looks like Memory Lane is now a cul-de-sac.' The man, a stallholder, laughed and peered through the doorway at the rubble and mess. The guts had been ripped out of the place. It stank of piss and shit. 'People use it as a toilet,' he said. 'This place has gone downhill big style.'

Hackney had gone the way of so many other London tracks before it. In the 1950s and 1960s the Greyhound Racing Authority had bought several tracks and continued to do so until the property boom of the early 1970s when the company renamed itself GRA Property Trust and started redeveloping many of its sites for residential and commercial use. West Ham and Clapton were early casualties, followed by White City in 1984 and Harringay in 1994?

Once upon a time, even a hippie haven like Glastonbury had a local unlicensed or 'flapping' track as they're commonly known. But in less than ten years, eleven NGRC tracks had closed down in the UK, mainly for financial reasons: Bolton, Bristol, Canterbury, Cradley Heath, Dundee, Hackney, Middlesbrough, Powerhall in Edinburgh, Ramsgate, Swaffham and Wembley are gone and others are earmarked for the chop.

The first innovation in gambling to hit the dogs was the legalisation of off-course gambling, which started the high-street betting shop revolution. Then in 1966, betting tax was introduced, which dealt a further blow to the dogs. The advent of television didn't help either, which seems ironic given the reliance sport now has on TV revenue, advertising and PR. By the mid eighties the industry was in turmoil and attendances had dropped to an all-time low of 3.7 million in 1985. In 1993 the high-street bookies introduced evening opening hours, once again putting the squeeze on the beleaguered track promoters.

The death of the London dog track in many ways ran parallel to the slow, grinding demise of the traditional working-class in the capital. Huge swathes of north, south and west London had yielded to the juggernaut of gentrification. Once upon a time you couldn't *pay* folk to move to Islington, Brixton or Notting Hill – nowadays a lock-up garage in these parts will set you back telephone numbers. But the property boom hit the east of the city first and hardest. Thatcher's fabricated eighties boom turned the Docklands into a yuppie citadel and spawned a generation of chinless wonders. It was out with the fishwives and in with the fish knives.

A decade later, much of what remained of the Old East End proletariat, with their two-up two-down accents, foreign tongues and exotica, was giving way to a New East End elite of artists' quarters in Hoxton and Shoreditch, writers' ghettoes in Stepney and Whitechapel, and actors' enclaves in Bethnal Green and Hackney. And as we all know, shit comes in threes. Where the workers and immigrants had blazed a trail for the artists and dilettantes, the corporates and moneyed classes would follow. The heart of cockney London was being priced out to the Far East End of Tower Hamlets, Waltham Forest and Redbridge to make way for the rich. The East End of the Cable Street Riots, the Blitz, the Krays, the Swinging Sixties and the Melting-pot Seventies was over. All that was left in its place was a soap opera.

The fate of the dog track in many ways mirrors the demise of many parts of my personal history. For instance, where I was born, the Mothers' Hospital in Lower Clapton, Hackney (E8), is now a private housing estate; my old secondary school Ruckholt Manor in Leyton (E10) is a car dealership; and my former primary school, an Edwardian edifice on the border of Leyton and Stratford (E15), is now scheduled for demolition too. And what would become of that? A shopping centre, a hypermarket? I bet Eton or Harrow never wind up as a fucking Tesco superstore.

But things are looking up, in some ways at least, for the dogs. According to the BGRB up to four million punters are going through the turnstiles each year, gambling an estimated £1.6 billion. Throughout Europe, the US, Australia and the Far East greyhounds race competitively and the explosion of internet betting means that a punter in Kuala Lumpur can now, in real time, lose his shalwar-qamiz on a dog running over 6500 miles away in Nottingham, Swindon or Sunderland. And Wembley plc has confirmed plans to build a £7 million stadium in Liverpool – one of the few new tracks in the UK for thirty years.

The government kept banging on about how it was going to liberalise the gaming laws to the extent that soon you'd be able to open a crap shoot in an infants school. It seemed pretty obvious to me that once gambling licences became easier to get than TV licences, and the archaic rules surrounding table and card games were deregulated, more casinos would open up. But what offered the infrastructure, gambling know-how, equipment, staff and space to invest in such a cash-intensive, growth business like a casino? A dog track of course. In typically schizoid fashion I was back to thinking I had made a smart move with this greyhound lark. With the expertise I was amassing, a couple of years down the line I would be making money hand over fist.

chapter 15

I lived in a rough neighbourhood. Two doors down from my flat was a knocking shop, crack heads and junkies fixed up in doorways nearby and on Friday and Saturday nights there was always some creep beating up his old lady. A couple of poxy-looking local drunks had taken up residency on the front doorstep of the flat. Throughout the summer, on sweltering days when the tarmac on the stoop would melt, the drunks would freak out as their beer cans, cigarettes and pants stuck to the steps. Leaning out of the sitting-room window, cursing, I'd shoo them away like flies as they looked up with their dirty, rodent faces, before skulking off down the street, scratching and sniffing. I was waiting, just waiting, for the opportunity to get medieval on 'em and throw a bucket of hot steaming piss all over their mangy heads. Man, I was born in the wrong fucking century.

The streets of Paddington were not paved with gold but littered with the detritus of human failure and misery. Sometimes I would look out my window and grieve for humanity. In another, virtual, movie life, I'd be Travis Bickle. *Some day a real rain will come and wash all this scum off the streets.* But on other brighter days, usually when I was sleepwalking or stoned, I'd look out the window at those same scumbags and go all Oscar Wilde: 'We are all in the gutter, but some of us are looking at the stars.' How quaint.

Now it was nearly time to say goodbye to all that. I was on the move again, the seventh time in four years. If I had had a tent, a top hat and juggling balls I'd be a circus. This nomadic lifestyle had to stop. Margot and I were going to try living together in a few weeks' time. Her father owned a swanky pad on the Thames, in Battersea. He agreed to let us stay there for a while, as a social experiment, to see if we could handle each other 24/7. If it worked out, maybe one day we'd buy a place together, settle down, have kids and go insane.

Kevin was running in the 19:30, the opening race at the Stow. Many punters never bother with the first or second race on the card, as it's always puppies and scrubbers at the start of the show. As you move down the card the quality of the dogs gets better, with the real triers and form dogs making up the meat of the schedule.

Anyway, Kevin was due a win. I was having a party at the flat that night so I couldn't make it to the track. Instead, I popped over the road to the bookies to watch the race on SIS. Seeing him up there on the screen for the first time was like seeing my daughter in a nativity play. I was filled with a goose-pimply pride as the kennel hand paraded him in front of Britain's compulsive gambling public. He opened out at 2–1. I had a score on him. Aw, fuck it. I stuck another tenner on the nose. He went to 7–4, then 6–4. The way the price was moving suggested he had 'connections' at the track. At the off he was evens. The boy was turning into a little steamer.

'*Hare's approaching* . . .' yakked the TV commentator. Kevin fell out of trap four like a drunk leaving a club on New Year's Eve. Jesus. He then clattered into the one dog like a 'screw' at the first bend but managed to make up ground down the home straight. 'Go on, boy, go on.' My fist clenched, as per, I willed him on as he closed in on the leader, Brickfield Fox. 'Oh, for fuck's sake Kev . . .' He finished second, three-quarters of a length behind the winner. If he'd trapped, i.e. had a good break at the start, he would've won. He ran on and was first to the pick up (the cuddly toy used to calm the dogs down after a race), which meant he had a bit left in the tank. Lazy sonofabitch.

That was six defeats on the bounce, three under my ownership. So much for him being a one in four dog. If he were a professional boxer, a human athlete with the same record, he'd be finished by now. Some dude with a big mouth, electroshock hair and sovereign-ringed knuckles would've turned him into a human punch-bag by now.

That night I put defeat behind me and partied like it was 1999. I'd hired a 1000-watt rig, busting speakers and decks – the works. A few friends spun some tunes and we drove the rats out from under the floorboards for a night. There was plenty of booze, good music and other shit to distract me. Around 4a.m. two Environmental Health officers from Westminster Council arrived and served me with a noise pollution notice. 'We've had complaints about the noise,' they said. 'Thank you,' I said, slamming the door in their faces. It hadn't been a bad day after all.

chapter 16

At the track, interaction with your dog is brief and usually immediately after its race. Once Kevin had done his thing, i.e. lost, I'd go over to the paddock and beckon one of the kennel hands to bring him out after he'd been cleaned up, given a rub down and a drink of water. He'd mince over to me, tongue hanging out as he caught his breath, and he stare at me with those doleful eyes as if to say, 'Who the fuck are you?' I'd pet him and chat with the kennel hand about his performance, or lack of, and for a moment I'd forget about the £2500 and the reality that, like a basketball team of pygmies, he'd never amount to anything.

Our post-race love-ins were very short. I'd get three, maybe five, minutes tops with him. The atmosphere in the paddock was always frenetic and the kennel hands were usually too busy to hang around; besides, security and safety are always an issue. The Stow will not, cannot, allow a greyhound to be out of the paddock while a race is underway. In fact, apart from Kevin and the other track fodder, pet dogs or animals of any description are strictly verboten on the premises. But on Sundays you can visit the kennels and hang out with your dog for a couple of hours. Here was an opportunity for Kevin and me to bond. I could take him for walks, give him a bit of cheese or some other treat, maybe some coke or PCP to perk him up, and generally act like I actually had something going on with him.

Going to the kennels was a bit like visiting a sick relative or a friend in a mental institution. Initial contact was always a bit clumsy. One of the kennel hands would fetch Kevin from his hutch, present him to me while I cooed, 'Come to Daddy,' with my arms outstretched. Kevin would give me that dumb look again, trying to figure out who the hell I was, stick his tail between his legs, and scurry behind the kennel hand, shitting himself, literally. However, as soon as I got hold of the reins, stuck that muzzle on, and gave a few reassuring rubs, baby we were flying, off down the lane into the Suffolk sticks.

'Don't overdo it now, David,' Linda would say if Kevin was racing within the next day or two. The dogs love to break free from the confines of the kennel and stretch their legs but too much exercise is not good for a greyhound. Being a sprint animal they need to conserve their energy so, technically speaking, giving a greyhound long walks is the easiest way to nobble it. 'In *theory*,' Linda told me, 'all you've got to do to slow a dog down is overwork it. But don't you go doing that, David.'

But why slow down your own dog?

Well, to speed a dog up *significantly* in the short term you have to blatantly break the rules: you have to dope it. Some form of amphetamine would work. But the problem with that is: (a) it's wrong; (b) it's wrong; and (c) it's wrong. Doping harms the animal, cheats the system, the punters and your competitors and, to be really officious, it 'undermines the integrity of greyhound racing'.

As for slowing down the other dogs in a race, well, even if you were that way inclined, pulling it off would require such sophisticated subterfuge that you'd probably be putting your Machiavellian skills to profitable use in some other field like politics or organised crime. That's not to say it didn't use to go on. I know a petty crook who claimed that back in the Sixties he was paid to break into kennels and dope dogs. These days people are too clued up and security is too tight at most kennels to get away with that sort of thing on the regular at all but the most provincial tracks. But overworking your own dog, now that is another matter. Alternatively, as one old boy I knew in Sheffield used to do when he owned greyhounds, you can 'lay it up', i.e. have it lie around for days on the sofa doing absolutely nothing, so it becomes listless and apathetic and ready for the fix.

Once you had slowed it down sufficiently, for say two or three races, its odds would lengthen with the bookies and maybe the race manager would drop it down a grade too. The most anyone who wasn't 'in the know' would think was that the dog was a bit peaky. After all, even a greyhound is entitled to have the odd off day. You would then start shaping it up, exercising it and massaging it in readiness for a big hit. When the right race came along you'd have a big punt and clean up with the bookies. All this of course is *theory*. Anything can happen in practice.

One trainer I met on my travels told me that he had slowed a dog down on the repeated insistence of a rich owner who had several dogs at his kennels. The trainer felt pressured by the owner and against his better judgement he overworked the dog for him. After a week of long, hard walks the dog raced . . . and won! The owner and his cronies lost several thousand pounds after backing another runner in the same race. To make matters worse the dog went on a losing streak despite being put back on a normal training schedule, costing the owner even more money.

To keep a dog or bitch in tiptop shape you can't let them shag either, unless you're into the mating game, in which case you let 'em have it plenty. The chances of Kevin getting his end away however were pretty slim. It would take a miracle for him to reach stud dog status. Only the best of the best dogs ever get their groove on. In the meantime he could only dream of getting his end away. Whenever I took the little virgin out for a walk down the lane, I would remind him of the carnal delights that awaited him if he bucked up his ideas and actually won something, anything.

'Hey, Kevin. I might be able to fix it for you to get a little, er, you know, *action*. But you have to help me out here. You have to *win* boy, *win*. Hey, Kevin? Kevin? I'm fucking talking to you.'

Kevin would just amble along the lane, sniffing, the ground, the air, my crotch. I'm speaking to the dog, trying to give him a pep talk and all he does is look at butterflies, flowers and shit. Belgian Patrick had dubbed him 'The Poet' due to his acute sensitivity and introspective airs and graces. I had gone in search of a Linford Christie and come back with a Linton Kwesi Johnson. Did he not realise I had competing interests on a Sunday? By rights, Kevin was at the bottom of a dominical food chain. Sundays were generally the only days I got a chance to spend time with my daughter. Then, as a season ticket holder at Spurs, many of their home games were on a Sunday. Moreover, I had to do the lovey-dovey picnic in the park routine, shopping, art galleries and all that girly shit with Margot.

Sundays, don't you just love 'em? Kevin and I would always take the same route: right out the compound's gates and down the lane, following the same path I took driving into Imperial Kennels. I never strayed into the adjoining fields for fear of giving some farmer a bit of target practice. I was also concerned about Kevin walking into sheep-dip or manure or eating a festering morsel of dead rat or badger pooh.

For safety's sake I'd usually keep Kevin muzzled while out walking. The common sight of muzzled greyhounds has helped foster an erroneous belief among the public that they are a vicious breed, but on the whole they're harmless. The muzzle is only there to stop them taking a nip out of each other while racing and eating crap off the ground.

So I'm walking Kevin. Maybe if he tried to take a chunk out of me he'd show a little gumption. When the odd wild rabbit darted out of the bushes more often than not he'd be indifferent. Sometimes he'd strain on the leash, I'd hold it tight and we'd chase after it. Other times, at the sight of a rabbit, his ears would prick and then flop down again as if to say, 'What, you again? Please!'

Despite being a sight hound Kevin could sniff like the best of them. He would walk the lane, burrowing his shiny little nose into the undergrowth, sniffing out a variety of scents from bundles of little critters. His ritual was to make a series of sniffs followed by a quick leak, so that the sequence would go something like: sniff-sniff-sniff-sniff-piss-sniff-sniff-sniff-piss and so on for more than an hour. And of course he'd keep snuggling in there, looking for love.

'See, this is your problem, Kevin,' I'd say. 'You're too soft. You need the killer instinct, boy.' He'd stop, look up at me with those puppy dog eyes and snuggle his schnozzle right in my schnitzel. 'Aw, you soppy little fucker.' I'd give him big hugs, rubs, cuddles and fuss. He loved that shit. So did I. But listen, I drew the line at that dog-licking-your-face nonsense though. Think about it. Even the fattest, most unwieldy mutt is capable of munching the living daylights out of its gonads, which is why you never see a dog renting a porno movie, reaching for the top shelf at Smiths or buying Kleenex. The fact that a dog spends 50 per cent of its every waking moment licking its crotch, usually after it's just relieved itself (which it spends most of the other 50 per cent of its time doing), means that at any given moment it could paste the Sistine Chapel with enough cack to keep *Location Location Location* busy for years.

We would walk down the lane, Kevin and me, me and Kevin, like a couple of old swells: one man and his dog. Sundays being a day of rest and reflection and all, whenever I took Kevin for a walk, I would often ruminate, meditate and philosophise and ask myself, *what in God's name, does he think about?*

'So, what are you thinking about, Kevin, you know, in general?' Blank look. Nose in crotch. Sniff of the air. Kevin did not really say much in response. In fact, he didn't say anything at all. Greyhounds hunt silently, which means they seldom bark. It also means they speak even less. This preoccupation with non-verbal communication and an apparent lack of emotion has also fostered a notion that greyhounds are aloof, unfeeling and detached from reality – a bit like the Royal Family.

The truth is, Kevin probably could not think further than his next meal, so psychoanalysing him was a waste of time. As one old Jewish proverb goes, 'What do hens dream of? Of Millet.' Alternatively, as the poet Rupert Brooke pondered, do fish believe in Heaven? 'Fish say, they have their stream and pond; but is there anything Beyond?' The answer is: no. For man nor beast, there is nothing out there except nothing. Zilch, nish, nitto. There is no heaven; there is no hell. God told me so in a vision I once had on acid.

My conclusion then was that greyhounds did not think in a logical, stream-of-consciousness way. It was important for me to come to accept that Kevin was a thoughtless, soulless mutt – nothing but a cuddly running machine, a 35 mph teddy bear. I needed to come to this conclusion to prepare myself for the time when he made the journey away from me, into the unknown, and possibly the Kitty Kat factory.

Apart from taking Kevin for a walk, Sundays at the kennels also gave me an opportunity to get the odd titbit of information or idle gossip from the other owners over a cuppa. One of Linda's favourite owners and close friends was Big Al. His daughter Kelly had worked for Linda at Imperial since the 1990s. Big Al was a twenty-stone retired copper and fulltime Yorkshireman who had a number of dogs at the kennels. 'I wanted to be a teacher when I was at school,' Big Al told me, 'but I thumped a prefect and was gonna be thrown out. I saw an ad for the Met on the careers board . . . wound up being a protection officer for twenty-eight years out of thirty-four years service.' As a young man, Big Al had obviously shown the requisite qualities of a copper.

After a stroke in 1983, he lost his 'licence to kill', switched to other duties and retired in 1996. Now he did driving for the military. When I say Big Al was big, I mean *very* big. Big Al was so big he could have had his own seat at the UN. His somewhat more petite wife, Mavis, made exceedingly good cakes and biscuits, which she would bring every Sunday to the kennels for Linda. No wonder Big Al was so big.

Big Al got into the dogs in 1993, via a circuitous route, after his youngest son bought a greyhound with a bunch of college buddies, who, just as I had, thought it would be a 'good idea'.

'He bought a dog with his mates and went with a trainer called Ernie Wiley,' said Big Al, 'and while she was running they were very happy. Then all of a sudden she went lame and was off for a little while. They didn't pay the bills and it started to mount up for a fair time. In the end they couldn't pay the bill and cleared off so Daddy here squared it up.'

According to Big Al, the dearly departed Wiley wasn't the best trainer in the world. 'We used to go to the kennels on a Sunday, feed 'em and Christ knows what else and then take 'em for a long walk, not knowing that they might be running the next day and we'd walked the legs off 'em. Ernie never used to say, "Oh don't take that dog out he's racing tomorrow" like Linda does. We used to take 'em for two-, three-, four-mile walks! We didn't know any different in those days.

'We went in at the deep end and bought two three-month-old pups from a litter but unfortunately one developed a hip disorder when he was only a babe so he went to the great man in the sky. Eventually I acquired his sister. Then my son decided he and another mate wanted a dog, so they bought Ridgefield Millie. And it went from there. My son knew more about greyhound racing than most of the trainers did, certainly about the breeding. He could name the dams and sires of every dog out there. He was only eighteen at the time. He studied greyhounds and got into it. He didn't gamble. He used to have a bet but nothing special. Eventually we went to Linda in '97. We got fed up of Wiley and messing about.'

Wiley's messing about had led to one of Big Al's promising pups, Crypal Pips, a.k.a Cassie, being seriously injured during an unauthorised schooling session.

'Honestly, Dave, you should've seen it. It were down to the bone, the muscle was ripped apart. I thought it'd be a miracle if she ever ran again. Wiley said it was a training accident but we had her checked out. You could see the teeth marks. She'd been savaged. The other dogs had turned on her and ripped her apart and Wiley tried to keep it a secret. He didn't have the guts to tell me. Anyway, we told Linda about it and she said, "You can't have that," so we picked her up and brought her home and then took her to Linda. And that was it. We moved everything to Linda's kennel. She even managed to get Cassie into such good shape she made the top grade at Romford.'

Big Al was not the first person to tell me about dogs being ill-treated or neglected, but I had not seen any cruelty at first hand, either by owners or trainers. The odorousness of animal abuse that trailed greyhound racing like a bad case of flatulence however was inescapable.

'There was a demo last night at the Stow,' boomed Big Al as Linda doled out another round of teas. 'Some old bag and around half a dozen of the great unwashed were outside, ranting about cruelty and that. They had a poster with a greyhound on it lying on the ground . . . dead I suppose, with a brick tied round its neck. They pull the same old pictures out every time and blow 'em up out of proportion. Bloody rent-a-mob.'

'We've heard it all before, David,' said Linda, shaking her head. 'Two sugars?'

'Yes please,' I replied.

'Talk of cruelty, banning racing and all that . . .'

'Go on. Go for a walk with your dad,' said Linda's mum, a.k.a. 'Nan'. One of the kennel hands had brought Kevin over to me for his afternoon stroll. 'When you get round the corner you can show him all those bruises I gave ya!' Nan was a sprightly silver-haired old bird, eighty-six going on sixty-eight. She was always at the kennels on a Sunday, mucking in and wisecracking. Her and Linda were a regular double act. Nan had a habit of often asking Linda a question she'd already given her the answer to. Linda would tut and roll her eyes while Nan carried on gassing. I don't think it was senility, just a sly wind up. 'Yeah, I had to give him a right good kicking this morning, right in the gut,' Nan added, playfully squeezing Kevin.

'Did you have your hobnail boots on when you did it, Mum?' piped Linda, 'cos it ain't the same with trainers on.' OK, I get the picture. Such is the sensitivity surrounding the constant charges of cruelty levelled at greyhound racing that dog people have to make a joke of it else they'd never stop flipping their lids.

'I wouldn't have a problem having a horse or a dog put down rather than send it to a bad home,' said another owner who cruised in and out of the conversation as Linda, Nan and me loitered by the kitchen doorway. She was a matronly woman who said she had once worked with 'unruly boys' and had met Frank Bruno as a fifteen-year-old. I was just about to find out how unruly Bruno had been as a kid when Kevin started straining on his lead, heading for the gate. All the talk of beatings and euthanasia finally was too much for his sensitive little soul, so I took him off up the lane to marvel at the Suffolk countryside, its pig farms, its piles of manure . . .

When I got back to the kennels Big Al was still there, this time with a little silver-grey Italian greyhound, no bigger than a shoebox. He was called Eric. Eric belonged to Big Al's son. The dog was a handful, lithe and slippery. They made quite a contrast – Big Al and Little Eric. For an ex-copper, Big Al was OK. And to think, there was a time when the only way I'd be in the same room as a cop was to have my fingerprints taken. Now I was being invited round for tea and biscuits. How times had changed.

chapter 17

Margot looked anxious. 'I think I'm going to freak out,' she said, grabbing my arm. 'Look at them: they've all got big ears and bald patches with crazy clumps of hair coming out of their heads.'

'Calm down, babe,' I said, almost reassuringly. 'Everything's cool.' The crowd was swelling rapidly, squeezing us in, pushing us forward towards the track. I downed my drink with the aid of someone's elbow and pulled Margot closer to me. Then I made a face and took a snapshot with my camera. I loved this cultural safari shit.

I needed to earn some Brownie points after a run of writing some 'controversial' material for the *Evening Standard*. My shit hadn't gone down too well with the ladies, especially Margot. Chicks are always blabbing about empathy and honesty and shit like that but when it comes to affairs of the heart most women I know prefer well-crafted white lies to brutally dark truths. Consequently, my self-confessional brand of journalism re women was interpreted as an anthology of misogyny. I guess with features entitled 'Giving Birth Turned Me Off' and 'I Could Never Be Faithful' what did I expect?

So I had to appease the woman. I thought a romantic weekend away would do the trick, so I booked a couple of flights and a room at the swanky Morrison hotel in Dublin. The interiors were designed by the fashionista John Rocha; and at £180 a night minimum for a double, I knew it would be somewhere approaching the lifestyle that Margot was accustomed to. As luck would have it, it just so happened that the romantic weekend coincided with the Paddy Power Irish Greyhound Derby, the world's richest greyhound race. Yeah, yeah, I know what you're thinking. Just call me Mr Lover Man, OK?

I looked at my watch: 9.15p.m. It was fast approaching the big race. Margot and I had been cruising around Ireland for a few days in a, er, Hyundai, and had reached the end of our road trip, Shelbourne Park Stadium, via the Ring of Kerry, the National Stud and the Irish St Leger at the Curragh. I'd landed a couple of modest winners on the gee-gees that afternoon and felt confident. Whether it was horses or dogs I didn't know one race from another to be honest. Betting on an animal still seemed absurd to me, regardless of a race's history, prestige or the prize money at stake, but a little flutter never did anybody any harm.

Three months earlier, even at the English Derby, I would've prided myself on being able to watch every race on the card and not bet a penny. But as a fully paid up disciple of the dogs it now felt irreligious not to have the odd punt, especially in a gambling Mecca like Ireland. In the run up to the Derby, Shelbourne Park bookie Ted Hegarty had laid one of the biggest bets ever at the track: €30,000–€4000 resulting in a winner, Fast Kodiak. The same punter who had that touch landed €16,000 for a €1000 stake. I could only dream about such gambles. I wouldn't even stake that kind of dough in a game of Monopoly.

I left Margot in the teeming crowd of *Father Ted* look-alikes, 'blown-ins' and Saturday night punters and headed for the bar. It was six or seven deep. Arms crawled over arms, people guffawed, multiple orders went in, cash tills rang as reams of newly adopted euros went back and forth across the bar. 'Who d'you have to sleep with to get a drink round here?' Wisecracks and asides flowed with estuaries of Murphys, Guinness and whiskey and cokes. Unlike the English Derby at Wimbledon, where people feel suffocated by the burgeoning crowds and scuffles break out, at Sherbourne Park, a far smaller track in comparison, punters hold their own, and their drink, in the cramped inebriated atmosphere. And love every minute of it.

'Where are ye from, big man?' asked a chap at the bar, his broad shoulders squeezed into a tight double-breasted blazer. 'I'm from London,' I said, craning. 'The East End originally. I'm about to move to Battersea, but now I live not far from Kilburn. D'you know it?' He had to know it. Kilburn was the Irish quarter of London, Little Dublin you might say.

'Ah Kilburn. I know it, I know it. I lived there for a while a few years ago. I was working in London you know. Not a bad place . . .' Then he leant into me and whispered. 'If you discount all the fucking Paddies! Ha ha ha . . .'

I have a lot of time for the Irish. In fact, I am something of an honorary Irishman. A year earlier, just for the hell of it, I had followed the Republic of Ireland to Iran for a crucial second-leg World Cup qualifier. There was no beer for love nor money in Tehran, all the women were dressed as Ninjas and you couldn't piss without some state security monkey inspecting your foreskin but it was great to hang out in a foreign country with a bunch of football fans who spoke your language but weren't into Nazi salutes and killing the locals.

I admire the Irish sense of positive cultural identity, pride and respect. When I was around sixteen or seventeen a big pikey paid me a tenner to smash his right hand with a paving slab, just so he could avoid a bare-knuckle fight with some meathead in a pub car park. 'As God is my witness,' he had growled, 'if I have to fight that man I'll fucking kill 'im.' I'd never met Big Pikey before – he just stopped me in the street. But I had no reason to disbelieve him. He had a face carved out of granite and fists of stone. He was built like Old Trafford. If he was a bottle job, what the beejaysus did the *other* guy look like? Big Pikey explained that it was bad form to back out of a fight for no good reason; it had something to do with the didicoy code of honour. A serious injury was a legitimate excuse not to scrap though. So I smashed his right hand with a 2ft × 2ft, inch-thick paving slab. And he gave me a tenner ... with his left hand. The right one was now completely fucked. Now I know what you're thinking, but look, £10 was a lot of money to a delinquent teenager back in the early eighties. Besides, it was an act of humanity. I'd saved one man's life and another from fifteen years in jail. Yeah, yeah, I know. I'm a regular Good Samaritan.

Of the many things I like about Ireland – the scenery, the hospitality and the easy-going pace of life – I particularly like the way the Irish have subverted the English language. For instance, if I am having a quiet pint in a pub in Skibbereen and someone asks, 'Are ya here for the craic?' this is not an invitation to free-base cocaine hydrochloride. See, us blacks and the Irish are on a level: we go back a long, long way – right back to the plantations of slavery, where the Micks held the whip and the niggers did all the fucking work. OK, let's forget that one. But there is an affinity between these two tough breeds of men, a shared earthiness and a collective 'soul'. We had both had our languages, land and culture raped, pillaged and plundered by successive English tyrants. Ordinary blacks and Irish had shared the same itinerant path for centuries, working like slaves, treated like dogs. As Mark Lamarr lookalike Jimmy Rabbitte reflected in *The Commitments*, 'The Irish are the blacks of Europe,' which is a touching, empathetic sentiment. The only fly in the ointment or 'nigger in the woodpile' with this concept is that *black people* are the blacks of Europe. But, hey, why be pedantic.

It was nearly the appointed hour of the final – 9.42p.m. I eventually got to the bar. Negotiating the crowd with a bottle of Moët, two flutes, a packet of dry roasted peanuts and a bag of ready salted would be too much, so I grabbed a pint, a G&T, forgot the snacks and headed back to the stands by the track.

I got back to find Margot still looking bemused. We had a modest punt on the final and waited for the bell. The stadium lights dimmed, the crowd exploded, the traps flew open and an almighty roar nearly lifted me off my feet.

Bursting out of trap five, the 11–8 favourite Bypass Byway was first to the bend, his sleek black frame a blur as Droopys Agassi challenged on the outside at the turn, a neck behind. By the second bend Bypass Byway had stretched his lead to a length over Droopys Rhys, with Droopys Agassi in third and Tyrur Bello, Heavenly Hero and Tamna Rose trailing into the back straight. POW! Bypass Byway put the pedal to the metal and kicked it down the back straight like he was on rocket-fuelled roller blades. Within nanoseconds he'd gone four or five lengths clear of the chasing pack with half the course blitzed. I'd never seen a dog move that fast. Correction: this wasn't a dog it was a goddamned Kawasaki 1100 in a dog suit. The pace was unbelievable. By the third bend the pack seemed to implode as they scrambled to make the turn, bouncing and checking their way out of the running, leaving Bypass Byway to romp home, smashing the track record, clocking 29.42 seconds over the 550-yard race and shaving 15 spots off the previous record. Now remember, Kevin was just about clocking 30.00 seconds at 475 metres. When I say that Bypass dog was fast I mean he was *fast*. (28 metres further in 0.20 seconds faster than Kevin's best time to date. Every dog certainly has its day.)

I had burned a score on Droopys Rhys, the second favourite, but in a way it was a pleasure to lose money to see such a display of speed and agility. It's not every day that you get to see some of the fastest creatures on the planet in full flight without the threat of them taking a chunk out of you. Cheetahs and impala just do not play ball the way greyhounds do.

When it came to handing out the trophy and cheque for a hundred big ones to the winner, there wasn't just some corporate lackey on the podium doing the honours. No sir. They had Bertie Ahern, the *Taoiseach* handing out the prizes. Bertie Ahern. The fucking Prime Minister! Can you imagine Tony Blair standing in the pissing rain at Wimbledon Stadium handing out the goods at the English Greyhound Derby? Admittedly, as my Irish connections later stated, Bertie Ahern would 'go to the opening of a car door' to get his ugly mug in the papers. He had had problems with the construction of an Irish national stadium, so he needed all the good PR he could muster. Across the pond, Tony Blair was facing his own problems in Parliament over the ban on hunting with dogs, a ban which incidentally could have serious repercussions on greyhound racing.

However, given that the Bord na gCon is a commercial quango, established in 1958 under special legislation by the Irish government, Bertie's appearance was not out of the ordinary. Irish greyhound racing is as much a state institution as a national obsession.

Ireland had embraced greyhound racing in 1927, a year after it had been introduced in England. The Irish too had fallen truly, madly, deeply in love with the sport from its inception and although the love affair was waning on the Sceptred Isle it was going from strength to strength on the Emerald one.

While prize money in Britain had hardly changed in twenty years, in Ireland it had grown progressively from €2.4m in 1995 to €7.4m in 2002. Right across the board the industry was booming. The number of race meetings was increasing annually and attendances had nearly doubled in seven years to over a million punters. Sponsorship was up and total betting turnover had gone from €28.9m in 1995 to a staggering €105.8m in 2002.

Having embraced the EU and all the lovely little euros that went with it, Ireland was undergoing a boom. Property prices were up, wages were up and many good old boys who had made big dough in America and Australia were coming back to the homeland with a lot of hard currency, further bolstering the economy. These factors combined with increased sponsorship and promotion meant the future looked bright for Ireland's greyhound industry.

However, this boom wasn't without its costs. Sadly, in Ireland, greyhounds are often treated like disposable dogs. The kindest trainers leave them in dog pounds to be put down on the cheap, but many are not so kind. The dominance of Irish breeding is a numbers game: the more dogs you breed, the higher quality you will produce; but you'll also produce more runts, dogs who just won't chase.

Some former racing dogs are used as resident 'blood donors' for other breeds at the Veterinary School in University College Dublin. What a transmogrification: from dice on legs to walking blood banks. An estimated fourteen greyhounds are dissected every year there so student vets can learn about animal anatomy.

I was biting into my toast in the Morrison dining room, thinking about how much Kevin would be worth as vet scrap when I had an eureka moment. *Why not buy another dog at an auction here in Ireland for, say, 200 quid, take him to Britain, change Kevin's race name to something like Electric Lovebox, change the new dog's name to Zussies Boy, sell Kevin (I mean, Electric Lovebox), recoup the £2500 I paid for him and pocket the difference.* My sleeping partners in the Headline Syndicate would never know the difference.

Then another thought occurred to me: not only was this idea ridiculous, it was also conspiracy to commit fraud. I could go to jail for just *thinking* about this shit. I'd lose my publishing deal, my livelihood and ruin what was left of my crumbling reputation. I'd never work in this, or that, town again. Aw, it was just the hangover talking. To assuage my guilt for thinking so *crudely*, after breakfast I decided to call Linda to see how Kevin had performed the night before. The news was shocking.

'He won,' said Linda. 'He ran really well.'

'Bloody Nora,' I said.

The result was typical of my role as his absentee father. There he goes, making his debut in the school play, scoring his first goal for the team, losing his virginity, and where's Pops? Knocking 'em back like an eedjit in Dublin. On the night that Bypass Byway won the Irish Greyhound Derby and pawed £100,000 into owner

Michael Kearney's pocket, Zussies Boy, at his ninth attempt of asking, won his first race. Things were looking up. I had just earned £65. Smashing . . .

chapter 18

Thanks to Kevin's first win and the few bob I had pocketed in Ireland I started to grow in confidence with my betting. Big mishtake. But I could only heed Linda's advice not to gamble for so long. I didn't want to stand on the sidelines like a kibitzer. I lived by the maxim 'experience teaches wisdom' and given that Kevin wasn't going to earn his keep in prize money I had to find alternative ways of financing his future. Gambling was the way forward. As long as I kept my stakes small I'd be safe. I just needed to earn enough to pay the kennel bills.

If I was going to be serious about gambling I needed to get myself organised. First up, I decided to set aside a modest bankroll of £500, from which I'd reinvest half of any winnings, gradually increasing my roll and stakes accordingly. As a safety precaution I'd only ever take £100 to the track with me to gamble, that way I could limit my losses at any given meeting. Furthermore, to be a dedicated punter you need a system. Any dummy knows that. So having bought myself a couple of idiot's guides to gambling I got down to work with a notepad, a calculator, the *Racing Post*, and a pen behind my ear.

The easiest thing in the world to do, if you want to call it a system, is to back the favourite. According to Tracy Cooper the Stow had the highest strike rate for favourites in the country – at least 35 per cent. In one of the books I'd recently purchased on 'betting systems that win' the author claimed that around 32 per cent of favourites win on average at every meet, with second favourites winning 22 per cent of the time. More tellingly, the underdog or rank outsider wins little more than 5 per cent of races on a card. Or put another way, he loses 95 per cent of the time. But you have to judge these percentages against the odds. While a good number of favourites indeed win at the Stow, many of them are short-priced. On a Saturday night there is so much action in the betting ring that open-race favourites will come in at evens, 1–2, 4–7 . . . crazy odds. Backing favourites indiscriminately is a false economy.

One way to overcome this problem is to be discerning about your favourites and second favourites or find a good source of tips and use a staking method, like the Martingale, which is designed for roulette and requires you to double your stake after a loss. The idea is, statistically speaking, if you stick rigidly to one selection, i.e. favourites or a trap number, eventually it must come up. Also, to always be in profit you have to back a selection at evens or greater. Betting odds-on doesn't work in your favour. Still awake? Right. Now all this is great on paper but in reality if you double a £1 stake over the course of a 12-race card, always backing the favourite, and no favourite wins you'll be £5595 out of pocket. Do the math.

Then there is the Fibonacci progression system in which you increase your stakes in units of 1, 1, 2, 3, 5, 8, 13, 21, 34, 55, 89, 144, 233, 377 . . . and so on after every loss; the Labouchère or cancellation system; the O'Hare Straddle or Ronnie Biggs – an alternate doubling scheme that works by borrowing a large amount of cash on a short-term basis, setting aside enough money for a ticket on the next plane to South America. Bet the rest on one favourite at even money. If you win, return the principal and retire on the rest. Otherwise, use the plane ticket. Or how about backing the second favourite with the field in a forecast? Alternatively you can 'play the numbers', i.e. bet the same two trap numbers religiously in a reverse forecast. Or what about working the win percentage of each trap?

The world and its aunt are full of sure-fire betting systems. The internet is the worst culprit. What a treasure trove of useless betting systems, strategies and techniques designed to separate the fool from his money with as little effort as possible it is. One example is the P=MCR system, which was either dreamt up by an acid-dropping twit or is an April Fool's Day joke that won't go away. This is how it works: (1) watch the first race at any given meeting; (2) subtract the smaller trap number from the larger one, i.e. 1 beats 3, 3–1 = 2; (3) back the resultant trap number in the next race; (4) if it loses, repeat: i.e. 5 beats 4, 5– 4 = 1, back the one dog next race, double your initial stake. The inventor claims that the system is 'so simple, I challenge you to find ANY meeting on the dogs where the system loses in any 12-race run'. What the numskull failed to mention was: (5) lose your bollocks. Such a system is illogical and financially suicidal. There are countless clowns out there peddling systems of one description or another and many more red noses buying into them. In the end I decided to stick to the basics and rely on good old intuition and inside information. Oh, and luck.

Whenever I went to the track in daylight hours I always felt like I was goofing off, like I should be somewhere else, doing something more productive, more important, more . . . grown up. The track affords adults the opportunity to act like children, to indulge in the bizarre, mindless, selfish and often unexplainable pastime that is greyhound racing.

One afternoon I was in the toilets at the Stow and overheard two punters bitching about the facilities. It turned out that the Stow was set to receive £100,000 from the BGRB to renovate their loos. Meanwhile there were plenty of broke-arse tracks in the country without air-con who had their dogs locked in kennels for up to six hours on long hot summer's days. It is amazing the kind of shit you pick up in a public toilet at a dog track. It is the sort of place where you might overhear someone plotting to have his factory burnt down or his missus bumped off.

I was starting to really obsess about this game now.

Eavesdropping on conversations in public toilets? Did I really hate my own company that much? Was there such urgency to get out of the house? Initially I'd go to the dogs only when Kevin was running but now I was hitting the track three or four meets a week. I'd also nip into the bookies when I couldn't make it to the Stow and have a punt, sometimes even on the gee-gees, which I knew absolutely nothing about. Then there were other bets . . . nothing much, a bit of football, draws, home wins, away wins, half-time results, correct scores, yellow cards, indignant arm waves and theatrical goal celebrations, that sort of thing. I'd do a few quid on the lottery too, no scratch cards though – didn't have that itch. I didn't bet in big hefty chunks of cash like the high rollers. I tended to make many smaller bets, parlaying my wins until, in snakes and ladders fashion, the cash went spiralling down to zero. I'd always had very little respect for money but I was nonetheless frugal. Now I was starting to slowly lose control.

In 1933 the Royal Commission defined a bet as thus: 'A promise to give money or monies worth upon the determination of an uncertain or unascertained event in a particular way. It may involve the exercise of skill or judgement.' What the Commission failed to add was that it usually involves luck. Luck or the belief in it is central to the notion of gambling. 'Chance governs all,' Milton said in *Paradise Lost*. And ever since the ancient Romans invented gambling with dice, luck has been a prerequisite of betting. I was running out of luck, fast. So I needed a system, a new system. And preferably one that worked.

My last visit to the kennels had been a week before the Irish Derby, the night Kevin had notched up his first success. He hadn't raced between that visit and his win, so was it possible that he had responded to my pep talk after all? It was a long shot, wishful thinking perhaps, but had positive energy, peace, love and all that happy hippy shit had a marked effect on his performance? Maybe he didn't need the killer instinct at all. Maybe all he needed was lurvvvvvvvvvvvve . . .

To test my hypothesis I returned to Imperial Kennels that Sunday. This time, however, I went doubly armed. I took my daughter with me.

'Ooh isn't she lovely?' crowed Nan. 'Ooh she's beautiful. Got lovely hair, ain't ya?'

Luca did her shy thing; we got Kevin and took him for a stroll up the lane. At first he was reticent about the little 'un, even more so than with me. But he soon changed his tune. Within minutes he was ignoring me and was all over Luca like a cheap suit. 'Hey, what about me?' I said. Kevin really got into Luca, snuggling and nuzzling. 'That's it, love him up,' I said. Oh boy, if he came good again after all this fuss I could really be on to something. I could see it now: a street, a ship, a Cambridge college named after me. 'That's it, give him a big cuddle . . .'

The following day at the BAGS meet Kevin flew out of the traps and pissed the race, recording a personal best of 29.84. That dog *ran*! Uncharacteristically he managed to stop licking his nuts and trapped well, bursting out of the boxes like a dog possessed. I couldn't believe it. The boy runs for *love*. Holy guacamole. This was a miracle. If Kevin ran within forty-eight hours of a visit he did the business. I had to test my hypothesis once more.

I went out to the kennels. The gang was all there, pottering about. It's a funny thing, training a dog, because ostensibly, once you figure out it's a goer, a chaser, all you do is feed it, walk it, massage it, pamper it, let it rest and that's it. If I'd had a garden of my own I could've saved myself £250 a month and kept him at home and done the self-same thing. It wasn't like he had to do ten miles a day on a treadmill or needed to bench press 250lbs or do pilates or the lotus position or jujitsu. He just needed to run and that's what he did naturally. Training. Bah! I was starting to feel a bit hard done by.

'These owners are always going on like they know what's best,' said Linda 'That's what I like about you, David. You keep your mouth shut and let us get on with it.' Little did Linda know I only kept my mouth shut because I didn't have a clue what I was doing.

'I've had owners in the past trying to tell me how to run my dogs or even try to 'influence' me, but I won't have it. One fella wanted me to a slow a dog down for him, cos he wanted to back him later and I told him I wouldn't do it. He insisted but I said 'no'. I put the dog out and it won. He didn't back it and was gutted. A few days later he came by and took all of his dogs out of the kennel. I won't have owners tell me how to run my dogs.'

Thanks to Kevin's improved track time the race manager, I think unfairly, penalised him for winning. Despite losing his next race, he was moved up a grade from A8 to A7. The supposed justification for this was that his times had improved: he'd managed to break through the 'psychological' thirty-second barrier.

When Kevin was in full flight, striding, leading, *winning*, he was a joy to behold. Of course such joy was rare, which made the win-seeking all the more addictive. He notched up three more mediocre runs before winning, as luck would have it, his thirteenth race. Kevin blasted out of the traps and won by a length and a half, having led right from the off. This was the shortest stretch he'd had to date between wins: two out of his last five starts, including a win early in October, as a 7–4 favourite, in which he scored a personal best of 29.80.

At the kennels I loved him up as usual, gave him some cheese and a good talking to. The following day he came third. Well, I was really clutching at straws. To make matters worse, in my haste to get back to the safety of London, I was tagged by Five-O doing 98 mph on the M11. Three points on your licence and sixty sheets, thank you very much. The following week Kevin came fourth. Then fourth again. The week after that, just for a bit of variety, he came last for the first time in his career. Fortunately I wasn't at the track to savour that little slice of history. I must've spunked a couple of hundred in between. The wins never seemed to amount to anything but the losses always did. Maybe someone was trying to tell me something . . . Anyway, Kevin then follows his dismal run with a win. The dog was a fucking yo-yo. There was no figuring him out, no determining what he would do from one race to the next.

Some three hundred dogs are contracted to run at Walthamstow. I'd come across dogs who hadn't had a win in sixteen races, so Kevin wasn't the worst. He was just, well, not very good. If a dog ever reaches a point where it can't get round the track without hailing a cab first, its racing days are over. There are no Eddie the Eagles or Eric the Eels at the Stow.

The strain of actually winning something must've taken its toll on Kevin as he lamed out of his next race, which earned him a three-week lay up. Fortunately it was nothing more than a little muscle strain, something that physiotherapy and some TLC from Linda cured. It did, however, put him out of circulation which, given his meagre earning capacity at the best of times, cost me money I could ill afford. I'd been struggling workwise and my bank balance was going down faster than a Bangkok whore on the Titanic. When things weren't going my way, which was most of the time, being a minor greyhound owner was a costly business. It was just disaster after disaster . . .

One time I was simply standing by the track rail, offering Kevin some words of encouragement while he was being paraded. 'Hey, hey. All right, boy,' I said with schoolboy enthusiasm. 'Go on, my son.'

One of the punters looked at me disapprovingly. Kevin came fifth, or second from last as we optimists like to say. 'You spooked him,' said Margot. 'Oh shut up will ya,' I said. 'Come on, let's go.' I stormed out of the track, sulking. It's surprising how much of your own ego you can invest in something as meaningless as a dog. If the dog wins, you win. But if the dog is shit, you are shit.

Despite the overall improvement in his times Kevin was still languishing in BAGS hell. This meant the opportunities to amaze my friends and family at the dogs had become virtually non-existent. It was a struggle getting them there on a balmy Saturday night in the summer, let alone a wet Monday afternoon in the bleak of mid-winter when Kevin was getting caned by five or six lengths.

chapter 19

Over in the Popular Enclosure, which I'd avoided since my coronation as an owner, Kevin had barely registered on Vince's radar. 'Susie's Boy?' he asked quizzically when I told him of my new acquisition. 'Never heard of him.' Vince knew every dog at the Stow by name. All serious punters keep a mental intelligence file on every runner. 'No, *Zussies Boy*,' I said, 'trained by Linda Jones.' Vince thought for a moment. 'Oh, *Zussies* Boy. I know the dog you're talking about. Bought it from Linda Jones, did ya? Hasn't done much yet, has it?' 'He had a result a few weeks back,' I counter. 'You picked a winner there,' he said with a toothy grin and a soupçon of sarcasm. Then, in a feeble attempt to mitigate my obvious failure, I blabbed, 'I *could've* had Twotone for four grand.' Vince raised an eyebrow. 'Like I said. You picked a winner.'

It had become apparent that Kevin wasn't going to set the world alight. Whether through my own sheer ignorance, a good old-fashioned bit of salesmanship by the Dog Lovers Syndicate via Linda Jones or a combination of the two, I'd been well and truly Tango'd. Kevin was a lemon, and as such the only place he was gonna get a squeeze was the BAGS circuit. Linda, like all trainers contracted to the Stow, had to provide her fair share of dogs for the BAGS. Kevin's name was now firmly in the frame. The man with the electroshock hairdo was moving in.

The dogs on the BAGS tend to be the more inconsistent or inferior performers at the track, which means betting on the BAGS is more of a lottery than evening meets. I'd often watched BAGS races and seen the favourite repeatedly blown out of the water. Some BAGS meetings, particularly at provincial or northern tracks can produce few or no winners at short odds, making me highly suspicious about the grading systems that were in operation.

As a sop to us poor minnow owners and to entice the feckless hordes and pensioners away from Oprah, Kilroy, Tricia and all that makeover shite on telly, entry to BAGS meets is free and the drinks are half price. Which is just as well because I needed a stiff shot or six at the end of an afternoon.

For Kevin to escape BAGS hell and save me from perdition his times and performances would have to improve and remain consistent. But on current form this didn't look likely. Greyhound racing is not a sport where one can say, 'It's not the winning that counts, it's the taking part that matters.' Bargain basement racehorse owners may get a buzz seeing their 1000–1 donkey ridden by a part-time milkman crawl home in eighty-ninth place at Aintree. But at thirty seconds a pop, a greyhound race is too fast, intense and expensive to cheer your dog home for anything other than a win.

As one owner told me, 'For small-time owners like you to stay interested, the race manager's got to get you an average of one win in six races. You get that and you're happy. But if you have longer losing streaks, there's no money in it, is there?'

Since its inception in 1967, BAGS racing has grown in popularity with high-street punters and now accounts for 27 per cent of off-course turnover, which at the last count was around £6.2 billion. But the BAGS isn't so popular with owners, trainers or independently owned tracks. Many fear that the Big Three bookmakers, who have a tasty 60 per cent of the off-course market share, exert too much influence over the dogs but few will speak out on record for obvious reasons. However, former Hove trainer

Bob Young once wrote in the *Racing Post*, 'Trainers live on the edge when supplying runners for BAGS racing, [and] fear being sacked if a greyhound wins and has been backed although no rule of racing has been broken.'

Like most stereotypes, the image of the swindling, money-grabbing bookmaker is largely founded on a few overblown myths. And the fact that the high-street bookmakers have the dogs by the balls. Approximately 8500 betting shops receive the BAGS service, of which the Big Three own almost half, and they also own 40 per cent of SIS. Of the £15 million the bookmaking industry paid to greyhound racing in 2001 the majority was for the BAGS service. Crucially, the bookmaker-controlled tracks supply anywhere between 40 and 50 per cent of the BAGS racing. Get the picture?

Every week the *Racing Post* groans with tales of woe from owners, trainers, promoters and concerned members of the public slamming the BAGS cartel for screwing the dogs. However, the tracks not owned by the Big Three bookmakers, owners and trainers have formed a shaky alliance under a BGRB initiative called the New Deal and are fighting back for a significant increase in the voluntary levy of 4 per cent from bookmaker profits and to stop them from recycling funds into their fat coffers. The points of the disputed, debated and protracted New Deal campaign are:

1. To ensure that only the highest standard of integrity exists throughout greyhound racing.

2. To raise prize money to levels where any greyhound that races once a week, and wins one race in four, is able to cover its owner's training costs.

3. To properly reward greyhound trainers for their expertise, dedication and commitment.

4. To provide the necessary funding for the Retired Greyhound Trust to enable it to strive to find a good home for every former racing greyhound.

5. To pay kennel hands a fair living wage that represents their

importance to the greyhound industry and offers a viable long-term career path.

6. To provide a platform for head kennel hands and assistant trainers to become professional trainers.

7. To take all necessary measures to ensure the wellbeing and welfare of every NGRC registered greyhound.

8. To ensure the race managers are free to provide fair and safe racing without undue pressure or influence from third parties or outside sources.

9. To ensure any conflict of interest in bookmaker track owner-ship does not prevent racecourses and betting-shop punters from betting on greyhound racing with total confidence.

10. To end bookmaking control forever, so that greyhound racing has the freedom to move forward independently and un-influenced for the sole benefit of those who are within or support it.

The problem, ostensibly, is about money. But the wrangling over percentages and slices of pies had turned political, which was my cue to go watch some paint dry. It was a complicated, messy and confusing issue but as Geoffrey Thomas, Chief Executive of the BGRB[4] put it, 'It has become increasingly clear as the New Deal has gained momentum that this deal is no longer just about money or politics but also about securing a future for the people who work in and support greyhound racing that is free from bookmaker control.'

Everyone in the game appreciates that bookmakers are a necessary evil. But, just as McDonald's has given the burger a bad name and Starbucks has taken the sting out of coffee, the chain bookmakers have fostered an image of corporate greed and faceless bean counters in suits. On-course bookies on the other hand enjoy a far different reputation. They are seen as

---

[4] Thomas eventually resigned over the New Deal issue after seven years as BRGB chief, following controversial comments made about the bookmaking industry which led to a £5000 fine from the NGRC.

lovable rogues, gentlemen hustlers, sly old dogs who could rob you blind but do it in a style that invited your willing acquiescence.

Dougie Tyler is one such character. He'd been at the Stow for years and was the granddaddy of the track's rails bookies. People showed Dougie respect. He drove a Bentley with a personalised number plate.

'I've been here since 1946,' said Dougie in a clipped cockney accent as he stood next to his pitch. If you squinted, you could mistake him for Arthur Daley's non-biological twin. 'I'm owed a fortune. I'll never get it. 'Ere, this is Gary but I call him Long Tongue,' said Dougie, introducing me to a deceptively youthful-looking character who acted as his floor man, giving him nuggets of information, starting prices and his take on how the market would develop in the ante-post betting ring frenzy. 'Very popular with the ladies is Long Tongue.

'Back in the old days there were loads of characters with funny nicknames: you had Odd Eye, One Arm Lou, Dead Body, Oily Rag . . . all of 'em used to work for the bookies. When I first started under the board in 1946 there used to be this tearaway where I used to bet. One day he says, "Give us three quid." "Got no money," I said. He looked at me . . . I could see he was dangerous. He had a knife in his jacket. "I'll cut your fucking ears off," he said. "I'll make you a dwarf." My heart was going bang bang. Anyway, he scarpered. But years and years ago there were some very nasty gangs and bookies. Them Krays never used to bother us; for others it'd be a £100 a week or turn it in. They'd blow your legs off.'

To be a trackside bookie you have to have charisma and a touch of the showman about you. Apart from Gary Long Tongue, Dougie ran the pitch with his two sons, a couple of new school characters who looked more like accountants than bookmakers. While his sons balanced the books and Long Tongue fed Dougie his information, the old master chalked up the odds and enticed the punters with his vaudeville banter.

'Too many favourites winning today,' said Dougie thoughtfully. 'I'm doing a lot at the moment. Normally, if the favourites win the bookies lose. Years ago people used to come just for the gambling. Now it's socialising.'

So how do the Dougies of this world make their money? Well, the statistical probability of a dog winning in a six-dog race is 5–1, which seems obvious on paper. But not all dogs are created equal. Acting on information, a bookmaker will calculate probabilities of each dog winning based on a number of factors. The starting point is time. Which is the fastest dog in the race? Then there's the health, fitness, age, running style and other variables to consider. Once he has an idea of how a race is likely to pan out he creates a book – a list of probabilities that he then converts into odds. In order for him to make a profit these odds must total more than 100 per cent probability. Why does the total come to more than 100 per cent? So the bookie can make a profit, stoopid.

Scientifically, it's impossible to have a greater than 100 per cent certainty of an event occurring. But bookies are mathematical magicians. A bookmaker *artificially* shortens the odds for a particular race outcome or, conversely, increases the estimated probability of a race outcome. Consequently, the odds offered for a race by a bookie are not true odds or fair odds. You can't bet on all six dogs in a race and expect to win. The difference in price between fair odds and the bookmaker's odds or mark-up is called the over-round: and that's how he makes money. The over-round can be anywhere from 116 to 128 per cent, depending on the size and location of the betting market and the greed of the bookmaker.

'You're always trying to guess what they wanna back,' said Dougie of the punters. 'Sometimes you're right, sometimes you're wrong. See that fella up there,' Dougie gestured towards a guy up in the stands dressed like Indiana Jones in a leather flight jacket, chinos and a trilby. 'He's an excellent, excellent judge. Professional punter. Very very clever. He turns a handsome profit every year. Some people you'd love to play against all day cos you'd finish up with all their money. But if you played against him every day you'd end up penniless. If there were ten more like him in the stadium I'd walk away.'

Probability is an interesting science. For instance, it's thought that if an endless succession of monkeys were set before a typewriter with limitless paper, eventually they'd create the complete works of Shakespeare, by chance of course. Now if there are fifty keys on a typewriter, the probability of a monkey getting Shakespeare's name correct for starters is raised to the power of the number of characters (letters and spaces) in 'Shakespeare' plus the adjustments of the typewriter needed for capitals and punctuation. On this basis the chance of the monkeys typing 'Hamlet' correctly is 1 in 15,625,000,000. To quote the probability of our simian cousins typing the Bard's complete works then involves an extremely large number. And a lot of patience. And coffee. And . . .

Christ. What had I become? I was approaching my very own John Nash/*A Beautiful Mind* moment, i.e. paranoid schizophrenia, characterised by delusions, hallucinations and bipolar manic freak-outs. I never was one for maths.

Anyway, against the pros, bookies like Dougie will protect themselves by putting a cap on their stakes. 'You've got to cut 'em down sometimes. When they come in for a grand you give 'em 200 quid.' Indiana Jones was part of a crew of big punters who I'd often see at the BAGS meetings, all of whom bet nothing less than a bottle, and often a grand, on most races on the card. They strutted around like they owned the place. In some ways, they did.

'Nobody in this world has seen more greyhound races than me,' said Dougie from behind his pitch. 'I've seen hundreds of thousands of races. I'm eighty-five years old.'

'No!' I said, with genuine disbelief.

'Well, eighty-four-and-a-half actually. I'll never retire. I wanna be carried out.'

'The thing about the game is,' said Gary, 'with people like Dougie once they give the game up . . .'

'They die,' said Dougie.

'They die,' repeated Gary. 'They just give up on life.'

'I don't drink, I don't smoke,' said Dougie, 'I can't handle women . . . well, I can't get no movement, can I? There's no movement!'

'He was actually on the front page of the *News of the World* years ago,' said Gary.

'I was definitely the Don Juan of the greyhound tracks in my younger days, but not now. Like I said, I can't get no movement. There could be a woman here stark bollock naked. Wouldn't make no difference to me!'

One of the other bookies trudged over, a fat, ruddy-faced old codger. ' 'Ere, this man's a personality in the game,' said Dougie, introducing me to 'Billy'. 'He's been about a long time . . . acts a bit stupid sometimes . . . but deep down he's quite a nice chap.'

'When I was in the army,' said Billy, 'I saved two hundred soldiers . . .'

'He did, yeah, he did,' chipped in one of the floor men.

'Yeah, I shot the cook!'

'This is a very big area for gambling,' said Gary. 'Chingford, Walthamstow, Leyton, Leytonstone . . . I think the game was a lot better years ago. It was crammed out here, d'you know what I mean? You just couldn't move, mate. But now it's a lot weaker. It's still holding it's own at the moment. There's been talk of William Hill taking over. How true it is, I don't know. But it's more than just speculation. What you have to remember is the Chandlers aren't getting any younger. They're all in their sixties.'

'But Thursday and Saturday nights are a licence to print money,' I ventured. Dog tracks are full of rumours. Why would the Chandlers want to sell such a cash cow? Gary played the 'bookies lose money too' card, claiming that while the Chandlers made money the bookies often took a hit. But I can't say I've ever seen a poor bookmaker. He said there was some confusion among many punters about the difference between the high-street bookies, many of whom owned their own racetracks, and the smaller, family-run operations like Dougie's.

'The game here for bookmakers isn't as easy as you'd think. Look, as far as punters and trainers are concerned bookmakers are the scum of the earth, the enemy, which is not the way to look at things. Some of it's tongue-in-cheek. But we're all human beings, we all have to earn a crust. They're out there to do as best they can to beat the book and you're out there as a bookmaker to try to beat them. That's what it's all about. You can't characterise people by thinking what you *think* they are.'

This view came from a justifiable cynicism towards the big bookmaking chains as opposed to the independents. 'We're not here for our amusement or theirs; this isn't charity, it's business. We're all here to make money so a lot of the criticism bookies get is unfair.'

A voice from the stands cried, 'Four minutes'. 'Right, business must prevail now, gentlemen.' No sooner had Dougie's son said the word than the old man turned his attention to preparing for the next race, chalking up odds on the board. Gary, ever the scout for information, started probing me about Kevin, who had come second two races earlier.

'So, what did you pay for him, if you don't mind me asking?'

'What would you say?' I said, feeling a lump of embarrassment forming at the back of my throat.

'I wouldn't pay no more than . . . he's only a puppy . . . I wouldn't pay no more than five or six hundred pounds.'

'Jesus fucking . . . Oh, I won't tell you what I paid. But it was a little bit more than that.'

'He's only an A5 or A6 dog,' said Gary. 'What did you pay for him? Over £1000?'

'Yeah, over a thousand.'

'You've paid a lot of money for him,' said Gary, euphemistically. 'I'm not being funny but he's nothing special. You've paid a hell of a lot of money for him.'

'Yeah, er, ah . . . tell me about it . . .'

With thirty seconds to the next race the usual organised chaos was well underway. The small band of big boys, the Premiere League of punters, who were too lazy, established and loud-mouthed to cover the twenty-odd feet from the stands to the bookmakers' pitches and physically place their bets, were barking out their wagers as the lower divisions of workshy, feckless, semi-pros and compulsive gamblers battled it out on the floor. Dougie worked the crowd like a snake oil salesman as the other bookies used their own spiel to liberate we band of fools from our money.

'Top, fifteen hundred quid, Doug,' cried one punter from the stands, a Bobby De Niro lookalike in regulation slacks and short-sleeved shirt. Dougie seemed otherwise occupied. Perhaps it was the size of the bet that made him turn his attention elsewhere. 'Fifteen, Doug. Doug! You switched the hearing aid on again or what?'

'No it was off,' said Dougie nonchalantly. 'Did you shout?'

'Fifteen hundred quid on top,' said De Niro, finally getting his bet on.

'To win a monkey,' replied Dougie, confirming the bet.

In the seconds leading up to the off things can get desperate in the betting ring. Punters want to 'get on' but the bookies can't or won't always play ball. Once that bell goes and the dogs are out the traps betting ceases and in the mad scramble to make a wager some punters get lost in the mêlée.

'That's fucking out of order.' The Indiana Jones man was remonstrating with Billy the bookmaker after failing to register his bet. In the event, the dog Indiana Jones fancied won.

'I've been coming to BAGS meetings here for donkey's years and I can't get on?' said Indy, his face reddening. 'There's fellas been here five minutes and you take their money, Bill. What's your problem?'

'No problem, Terry.' Billy looked embarrassed. He offered some lame excuse about not hearing Indy's, a.k.a. Terry, bet before the off, but Indy wasn't having it. Now it was handbags at ten paces. Billy, head down, rummaged through his moneybag and paid out a handful of lucky punters, ignoring the increasingly agitated Indy.

'That's out of order, Bill. Bang out of order.' As Dougie had said, if a bookie doesn't fancy the odds against a big-spending punter he won't accept his bet. But for the sake of business and gambling etiquette at the very least the bookie should offer to take a reduced bet. But bookies love a bit of gamesmanship with punters and if there is a way of wriggling out of an awkward situation by playing dumb, they'll take it.

'Terry, I didn't hear you, mate.' said Billy, repeating his defence.

'Didn't hear me? You must be fucking joking.' Indy had lost out on around £500 or so in winnings. As the wheels of the betting ring started turning again in readiness for the next race, having taken enough stick from Indy, Billy finally had a crack at his expense.

'Yep, *you've* got plenty of time to get on, John,' he joked as one of his regulars stepped up to place a bet. A ripple of laughter went round the betting ring. Indy was incensed.

'You're making yourself look a right cunt in front of all these people, Bill,' snapped Indy.

'Watch it.'

Ooh! A collective groan went round. And greyhound racing was meant to be fun? Maybe there were too many negative ions in the air or something. Tempers were running high. I was starting to feel pretty pissed off myself after yet another loss-making day at the track and Gary Long Tongue's revelation that I'd been stung over Kevin.

I slipped up to the bar to have a quick one, and then headed for the kennels to see the Boy Blunder, but his handler Kelly had already gone. Just as I was slinking out of the stadium, licking my wounds, Dougie spied me walking through the betting ring.

' 'Ere, if you wanna buy any more dogs, you better come and ask us first,' shouted Dougie.

'I think my dog-buying days are over. The dog-selling days are coming though . . .'

Gary had evidently told Dougie about our earlier conversation. 'Tell me the truth, what d'ya pay for the dog? C'mon, tell me the truth. What was it?'

I made a finger-twisting gesture, indicating an unspecified amount.

'*Sixteen hundred quid?*' whispered Dougie, before shaking his head. I think I may have said, 'Yeah'. Well, if I had told him the real price he'd have had kittens. And I'd feel like an even bigger schmuck.

'Still . . .' and Dougie took the words, to add to the money he'd earlier taken from my pocket, right out of my mouth. 'You learn by experience.'

'Exactly,' I said.

'You won't do anything silly again.'

'Exactly, that's for sure. That's for sure.'

The word had really gone round that a sap was in the house.

' 'Ere, if you're looking for something, he's got some lovely dogs,' said Billy, nodding towards a wide-boy floor man leaning against the rails.

'I got one for sale *at the moment*,' the fella said, his voice lifting at the end of the sentence, as if to suggest it was *my lucky day*.

'Oh *really?*' I said, putting on my best mug-punter air of optimism. Like I needed to fake it.

'He runs at Romford. He's running tonight.'

'What's his name?'

'Car Car Kid.'

'Car Car Kid?' I said.

'Car Car Kid. He's in the second race tonight. He's up for sale for *three grand*.' The wide boy put the stress on the end of the sentence this time to emphasise that three grand *was not a lot of money*.

I asked a few more bullshit questions about Cack Cack Kid's form, just to string the guy along. What did they take me for? A mug, I guess. Wide boy's mobile rang, he answered it sheepishly, turning his back on me, so in the time-honoured tradition of a journalist, I made my excuses and left.

chapter 20

December 2002. I had given up keeping any serious record of my bets. Well, what was the point? For one, there were too many to record, but more importantly it was too depressing looking in my little black book and seeing all that red ink and minus signs. Most of my 'odd flutters' these days were at the bookies as opposed to the track. With Kevin stuck on the BAGS circuit it was becoming harder to see him race, in the flesh at least. It was easier to pop into the bookies and see him 'live' on SIS.

One afternoon I was in my local bookies waiting for Kevin to make his grand appearance. I felt confident. He looked in good shape. When I had asked Linda a couple of days ago, 'Is he well?' she'd given me the nod. He was favourite for the race, so I decided to have a score on him at 5–2. He soon moved to 2–1 and stayed there at the off. BANG! He's out of the traps like Linford. An old brother standing next to me was 'riding the betting shop pony', making like Frankie Dettori, clicking his fingers in a whipping motion and urging on the one dog, who was bumped by Kevin at the first bend.

'Go on, my son!' I shouted in retaliation. 'Go on, you little beauty.' The sonofabitch led all the way, baby. I collected my £70 from the cashier. 'Pleasure doing business with you,' I said sarcastically. Getting one over on the bookies, particularly William Hill, was something to savour. As they showed a re-run of the race I turned and said to the old brother, 'See that? That's *my* dog that is.' 'So why ya na give me a tip then?' he said, looking me up and down. 'I didn't want to jinx him.' I walked out of the door clutching my £50 profit. Nice. When Kevin won I was a winner and basked in his reflected glory. But when he lost I was a loser.

Things just hadn't gone the way I planned. Correction: I hadn't planned anything and things had gone the way you'd expect when you don't have a plan. I'd always prided myself on being a bit of a smart cookie but I'd been had. Fucking dogs. I wanted out. This business didn't make sense: a bunch of dogs chasing a windsock, and I'm doing my bollocks on it? The 'winnings' barely covered half the expenses. I spent more on that stupid dog than I did on my daughter. This was bullshit. People just didn't 'get me' any more. I suspect my friends thought I'd really lost it this time. I used to joke about being a loner, an outsider. Now I had become one. I could float in and out of circles, networks, crowds and worlds and feel no attachment. I was a chameleon. I was an invisible man.

We took off after Christmas for Barbados, Margot and I, for some much-needed winter sun. Boy did I need a holiday. I'd been writing some heavy shit for the *Evening Standard* and was now on the hit list of every fascist, feminist and black power organisation in the country. I'd been keeping a low profile for a month or so, slowly going stir crazy.

While in Barbados I tried to forget about work, money and the dogs – all the things I was meant to enjoy but invariably had conspired against me. Then, one evening, while pondering the meaning of life over a margarita, I came up with the smart idea of importing greyhound racing to Barbados. They had a lovely little mile-long track on the edge of Bridgetown called the Garrison. It was a simple oval turf course with a shorter sand track on the inside, which could easily be modified for dog racing. Barbados was the perfect place for it: a sporty, outdoors culture with lots of well-heeled ex-pats and locals. All I needed was a couple of mil, a few dozen dogs, some trainers, kennel hands, bookmakers and I was in business. I then woke up, ordered a rum punch and let sleeping dogs and mad ideas lie for a while.

When I got back from Barbados at the end of January, Britain had come to a standstill. For a change, it wasn't the wrong kind of leaves on railway lines that was responsible, or petrol protestors, or baying mobs hounding paediatricians mistaken for paedophiles but simply Mother Nature. Substantial bands of snow had shut down the south-east counties, East Anglia, Essex, Bedfordshire and Hertfordshire, lying between 5 and 12 cm deep in most places. North and north-west suburbs of London also experienced a late period of heavy snow. There was major disruption and gridlock on motorways in Essex and Hertfordshire; some tube networks were also affected.

After nearly eighty years of dog racing there is still no safe, uniform all-weather surface. In days gone by, many tracks were grass, others were a combination of grass and sand and now most were just sand. At Peterborough dog track the wrong type of sand had once led to greyhounds suffering blisters on their paws. A mix-up meant the sand used to fill in gaps and cover bare patches was too gritty, so the track's managers had to stump up £9000 for 530 tonnes of the right type of sand.

The Stow had the right kind of sand but the wrong kind of weather for a lightweight like me, just back from the Caribbean. The heavy snow meant conditions on the track were ranging from minus 30 to minus 60. Apart from the very severest of conditions the show always goes on regardless. But even when the show can't go on there are alternatives.

Computers, robots and the machines, like H.G. Wells had predicted, are taking over the world. Sports leisure is no exception. The machines are taking over greyhound racing. Some bright spark had ignited a forest fire of fantastical high-street bookmaking the previous year with the invention of 'virtual' racing. Along with BAGS, the gee-gees, 49s, Heads or Tails and a bunch of other garbage, computerised horse and dog races, producing apparently randomly generated results are being piped into the high-street chains via SIS. While the gee-gees have the fictitious 'Portman Park' and 'Steepledowns' racetracks, the dogs have 'Millersfield' and 'Brushwood', where the yapping, pixel-fixed greyhounds bound 'over the sticks'. Like the ad in my local bookies said, 'There's nothing virtual about a winner.' Of course the same could be said about a loser – in fact, more so. Virtual racing is gambling for the Playstation generation.

In virtual racing the odds are fixed before the race, so the market never changes. But people do make big scores playing it. Ladbrokes once took a £10,000 bet on a virtual 6–4 favourite which won, while Hill's have taken bets of up to £4000 on totally fictitious animals, which just goes to prove there's one born every minute. That said, I've actually won a few quid on virtual dogs, obviously by sheer luck. Only the odd fiver or so, but my hit rate at predicting virtual winners was actually higher than with real dogs.

In my eternal quest to find an 'edge' and avoid ever having to work again I came across a variety of software programs available for the 'professional punter', most of which were utter rubbish. One intriguing innovation was the 'Greyhound Predictor', a computer program that promised to simulate the running of a greyhound race after you input data into it. Using the results from old copies of the *Racing Post*, I tested the software. And every time I punched in the necessary info, using my historical data – dog weights, best record times, running style and so on – the results never matched the outcome.

Then there is that other ruse, internet betting, which is as virtual as virtual gambling in the sense that, by using a computer screen and a credit card the bookies hope you won't realise you are actually gambling or, more accurately, losing your money. All these gimmicks are aimed at people just like me: the computer-literate, pre-middle-aged punter. The old school gamblers and technophobes wisely don't have time for such nonsense, preferring good old cash to credit cards and computer chips.

Internet bookies entice you with the offer of free bets, just like the £750 one that reeled me into this mess in the first place. For one, you never get the complimentary stake back and as the odds are always against you, the chances are the free bet will fizzle out like a damp sparkler. Even if you win, you'll plough the winnings back in. And that is how they get you.

chapter 21

The city droned in the winter. All that grey concrete, the traffic, the fumes and the bad manners were in stark contrast to the azure sea, golden sands, palm trees and post-colonial civility of Barbados. One of the many long-dead white men that I'm fond of often quoting once said something about, 'When a man is tired of London, he is tired of life.' I needed to get out of the Smoke urgently, before London ground me down and into a slipknot of rope slung over a balustrade. I needed to see green fields, go rambling on towpaths, bird watching, or maybe even hunt small defenceless creatures with packs of scavenging dogs.

An old boy called Brian Coleman had asked me to join him as a 'foot follower' on the Puckeridge Hunt in Hertfordshire, to give me a flavour of what country life is like. Brian was a retired terrier man, which is an adjunct assisted by terriers who rides on horseback or on a quad bike with the hunt in order to sniff out a fox if it goes to ground. An old mutual friend called Tamara, whose family had long been into foxhunting and various equine pursuits, had introduced me to Brian, who worked as a steward at the car boot sale at Hackney Wick Stadium.

It was a cold, misty morning, and drizzly, which was apparently bad news for the hunt but good news for the fox. Around twenty-five to thirty brace of hounds were 'speaking', not barking, as they jockeyed their way round the courtyard of the Barclay spread. The Barclays ran the Puckeridge Hunt. They had proper dough. 'See him over there,' said Brian casually, nodding towards a character who looked like he'd just rode out of a Stubbs. 'If I tapped him for £100 million he'd still be a billionaire.'

'But people have got hunting wrong,' chipped in Tamara. 'It's not all toffs and la-di-da.' Tamara was always at pains to explain that hunting is not an elitist activity. She had recently dragged me off to a Countryside Alliance demo in Parliament Square and insisted that I couldn't get involved with greyhound racing without looking at hunting. 'Yeah, yeah,' I'd said, at first dismissing the links between city sport and country sport as tenuous. But there were links.

Despite living not far from central London, Tamara was a big supporter of the Countryside Alliance. Her family hailed from Chigwell but like many people in that part of London they had made the exodus eastwards from Bethnal Green decades earlier. I knew Tamara's dad George pretty well too: salt of the earth geezer and all that. George had done the whole East End rites of passage thing, from being an amateur boxer to running a stall and grafting at Billingsgate fish market, with a few scrapes and adventures in between. He was also godfather to the actor Ray Winstone and knew the boxing promoter Frank Warren in the days when he was just starting out with characters like Lennie 'the Guv'nor' McLean.

All of this cockneyology is intriguing but largely irrelevant to greyhound racing, I agree. But it just illustrates that you don't need six degrees of separation to join the dots between town and country. It is the people and their attitudes rather than the physical environment that has created a new spin on what Disraeli called Britain's 'Two Nations'. Nowadays the barriers between people are not just economic, cultural or racial; there is a huge divide between town and country. Tamara had taken me to demos where police had baton-charged protestors dressed in plus-fours and anoraks and men with thick Cornish accents had looked me square in the face and declaimed the genuinely held belief that they were 'ethnic minorities' being oppressed by the state.

Like country folk and city folk, foxhounds and greyhounds are two different branches of the same species. While foxhounds are bred to hunt by smell, greyhounds, of course, chase by sight and with silent stealth too. One of the reasons a fox can outsmart a sixty-strong pack of bloodhounds is because, like all dimwits, they blow a lot of hot air and make a lot of useless noise. Greyhounds use guile and agility to nail their prey while foxhounds rely simply on brute force and numbers. They're mangy, semi-feral creatures, oafish and clumsy – a good few notches down the food chain from greyhounds.

Standing around a pack of hounds or, more correctly, twenty-odd brace of hounds, helped me to develop a degree of superiority as a greyhound owner. Greyhounds aren't known for being smart like Alsatians or mongrels, but there was always the outside chance that Kevin could be taught at the very least to sit, fetch and heel. Judging by his results, rolling over and playing dead already came naturally to him. Foxhounds on the other hand are beyond domestication once they've hunted. As Tamara kept telling me, 'If foxhunting is banned every hunting dog in the country will have to be put down. Where are the animal rights in that?'

Indeed, what little intelligence a foxhound has is devoted to its stomach and how to line it. 'I've had to pull hounds out of restaurants, clubs, even a pet shop, to get 'em away from food,' said Brian, pointing out that when they get loose they head straight for the catering. I felt there was something sinister about foxhounds. Maybe it was just what I thought they symbolically stood for. Or perhaps it was because two or three of them sauntered over to me and sniffed at my crotch while I was drinking my mulled wine and eating my fruity biscuit. 'You'll be all right,' whispered Brian, 'as long as you don't make a sudden move. If one of 'em goes for ya the pack will follow, and that's it. They'll rip you to pieces.'

I kept still, sipped my mulled wine and nibbled the biscuit. The

Barclay matriarch eventually saved my bacon by announcing it was tally-ho time. Despite Tamara and Brian's insistence that foxhunting was a people's sport, the red tunics, rat-catcher tweeds, jodhpurs and odd billionaire gave the event a decidedly toffee-nosed air. I'd dressed like a hunt saboteur for the occasion, you know, to get a reaction, but none of the forty or so riders and followers gave me a second glance. Snobs. I wondered what would happen if little Emily or Charlotte took me round to mummy and daddy's for Sunday lunch? I'd wind up as fucking desert, that's what would happen. I thought of England, knocked back another glass of mulled wine, pocketed two biscuits and set off for the hunt.

We trudged through mud and grass for half an hour. It all seemed like a harmless jolly until I made the mistake of being the first person to spot the fox. 'Here, what's that over there?' I said quizzically, peering some three hundred metres into the distance. 'That's it, isn't it?' Bounding across the horizon was a bushy clump of crimson and brown. At first I was excited. Here was a proper, well-fed, Disney-coloured fox not a manky urban critter like the ones I'd see lurking around the bins of my local Tesco. But my excitement soon waned. Without batting an eyelid, Brian let out an almighty cackle that sounded like an emu having its nuts crushed in a vice. 'Aaaaaaaaaaarrrrrrrrrrk . . . Aaaaaaaaaaa aaaaaarrrrrrrrrrrrrrk . . . aaaaaaaaaaaaarrrrrrrrrrrrrk!!!!!!!'

A bugle sounded. The field emerged from some woods far off in the distance, headed by the master of the hunt. Brian waved his arms frantically and pointed to a dell into which the fox had seemingly disappeared. We headed over to the dell, where the master of the hunt and the whip master met us. 'Have you chaps been here long?' the hunt master asked Brian, while Tamara explained to me that the field was kept out of sight of any potential kill, which I thought was rather civilised. There were a couple of young teenagers in the field and a boy no older than eight on what looked like a seaside pony. 'Very few people see a kill,' said Tamara. 'The RSPCA kill more animals each year than all the hunts put together. Most people go for the chase, because it gives them a chance to put some air in their horses' lungs. Riding over fences and hedgerows is better than beating tarmac at two miles an hour.'

I felt crummy. I'd fingered the fox. For the first time in my life I'd been an informer, a grass, a rat. I had turned Queen's Evidence on one of Aesop's little chums. The hounds went into the copse, turning over the joint like Feds on a manhunt. The master of the hunt mentioned something about the holes in the ground being bunged up the night before to stop the fox from going to ground, you knew, just to make it a fair hunt. But after ten minutes or so they gave up looking in the copse and rode off into the distance. From that point on I spent the next eight hours traipsing around the Hertfordshire countryside, praying the fox would get away, while Tamara extolled the virtues of country life as yet more foot followers, cars, quad bikes and of course funny-looking people on horseback galloped around the countryside in search of that sly old Mr Fox. As luck would have it, by the end of the day they still hadn't caught the little fella, so I was in the clear. Phew. The fox, the man and the guilty conscience. Aesop would've dug that one.

chapter 22

I just couldn't get enough of rural Britain and charming cunt'ry folk these days. Taking Kevin for idle walks in Suffolk, meandering through the rolling hills of County Kerry and badgering foxes in picture-postcard Hertfordshire had renewed my faith in nature. For the first time in years I felt comfortable venturing out into the sticks without fear of odd stares, harassment or a starring role as wicker man at ye local village witch-burning fête. Why, I even started buying the odd copy of the countryside bible *The Field*. But only for the sport, mind you.

I felt it was time to go further afield. It was time to go back to my roots – well, Kevin's roots really – in search of the ancient origins of greyhound racing, that soon-to-be-outlawed forerunner of the track and quaint county ritual: hare coursing.

It's 8.30a.m. and the final of the one hundred and fifty-sixth Waterloo Cup is due to kick off in an hour's time on the late Lord Leverhulme's estate at Great Altcar, a misty plain on the outer regions of bleakest west Lancashire. An enterprising Liverpool hotelier named William Lynn inaugurated the annual three-day event in 1836 as a way of promoting his establishment, the Waterloo Hotel. In the late 1800s crowds of up to 75,000 flocked to the Waterloo Cup, earning it a reputation as the Grand National of hare coursing. These days it was more widely recognised as the most controversial event in the British sporting calendar.

Mingling in the crowd of early risers I could feel the tension wafting through the dawn air. My initial attempts to make idle conversation with the locals were met with grunts, groans, and general indifference. People were eyeing me suspiciously. I was the only black man in a crowd of four thousand-odd rednecks; and I was talking into a Dictaphone and scribbling in a notebook. And I was dressed in a black leather jacket, black woolly hat, shades and combats, rolling like one of the Panthers. I knew I should've brought wellies and an Ian Duncan Smith rubber mask. Now was not a good time to stand out in a crowd.

The opening day of the event had been marked by around two hundred placard-waving animal rights protesters crying 'murderers' and 'scum' at the coursing fans; consequently, a number of surly looking cops were on standby in riot vans parked on the site. The news media had had a field day with the city v country, civilisation v barbarism narrative of the Waterloo Cup. Depending on which paper you read, what you ate or who you voted for, hare coursing is either a quaint English tradition essential to the fabric of rural culture, or an a evil, mindless, oafish, barbaric act of cruelty. If the hunting bill, which had been debated in the Commons the previous day, became legislation, the Waterloo Cup and all forms of hunting with dogs would be consigned to the knacker's yard.

Hare coursing is one of the world's oldest field sports, dating back to the time of the Pharaohs. The Greeks introduced it to the Romans who in turn introduced it to England. Then in 1014, King Canute enacted the Forest Laws, which decreed that only noblemen could own and hunt with greyhounds. However, it wasn't until Tudor times that it became popular in England.

Lord Orford, the same chap who bred the modern greyhound, founded the country's first coursing club towards the end of the eighteenth century. So this wasn't some fly-by-night badger-baiting cult. The advent of greyhound racing in 1926 saw a decline in the numbers of coursing spectators, particularly from the cities; but the pro-coursing lobby still had history on its side. Coursing, they argued, was an English tradition, like the Changing of the Guard, dancing round the maypole and noncing. But as Marx had said, 'The traditions of the dead weigh like a nightmare on the living.' People are too caught up in tradition, defending it, fighting for it, dying for it. Sometimes you just have to move with the times.

I kept circulating. Half an hour had passed and nothing much had happened. A small contingent of rails bookies was taking odds on the first course. Punters were digging into hampers in car boots – some with champers from buffed-up Range Rovers, others with cider from beat-up Escorts. Kids darted in and out of the crowd and old men in flat caps and oilskins chatted idly.

'Number seventeen, South Shore, is withdrawn,' came an announcement from a stuffy voice over the PA. 'We remind you that we will be *ruthless* with any member of the public having a dog on a lead, in their coat or in any other fashion,' continued the voice à la *1984*. 'They will be either removed or the dog will be put in the car. It'll be your choice. Can I also remind the public that when the hares are getting close to the dogs, please do not impede any escape routes. Yesterday, er, there were a couple of times when the enthusiasm of the crowd might well have turned a couple of them. Please let the hares escape through any gaps.'

If a hare could out-manoeuvre the dogs for more than forty seconds, chances are they'd run out of steam and give up, leaving the hare to escape into the thicket at the other end of the course or through refuges called 'soughs'. However, if the dogs caught the hare, it'd be turned into a Christmas cracker faster than you could say 'Jack Rabbit'.

I walked along a row of stalls of country apparel and dog paraphernalia thinking I might find a wee present for Kevin. Trophies, leads, collars, jackets and all sorts were on sale. As I was fondling a rather fetching leather riding crop I thought of Margot and then noticed an old pikey, dressed in a cheap two-piece suit, leaning against a low wire fence behind me. He seemed in distress. 'You all right?' I asked. 'Urgggghhhhh . . . . Urrrggg gghhh . . .' came the response as the man threw up on to the grass. A bunch of spotty-faced lads no older than fourteen strolled by swigging cans of beer, laughing. 'Urgggghhhh . . . . Urgggh hhh . . .' *Sod him. He'll live.* I left the old duffer straining to regurgitate what looked like a cross between half a pint of pina colada and a tin of pea soup and headed for the heart of the action.

Sixty-four greyhounds had started the knockout competition in pursuit of the Waterloo Cup and the £5,000 first prize, now down to the last sixteen on the third and final day. The runner-up would receive £1500 and a trophy, the next two £650 each, the next four £200 and the last eight £100, pretty shite prize money if you ask me.

As I got nearer to the course, I noticed the judge of the competition, a short fat stump of a man with a gammon ham face dressed in full hunting pink, having trouble mounting his horse. 'Give him a swift kick in his fookin' knackers,' cried a wrinkly old mare to the assembled crowd, as a stable hand gave the judge a face-saving bunk up. 'I'll give ya a fiver he falls off.' The assembled crowd roared with laughter as he finally worked his ample girth into the saddle. It was the judge's job to award the dogs points for speed and agility. Thankfully no one was judging him.

It was fast approaching 9.30a.m. The crowd seemed restless. I jostled my way deeper into the mass of bodies towards a gully separating the course from the southern bank of spectators. I felt increasingly uncomfortable, surrounded by hordes of Jacobean runts in flak jackets, khakis, combat pants, oilskins and fatigues. It was like dress-down Friday at a Ku Klux Klan convention. No surprise, then, that Lancashire was the heartland of the British National Party's 'political' activity. In 2003, of the seventeen council seats held by the BNP, ten were in Lancashire. This was not my kind of country. I caught a few choice stares and saw in some of the dark eyes of those rednecks an ancient truth: once upon a time the ancestors of these self-same characters would've hunted *my* ancestors through the rain forests of Africa and the plantations of the West Indies.

'They're now in slips, now in slips,' said the announcer. 'On the red collar, More Harry and on the White Collar, Judicial Best.' The crowd had swollen above five thousand and it felt as though every one of them was standing behind me, peering over my shoulder and watching my every move.

More Harry and Judicial Best were the first brace, in the first 'slip' or race of the day. They were competing in the Waterloo Purse, one of two warm-up acts before the Waterloo Cup final. The wind was picking up across the field. I rubbed my hands and felt my feet tighten with cold. The crowd grew ever more expectant and agitated. It was a long waiting game.

It passed 10a.m. My feet had frozen. My balls were as hard as brass. One scrawny hare appeared but was given free passage across the field and the dogs, chomping at the bit, weren't let loose. I asked a man standing next to me if he knew why the hare hadn't been coursed and he ignored me but for a shrug of the shoulders. The bookies were trying to work up the crowd: 'treble the field' and 'six to four the red collar', they kept calling, but the action was lacklustre. I was about to throw a tenner to the wind when *Henry V* got in on the act:

> I see you stand like Greyhounds in the slips,
> Straining upon the start. The game's afoot:
> Follow your spirit; and upon this charge
> Cry 'God for Harry! England and Saint George!'

Distraction. The spectators at the far end of the course caught sight of the hare first. The beaters had driven it from out of the surrounding bushes and on to the course. Game on. A ripple of anticipation went through the crowd, then a breaker, and then a tidal wave. I was standing in front of a group of old yokels who reeked of either very cheap scotch or cough syrup. 'Here we go, boys!' yelled one of them, a Welshman. The hare came into view, its feet a blur, its marble eyes bulging with utter panic. 'That'll do us, that'll do us, that'll do us,' squawked a ruddy-faced stoat in a deerstalker, followed by an enthusiastic cry of, 'Go on, pussy.' As the hare fizzed past the small screen in the middle of the course, behind which the slipper held the dogs, voice after voice barked, 'Let 'em off, let 'em off.'

The hare was given the requisite eighty-odd-yard head start ahead of the screen before the slipper let loose the baying dogs. Within seconds they'd closed in on the hare but it then made a sharp right turn, losing More Harry in the process. 'He's in bother, he's in bother,' hollered a Cornishman. 'He's on line, he's on line,' came back an Irishman as More Harry corrected himself and rejoined Judicial Best in the chase. 'He's up and turned him,' said the Cornishman behind me. The hare bobbed and weaved as the dogs fought to keep track of him; he had too much in the way of guile, speed and technique for the dogs and bolted off towards the thicket at the other end of the course, leaving the greyhounds trailing behind. 'All right, pussy, all right, lovely,' mumbled the Deerstalker Man, cryptically, as handlers rushed on to the field to retrieve the dogs.

The announcer pronounced Judicial Best the winner. Clearly the hare should've got the decision. The next course was equally, if not more, barbarous than the first, as this time the hounds gained on the hare much faster than their predecessors had. One of the dogs buckled as he made a wide turn in pursuit of the arcing hare. In such an instance, a hare can literally run rings round a greyhound as its lower centre of gravity, lighter weight and smaller frame make it easier for it to negotiate tight bends, which is why, I guess, they always pass the finish line first at the track. The hare disappeared into the thicket and survived, but only just. Hares 2, Greyhounds 0.

Just as I was debating whether to stay for the inevitable slaughter of one hare my mobile rang. It was Dr Paul. Dr Paul wanted to know what had gone down. I gave him an appraisal of the last slip.

'So what happened to the hare?' asked Dr Paul.

'Oh, it's probably being ripped to shreds right now,' I said jokingly, to which Deerstalker Man interjected, 'Na, na, na, na, no, no, no, no, don't say things like that. That hare went straight away, straight away.' What was it with these inbred freaks, repeating word, after, word, after, word, after word?

'That doesn't happen, that doesn't happen at all,' continued Deerstalker Man, now supported by a small mob of equally touchy-filthy friends. 'Don't give the wrong impression,' he added. 'Forgive me,' I mocked, barely able to conceal the cry of 'wankers' in a forced cough. The mob gave me the eye. I gave them the eye back. *Go on, make a move, you freaks.* The first half a dozen or so wouldn't be a problem: a left hook here, a straight right . . . it'd be fun. The other four thousand would be a bit of a handful though. Now they were all piling in. 'Ripping it to fucking pieces?' moaned one. 'Attacking hare coursing again, eh?' said another. 'For fuck's sake . . . unbelievable,' groaned another still.

'What's up?' I said, shrugging my shoulders as I made my way through the gauntlet of angry yokels, keeping a watchful eye on their fists, just in case someone fancied their chances. The cops weren't far away but they'd probably pile in too if the crowd turned nasty.

'If you don't like hare coursing, why don't you fuck off?' said one banjo-playing specimen as I walked by.

'Make me,' I snapped, stopping to glare at him. As Sophocles, or perhaps Chris Eubank, might have said, 'A short saying oft contains much wisdom,' so I told Banjo Boy to 'fuck off' for good measure. He gave an embarrassed grin, glanced round, looked me up and down and disappeared into the crowd. I could hear murmurs, words of disquiet: the prelude to action. I edged along at a skewed angle so I could keep an eye on my back and simultaneously keep an eye on the local pond life, in case they fancied giving me the bum's rush. I passed through the crowd, bumping a few shoulders and exchanging sneers and snarls, playing up to the sort of big bad black bogie man stereotype that freaks the shit out of white folks. Well, if you've got it, flaunt it.

I decided that two courses of wild hare à la frustrated grey-hounds was enough and split before I became dessert.

Most of the time greyhounds are docile, passive creatures. But they have a dark side to their character, a vicious mean streak essential to their pathology which is easy to ignore on the racetrack or when out for walks. Thousands of years of progressive breeding, crossbreeding, rearing and schooling have made them fundamentally highly trained assassins. That's why they race. The only reason they race. For a greyhound, chasing a plastic hare round a track is like a sniper taking pot shots at tin cans. Once faced with live bait, something tangible to aim at, the temptation to kill is overwhelming.

As for the hares, the National Coursing Club, in its glossy promotional literature, argues that the little buggers enjoy nothing more than a good day's coursing:

> Opponents of coursing admit that the sport ensures the preservation of the hare and that few are killed, but claim that the hares are terrified. Research carried out on behalf of the RSPCA by Dr Stoddart has shown that the flight of the hare is a natural, instinctive and routine response to danger. Dr Stoddart concluded that the hare would've become extinct years ago if it was not capable of escape from pursuit. For the hare, it's all in a day's work.'

I particularly love that last line about it being 'all in a day's work', as though dodging the snapping, salivating chops of two 34-kilo greyhounds is something a bad-ass hare's just gotta do to make it in the hood.

The seventeenth-century philosopher Thomas Hobbes could've been referring to hare coursing when he said famously, 'Life in an unregulated state of nature is solitary, poor, nasty, brutish and short.' It was precisely this idea, according to Hobbes, that caused humans to enter into social contracts, gladly accepting the moral constraints of civilisation to its alternative, the law of nature.

Morality, as an extension of that contract, is a way of protecting ourselves from the brutality of living in a world where people simply do what comes naturally, i.e. kick the living shit out of anything that moves.

A hare or a greyhound can't change its spots. But with the use of Oxy 10 a man can. To the uninitiated, coursing hares just for a lark was sadistic. Sure, farmers kill or cull foxes, hares, crows and other pesky critters all the time – but that's to protect their livelihood, which ultimately is in the food-buying public's interests. Animal husbandry is one thing; hunting for sport or, more accurately, to stiffen an erectile problem, is something else. Just because some weird practice has been around for centuries doesn't make it morally justifiable. Man will always try to rationalise bad behaviour by making a cultural virtue of it, especially if he gets a hard on to boot.

By the end of the day, Heneritta, a three-year-old greyhound bitch trained by Irishman Joe Walsh, had beaten Goodbye Joe to become the Waterloo Cup Wonderdog. No sooner had the rosettes, laurels and crowns of thorns been awarded than a war of words erupted between the RSPCA and the event organisers. The RSPCA said that in the last four events, 76 hares had been killed and claimed that one in 3.6 slips – the highest ratio since the charity had started keeping records – had resulted in a kill. But the National Coursing Club hit back, accusing the RSPCA of 'concocting the statistics' in order to boost opposition to the event. Liz Mort, spokeswoman for the National Coursing Club, told anyone who'd listen that the RSPCA's figures were 'pure fantasy'.

'These statistics are all wrong,' said Mort. 'There were a total of 109 slips and under 20 hares were caught.' The RSPCA was appalled at the suggestion that their officers had lied. There had been demos and counter-demos by outraged opponents and supporters alike. The Countryside Alliance claimed only one in eight hares was killed and said the crafty little buggers, much like the fox, had a good chance of escaping the hounds. The

International Fund for Animal Welfare (IFAW), on the other hand, insisted the death rate was nearer to one in five and said that one of its undercover investigators had witnessed Waterloo Cup organisers shipping in at least seventy hares two nights earlier. A few tweeds cried, 'Hear, hear!' and a few crusties yelled back 'Fuck off' and so the debate ding-donged in time-honoured fashion until all was forgotten, at least for another year.

Like *The Mousetrap*, the hunting issue was set to run and run. The day before the final, Westminster's Politburo had ended its consideration of the hunting bill, which was aimed at bringing about an effective ban on foxhunting and hare coursing in England and Wales. The rural affairs minister, Alun Michael, condemned hare coursing as an 'unnecessary and cruel activity' that failed the utility test set by the hunting bill. It was widely expected that when the bill returned to the Commons the following month many MPs would get tough and seek an amend-ment calling for a total ban outlawing *all* hunting with dogs. But why stop there? Having smelled blood, the animal rights lobby, spearheaded by the League Against Cruel Sports, was clawing for a ban on greyhound racing too, effectively outlawing the hunting of plastic bunnies and smelly old rags.

The abolitionists talked a good fight. But I had little faith, and less money, to back on New Labour coming to the rescue and actually standing by one of its manifesto commitments; there'd never be a ban on hare coursing and fox hunting, let alone greyhound racing without a bunch of limp-wristed provisos and get-out clauses attached.

To paraphrase John Gray, Professor of European Thought at the London School of Economics and author of *Straw Dogs: Thoughts on Humans and Other Animals*, for much of human history and all of prehistory, we did not see ourselves as different from any other animal. In fact, hunter-gatherers, to which hare coursers may claim a relation, saw their prey as equals, if not superiors. Ancient peoples worshipped greyhounds, like many animals. 'The humanist sense of a gulf between ourselves and other animals is an aberration,' says Gray.

I had tried to go hare coursing with an open mind. I'd seen *Snatch*. But fuck it. I was glad I hadn't seen a hare pulled apart at the seams. If greyhound racing was anachronistic, hare coursing was positively antediluvian. Lacking the high drama and brutal aesthetic of, say, bullfighting or boxing, and the genuine competitiveness of greyhound racing, it was hard to accept any argument in favour of hare coursing. This poor excuse for a 'sport' was a cheap and nasty little pastime that appealed to graceless drunken oafs who had nothing better to do than stand around a soggy field all day dressed up like toy soldiers, waiting with baited breath for the odd rodent to be devoured by hungry dogs.

We put animals in zoos and goldfish bowls and ring-fenced fields because we want to play God. We imagine that somehow we are subverting the Universe through such acts. We can peer, meddle, feed, love, withdraw love at our mercy. The animal looks up at us and prays in its silent way that today we are benevolent. A dog wags its tail and hopes we'll just carry on drinking, smoking, dancing away in our semi-detached Pantheons and not deliver an avalanche of hate or a psychological earthquake into its little world. When man hunts, he trades in God for the Devil. In such instances we still command divine control but we do so with a sadistic edge. There is the theoretical possibility of escape. Of course, like a bookie, we have adjusted the odds so that the experience is over-round: one way or another we can't lose. If the quarry has the good fortune to escape, we have still derived pleasure from the 'thrill of the chase', the foreplay *and* in-out, in-out of the act. If and when the kill comes, so much the better, for herein lies that essential ejaculatory moment.

The Devil gets all the best lines because of his unpredictability. This is what hunting is: a set of pre-arranged factors wrapped up in the fancy dress of apparent randomness. The 'laws of nature' apparently even things out. Trouble with that axiom is there are at least six billion people on the planet. Even if all the lions, tigers, cheetahs, crocs, black widows etc. formed their own G7 or NATO and massed ranks to take on the global enemy that is mankind, we'd take them out in no time. Gnashing teeth and a good line in stingy tails are no match for weapons-grade plutonium and Stealth bombers.

That said, what the hell do I know? While I found hare coursing and the people who practised it repugnant, my disgust didn't give me the moral ammunition to join the prohibitionists. I'd sit this one out and maintain the best position a journalist can ever occupy: smack bang on the fence. Rural Britain was another country and one that I felt I had no business troubling. Let them eat cake. Or as the nineteenth-century essayist William Hazlitt put it, 'There is nothing good to be had in the country or if there is, they will not let you have it.' Too fucking true. I hit the dirt road out of Great Altcar, did a wheel spin, turned left on to the B5195, left on to the A565, then the A5207, the M6, the M1 and kept right on driving with my foot to the floor, back to the relative civilisation of Londinium.

chapter 23

'Once upon a time you had White City, Wimbledon, Hackney, Wembley . . . and punters came in their droves.' Gary Long Tongue scanned the stadium mournfully. 'Now look at it.' It was a damp, listless Thursday night. I was down to my last score and searching the Stow for life. Drained of the chattering, raucous bodies that had been its lifeblood during the summer, the Stow had the ghostly air of an out-of-season seaside resort. There was still a crowd, still action, a few 'kiss me quick' revellers, but the greying cynical diehards had the run of it, not the party hearty six-packers.

'Greyhound racing's going down the toilet, mate,' said one punter, another lonely fool who was evidently eavesdropping on my conversation with Long Tongue. 'In the summer you'd be fooled into thinking the game's healthy but it's fucked. Once the weather turns it's empty here. Many owners don't race their dogs any more . . . same with trainers. Can't make it pay, can they?'

I certainly couldn't make it pay. But that didn't stop me coming back again and again. How had I become hooked by such a godforsaken, grimy, low-rent pastime like the dogs? Why is it so easy to become addicted to crap? Whether it's smack, crack, junk food, dogging, booze or tobacco, man's addictions have one thing in common: they're all based on a predilection for utter rubbish. Gambling is addictive because it's bad for you. And gambling is bad for you because, get this, *you lose*. And the more you lose, against all reason and better judgement, the more you're sucked in. Why? Well, apart from the subconscious need to beat yourself up, there are a number of reasons, but one other major factor is ego. Every time you lose, someone, somewhere has taken your money. They've bent you over a counter, pulled your pants down and given you a right good seeing to. And you want to get your own back. Gambling preys on the need for men to get their own back, to get even. One thing that boxing taught me is that you learn a lot more about life as a loser than as a winner.

We losers love gambling because it tempts us with the prospect of being a winner, a prospect that ultimately is never fulfilled. We always lose more than we win. Which reinforces the fact that we're losers. Which makes us feel good. Cos that way we wind up knowing we were right all along. We get *validation* through losing. Many gamblers are losers because they are addicted to gambling, not making money. If they were addicted to making money they'd engage in an activity that could yield them a greater profit, like a job, a rich wife or a career in the porn business. Unless you can turn gambling into something other than gambling, i.e. book-making, you're on a hiding to nothing.

A dictum of philosophy is that anything taken to an extreme turns into its opposite. I thus spent many hours, days, weeks and months pondering the probability of turning my increasing debt into a profit . . . with little success.

Having come through two hard races third and second, the formbook suggested that Kevin should've been a good bet as an 11–4 favourite in the previous day's BAG'S meeting. Just as well I didn't run the A406 gauntlet to see him race in the flesh. Instead I opted for the relative comfort of a smoke-filled betting shop in Portobello Road. As craggy-faced punters hacked their way through several tons of B&H, Silk Cut and Lucky Strike, I saw fifty quid on the nose sail down shit creek as Kevin feebly weathered the storm of another rocky race to finish fourth. That dog was a weed. He was over two years old now; he should've been bullying his opponents by now, instead he was still acting like the runt.

The BAGS was killing it for me, like it had killed it for a lot of small-time owners. Where was the joy, the pleasure, the excitement of watching your dog limp around on a freezing Friday afternoon while you ate a soggy meat pie and drank warm beer? So much for the glamour of racing. As far as I was concerned the little guy was getting shafted left, right and centre. Not only did we provide a service for the Big Three bookmakers to get fat, we had to do so at a time of day that was not conducive to us. I had a lot of time on my hands but I couldn't afford to spend it wiling away the daylight hours at a dog track.

On a lighter note, while Kevin was slumming it with his fellow scrubbers, his old buddy Twotone was in the UK Packaging Arc, second round, heat three, at the Stow. Second round, heat three! I could've owned that mutt. The top prize was £15,000. If he got to the final and won it I'd ring his little brindle neck! But I wasn't bitter.

'You would've been better off buying a dog from a sale than a trainer,' said Ginger, his eyes darting from me to the race card to the track. 'If it's any fucking good the trainer won't sell it to you, he'll sell it to one of his big owners, do you know what I mean?' Ginger laughed. My height decreased an inch per swipe, as he told me at a rate of knots what I'd known the moment I'd got knee deep into the dogs: I'd mugged myself off. 'And you went in at the deep end, didn't ya, with Linda Jones? You could've gone to someone small and got a cheap dog. I'd never buy a dog from any trainer. Ever. I don't see it run, I don't wanna buy it, simple as that. 'Ere, let's watch this race. I think six might lead five up. I make it a match five and six.'

What did Ginger know? He was currently lying third from bottom in the Tipster Challenge out of 25 tipsters, on minus £155, way behind 'The Fox', 'I Used To Wear Trousers' and 'Manface.' The Tipster Challenge was a monthly competition that cost £100 to enter but paid 80 per cent of the pool to whoever picked the most naps and next best selections on the evening cards. (The other 20 per cent went to the Owners Association.) With a payout of £800 to £1500 a month, it was a nice little earner and as a pool competition it didn't cost the Stow a penny.

What *did* Ginger know? A damn sight more than me, that's for sure. I'd come to know him through Tracy Cooper. He was one of the bigger punters I'd met at the Stow. Ginger always sat in the same seat in the main stand, usually with the same bunch of lads. And always had the same expectant look on his face. A youthful forty-five, he was more strawberry-blonde than ginger, well-fed but not a cholesterol factory like many punters I'd seen.

Ginger didn't get the forecast but he still picked another winner. Five beat one. 'One of the biggest owners at the Stow owns this,' he said, pointing to the five dog's form in the next race. 'Mr Correll. He's got about fifty-two dogs ... about half a million pounds' worth. And he pays MONEY. Never mind two-and-a-half grands. He pays twenty grands for his dogs. I saw him here earlier so I knew it was a runner.'

Ginger wasn't big like Correll but he had money invested in 'a few bits and pieces' of dogs scattered around and a promising pup at the Stow. 'It's had four runs, we bet it three times and it's won three times.' Ginger grinned. 'It won six-and-a-half on Tuesday – first time over the distance ... Patience is a virtue in this game. You've got to be patient.

'Me and the boys went to Ireland a few weeks back, just for a weekend of racing, and we picked up two young dogs there. They've both come out and both won twice for us. If they were with a big trainer, they'd be dear. You wanna buy something from Linda Jones, you're talking telephone numbers. But if you go to a little trainer in Ireland you can buy quite cheap. About ten years ago we bought twelve dogs for a £1000, took the whole lot. And every one of them dogs won.'

Ginger had been in the game since he was four, so you could say the dogs was in his blood. I was getting the feeling I was thirty-something years behind the competition. 'Me mum used to work at the dogs,' he told me. 'Me dad left when I was small so me mum used to take me across in the pushchair. I've been to nearly every track in England.

'I grew up with the dogs. Some people like to go discoing, drinking . . . I just like the dogs. I love the dogs. I *study* the dogs. When I finish the card tonight, I'll go home and I'll be studying till three, four in the morning for Saturday's meeting. I'll have people ring me up saying, "What d'you fancy, Ginge, what d'you fancy?" I know all the races already. I've read 'em so many times . . . I mean there's a dog running tonight, it'll be a big, big price, 33–1. I was gonna bet this next time up in an A7 but they've thrown it in an open race now – much too hot for it. Sometimes they do ya like that. But the dog'll come out *flying* and go straight for the rail. Could cut one off: 33–1? Maybe I'll have a few quid on it, take a chance.

'Once those traps open, mate, you're on your own. But horses are harder. You've got to get the horse to be right, the jockey to be right . . . Ain't no jockey pulling up a dog. Dogs run more to form than horses. A dog can only make its own mistakes but a horse can make a mistake *and* a jockey can make a mistake. You get much more value in a dog. I don't play the horses much. I might have a bet if I'm at home on a Saturday but I wouldn't go out of me way to bet a horse.'

Ginger had all the moves, all the ideas, all the lingo. He'd call Maxi Rumble, the darling of the Stow, a 'fucking aeroplane' but if a dog was a dead duck it'd be 'a fucking screw'. 'Dodge pot' or 'cripple' were others.

Punters throw insults at the dogs as a means of expressing anxiety or frustration rather than genuine malice. 'It's fucking paralysed,' they'll scream when a dog fails to make the turn or 'Die you fucking mutt,' they'll holler at any dog that's gaining on their selection, which does sound a bit strong. I even indulged in a little sledging myself but I never thought ill of a dog, no matter how useless it was. Linda, however, didn't care about the intent. To her, people who dissed dogs were scumbags.

'I hate it when people insult and swear at the dogs. It's not on. They do their best for these people and all they can do it slag 'em. There was a fella over the Stow recently started having a go at a dog. I said to him, "Why don't you fucking get down there, then, and see if you can do any better?" He shut right up. Ooh, it makes me mad.'

Still, dog people are dog people. They are entitled to their little grunts and gripes; after all, they've served their time. But the more dog people I met the more I felt like an outsider.

'I've been everywhere,' said Ginger, now clearly on a roll. 'I've had dogs on the flaps, Silver Salver, er, Aldershot, Derby, everywhere. I can do the tic-tacking, I can do it all, look.' Ginger started waving his arms around, wheeling and turning, just like a pro. 'One, two, three, four, five, six . . .' Clap, click, clop, click . . . '. . . Evens, eleven-a-ten, five-a-four, eleven-a-eight . . . Cos you grow up with it. Once you grow up with it you get used to it.

'This is racing. Everything's a challenge. You're always out to see if you can beat 'em. This geezer here is one of the best grading managers there is. He's *mustard*. He's mustard. But every now and again you think, I've got him. You won't find a better geezer at grading dogs up. The boys here buy videos of every meeting. I never bother with 'em. I believe what I see with me eyes, don't watch the telly. I see what I see in the race and I remember it. Cos if you start relying on the video you start seeing loads of things and doubting yourself. But that race manager is mustard.'

Not all race managers got the kind of respect Chris had. I heard many punters at the bookies grumble about the standard of grading at other tracks, particularly in the provinces. I usually avoided backing dogs at northern tracks for this reason. At many BAGS meetings I had watched on SIS, plenty of races produced finishes where the dogs came home in Indian file, indicating poor handicapping.

The race manager holds all the aces at a dog track. He has the power to disqualify, fine or ban a dog or its trainer or kennel staff for anything suspicious, he records track times, does the weighing in and officiates over disputes. He also has to keep an eye out for dogs with an attitude problem. Fighting is frowned upon and the NGRC operates a two-strikes-and-you're-out rule. If a dog is caught twice for biting another dog it is banned from racing, end of story. 'Aggressive interference' they call it. Some banned dogs invariably fall into the twilight world of flapping, where such rules and regulations are not enforced. Others that have been sanctioned just once or been a bit unruly in the kennels are put into hurdle races. Hurdling gives a dog something else to concentrate on rather than its competitors' jugulars. That's not to tar all hurdlers with the same brush. Many hurdlers have switched from flat racing for a number of reasons.

The race manager knows all the dogs at the track and as such allocates their races and trap numbers in accordance with their times and running styles. The last thing punters want is a wide runner in an inside box, careering all over the place. The race manager is to dog racing what a handicapper is to horseracing. His job is to match six dogs so that the statistical probability of a dead heat is raised. That's the theory at least. In practice this doesn't happen, simply because greyhounds have their own minds and occasionally, just occasionally, like to do their own thing. But punters want to see properly graded races where every dog is given at least a theoretical chance of winning.

Ginger could talk dogs until the cows came home. He'd had chunks on dogs here, lumps on them there. Three, four, five hundred quid straight bets were the norm. He liked the forecasts and tricasts too. He said there was hope for me yet, that knowing sweet FA wasn't a barrier to making a few quid.

'If you come here every meeting and you watch the dogs run and don't listen to people and do your own thing, you'll pick winners. But if you wanna be like me and bet every race, you can't do it. If you stick to a couple of races you can make this game pay. But never bet a dog odds on. Never. Even if it's first past the post I won't bet it. Quickest way to the poor house.'

And boy was I on my way there.

chapter 24

Today was the moment of truth, the day of judgement, the day of reckoning, the eleventh hour . . . The war in Iraq was on its way; but I had more important things to think about, namely would Kevin win the 4.18 that afternoon at Walthamstow. If he didn't win that was it, it would be over. I'd be out of the dogs, for good.

'I didn't want him to see me,' I said to Felix, as we strolled back from the traps. I had cajoled Felix, an old college buddy, into taking snaps of Kevin with his swanky digital Nikon camera. 'He might catch sight of me, you know, recognise me. Well, I'm easy to spot, aren't I? You don't get many black people at the dogs, do you?' Felix murmured, then carried on taking pictures of the crowd and the sun-kissed track, impervious to my armchair sociology.

' 'Ere, that's right,' said one of the floor men in the betting ring, sidling up next to me. 'One in five, I'd say . . . less probably. But at the bookies it's at least 50–50. I wonder why that is?'

'I've got no idea,' I said. I did have an idea but it was pointless trying to explain it with under thirty seconds to go to the race.

Once again, Kevin flopped. Fourth. It was his twenty-ninth race and the twelfth time he had come fourth. He did a 30.21, his slowest time in eight weeks. Whatever. The numbers didn't add up.

'Silly fucker.' A fella in the betting ring was whining about the five dog, a.k.a. Kevin. He ripped up his ticket and threw it on the floor dismissively. 'If it'd trapped instead of shitting itself it'd have had half a bloody chance.'

'Hey, that's my dog you're talking about,' I said, trying to make light of what was a shitty situation for me too.

'It could be your missus for all I care,' said the punter, walking away. 'I just lost fifty quid on that mutt.'

That mutt. How dare they talk about my Kevin like that! This was the problem with owning a loser. You became a de facto loser yourself. Loser, loser, loser. I went over to the paddock for the customary slap on Kevin's back. Belgian Patrick was cleaning him up. He brought him out and Felix started snapping away again. Kevin was panting and giving me a forlorn, dare I say, hangdog look.

'Eh, you could've bought Twotone, couldn't you?' said Patrick as I commiserated with Kevin. Not another one. Why bring that up? If I heard any more about Twotone I swore I'd head for Imperial Kennels and slip him a Mickey. Twotone this, Twotone that. I was sick of hearing about that damn dog. When I had told Tracy Cooper that I had had the opportunity of buying him her face had lit up like a Christmas tree.

'Really,' she said. 'For how much?'

'Four grand.'

'Four grand. Really?'

'Four grand. Why, what do you think he's worth now?'

'Oh . . . I'd say about . . . twelve to fourteen thousand pounds.'

I nearly choked. That dog was earning more money than I was. I had been monitoring him over the months, measuring and comparing his performances against Kevin's. The results did not make happy reading.

At this point in their careers Kevin had just run his thirtieth race and Twotone had twenty-six starts under his belt. Kevin had secured a mere four wins compared to Twotone's ten but I took some sadistic consolation in the fact that Twotone hadn't had a win in nine races. This was down to the increasingly competitive races he had to compete in. But where his form had started to dip in recent weeks, Kevin's had remained mediocre for months. My boy was consistent if nothing else.

When Twotone was on the up I had imagined him dressed in a smoking jacket and cravat back at Imperial Kennels, sipping on fine wines, chugging on a Cohiba, eating caviar and regaling the other keen-eyed greyhounds with his stories of derring do at the track, while Kevin sat in a corner, brooding, jealous, sensitive. At various points in his career Twotone had had an impressive 50 per cent strike rate compared to Kevin's 1 in 7.5. For the sake of 1500 measly pounds my fortunes could've been radically different.

I didn't need this. I had spent a small fortune in this game and for what? I had to stop this life-imitating-art-participatory-gonzo-journalism bullshit. The previous night I had been at the Stow and blown £150, after going £75 up on my roll. In a good week I could recycle several hundred pounds in bets yet I felt inadequate, totally out of my depth compared to most punters. The only time I felt equal to the guys at the track was when they lost. Vince had offered me some kind words to stem the tide of my growing cynicism. 'Once he gets the sun on his back, a shine to his coat, he'll come good,' he said reassuringly. God I hoped he was right.

'What d'you fancy?' Vince had asked as I peered dreamily at the race card.

'I dunno,' I replied.

'It'd help if you look at the right race,' said Paul, turning the page of my card. Jesus. Where was my head at?

As a visiting university lecturer, with an MA, I was practically an academic. I was a man of letters, a published author and award-winning journalist. The previous week I had given a speech at the Mansion House in front of the Duke of Edinburgh. I was *this* close to the fucking king of England! Last year I'd met Bill Clinton. Damn. That dirty ol' dog has one big-ass Cro-Magnon man-sized head. I had the mobile phone numbers of at least two D-list celebrities.

And I knew Vinnie Jones.

Ann from Marketing had introduced me to Vinnie one night

in the Paddock Grill, the Stow's 'prestigious restaurant'. The Chandlers, Dougie Tyler and all the big-time owners and corporate types hung out there. 'Hi, Ann, how are ya?' Vinnie gave Ann a warm kiss. He was wearing a white open-necked shirt and grey slacks. He looked like any other white boy wide boy with money rather than an ex-footballer turned Hollywood hard man.

'I'm fine, thanks,' said Ann. 'Vinnie, this is David. He's writing a book on greyhound racing.'

'Hello, David,' said Vinnie, giving me a soft handshake. I appealed to Vinnie's vanity and told him we shared the same publisher. He liked that. Without giving him the pitch, he knew the score.

'Get my number from Ann and we'll sort something out,' he said, giving me a knowing nod. 'I gotta go, see you later.' Vinnie was in a hurry. Ann gave me a wink. Nice PR.

Vinnie had been into the dogs since he was ten or eleven. He famously introduced Brad Pitt to greyhound racing when the pair were filming *Snatch*. At the last count he had 53 racing greyhounds and puppies, including a brood bitch named Smoking Barrels, twenty of which he raced at Hove under Derek Knight as well as the Stow with Gary Baggs. Jones had a dog that had come fourth in the Derby. Not bad out of 143 original entrants. He also had a horse called Sixty Seconds.

The Vinnie Joneses of this world were unofficially mandated with the responsibility of taking greyhound racing to the trendy masses, making it more attractive for a younger, funkier audience. Celebrities, always keen to get in on the next big thing, had followed the former Wimbledon hard man into greyhound racing like he was the Pied Piper. Brad Pitt, Damon Albarn, that geezer from *The Bill*, they all got in on the act. But rather than reinventing the wheel, this new generation of faces had only followed a long-established tradition. Outside the Paddock Grill was a rogue's gallery of celebrity photos: Mike Reid, Raymond Chandler, that geezer from *The Bill* again . . .

Following my brief encounter with Vinnie I called his people. I spoke to his agent's assistant, Cecilia. As her name indicated, she was posh totty.

'Vinnie's in Atlanta, then he's off to Prague for two weeks. May's chock-a-block and I can't commit to anything after that, sorry.' This is known in the business as the executive brush off.

But so what? I had better things to do than star gaze . . .

chapter 25

Chrome, plastic, synthetic fibres and a kaleidoscope of gaudy colours spewed together like a Saturday night pool of vomit; fruit machines, soggy chips, OAPs smoking for England; flat beer, flatter cola, chewing-gum stuck on the seats, translucent faces and empty heads . . .

Sitting in a bingo hall is like dropping acid without the threat of permanent psychosis. Not only is it a mind fuck, the cumulonimbus of carcinogens wafting through the room doesn't do much for your lungs either. The public didn't come here to play games; they came to smoke. If 80 per cent of the cost of a packet of fags went to the government in tax, I wanted a rebate. I must have got through 20 tabs just walking to the lavatory. Smoke and be damned.

My eyes were aching from looking at the carpet and wallpaper, let alone from staring at page after page after page of random numbers, while dabbing at them furiously with a marker pen. Never had the mundane required so much concentration. 'Seven and three . . . seventy-three. Number twelve, one and two. One and three, thirteen. Number four on its own, number four. Sixty-six, all the sixes . . .'

'Oussssse!'

'Sixty-six. A line one sixty-six . . .' Bollocks. So near and yet so farcical.

My mum had invited Margot and me to the Mecca bingo

hall on Hackney Road for a chance to win thousands and thousands of pounds, but the certainty of winning fuck all. We were also there to bond. When most parents want to meet their son with their 'partner' they invite them over for Sunday lunch or a night out to a bijou restaurant. But such niceties didn't happen in the Matthews family. No sir. When my mum wants to check out her next ex-daughter-in-law, she takes her to the bingo.

The old girl treated us to the festivities: about thirty-three quid on an assortment of bingo games, including the National, the Link and the American – potentially paying out from £20 for a line to £95,000 for the national game, which was linked to Mecca's cross-country bingo network.

'You've got to move faster, faster,' my mum kept saying as the caller reeled off digits like Mecca had just bought a job lot of prime numbers, odds, evens and 'fat ladies'. 'Christ. I can't keep up,' I said. 'How the hell do you do this at your age?'

'You gotta move, move.'

The game is surprisingly fast, and strangely addictive. If you can handle being used as a human beagle for cancer research, smoke-filled location aside, bingo is quite a compelling game. The addiction comes from the repetition, the knowing that the same thing will happen repeatedly. In essence, this is what addiction is all about: the need to repeat. The predictability of doing something until your fingers fall off is reassuring for many people. And occasionally, just occasionally, ye gods shine on you and hand over some moolah. Just like at the dogs.

The losing is the predictable bit, the meat and drink of gambling. It's also part of the working-man's philosophy that 'Everything else is a bonus,' which is a bit like contracting lung cancer and thinking, *hmm, well at least it wasn't testicular*. It was slowly dawning on me that *I didn't have to be a loser all my life*.

Winners, many of whom I have had the privilege and misfortune to know by the truckload, don't think that 'Everything else is a bonus.' To a winner, losing is the bonus or, put another way, it is the *slim* possibility of defeat that gives their calculated odds of winning the necessary zest to make the game interesting.

Since the introduction of the Lotto, née National Lottery, in 1997 ('It Could Be You' but it sure as hell won't be), it was now beyond doubt that Britain was a nation of losers, for to gamble excessively is to lose excessively. The Lotto, as Billy Connolly pointed out in an aggressive ad campaign, is, for a paltry pound coin, an easy tease. Why live on a rundown council estate existing on month-old bread and rusting tins of Spam when you can take your 14,394,367–1 chances and pocket a few mil?

In all my days of growing up, my dear mother had never been a gambler, unlike my father. But lately even she had joined the bandwagon, thanks to the convenience of the modern gaming industry. Twice as many women in Britain as men play bingo. It's the only gambling proposition where female punters outnumber males. Chicks love it, probably because it gets them out of the house and away from their grumpy old men, the screaming kids and the barking dogs. Judging by the 'talent' in the hall, though, I think many a husband and boyfriend appreciated the space too.

The dogs may be a guy thing and bingo a chick thing, but everyone is playing the wheel of misfortune these days: geriatrics, teenagers, black, white, rich, poor . . . no, scrub the rich . . . compulsives, impulsives, repulsives, everyone has a game of choice. Millions are hooked on scratch cards, text competitions, pools, sports betting, spread betting, bingo, bookies, dice, cards, quiz machines, fruit machines, one-arm bandits, two-horse races and three-card Monty, all of which amount to a massive five-knuckle shuffle for the punter. Britain is in the grip of gambling fever.

In Las Vegas, they have slot machines in the backs of cabs, just in case you get withdrawal symptoms travelling between the crap tables at Caesar's Palace and the poker room at the Sands. And you know that we're twenty years behind America. Actually, that's not strictly true. We're twenty years behind them in terms of the shitty stuff but fifty years ahead on everything else, like fashion, art, culture, civilisation, that sort of thing.

Soon, Britain's gaming laws would be liberalised and then it'd be open season on gambling. And the dog tracks were better placed than most to capitalise. Unlike racecourses, dog tracks tend to be in or around big cities and towns, have ample capacity for man and car alike, are easily accessible and have the gambling experience and floor space to accommodate their own casinos, just like Sheffield's dog track, Owlerton Stadium, who helpfully note in their programmes that, 'No strippergrams will be allowed on these premises.' Very post-*Full Monty*.

Just as I was getting into the swing of things my flow was interrupted by a commotion a few tables away from us. A greying old man in his sixties had collapsed with a suspected heart attack. Mum reckoned it was the stress of playing bingo. Margot thought it was to do with the oppressive heat in the hall and the result of the scores of high-wattage lamps designed to help people see the cards. I thought it was simply because he was old, as that's what old people do: they roll over and die and SPOIL YOUR BLOODY EVENING.

'Can someone call an ambulance?' said a fishwife sitting across from the heart-attack man. A small crowd flapped round him and one woman kindly dialled 999 from her mobile, as emergency calls don't cost anything, even on Pay-As-You-Go. But as soon as the caller started up again with, 'Eyes down,' they fled back to their bingo cards, leaving the man propped up against his table, wheezing like a semi-deflated blow-up doll. People are so selfish. Of course *I* would have helped the guy out but I needed 'one and four, fourteen' for a full house and I was damned if some bird with no teeth called Eileen was gonna beat me to it.

chapter 26

Spring came late as usual, or perhaps summer had come early. Winter stood at the new season's gates, shaking its fist like a miserable old git. The winter months at the track had been bleak, and made bleaker by Kevin's mediocre form. He'd had something like thirty races to date and five wins. There you go: the magical 'one-in-six'. I hoped that the fair weather might improve Kevin's chances.

I was spending an unhealthy amount of time at the track. Every opportunity I had I was down there. My problem, apart from not being able to pick any winners, was that the frequency of my betting had increased steadily over the months. The most I'd bet on a single wager was £100, but nevertheless all those little bets were starting to mount up.

When I had cash in pocket (ha!) I'd have straight win bets. When I was on my uppers I'd chance my arm with a few quid on reversed forecasts and tricasts. But I had to have a bet in some form. I needed that fix. However, I only ever seemed to recycle my money. If I were up £200 one week, I'd be down £300 the next. My form was as unpredictable as Kevin's.

Thanks to an epiphany of 'professional integrity' I had decided to stop writing rubbish for the tabloids. However, not writing rubbish and concentrating on serious issues reduced my income by about, oh, 100 per cent. My outgoings were killing me. The payments on the Porsche, the yacht and the villa in the South of

France would, er, have to wait while I concentrated on paying parking fines, rent and utility bills. I knew I'd spunked a few grand but was unable to account for any of it.

The sum of my gambling was a bunch of old betting slips, illegible notes of results and bets and systems scrawled over race cards, envelopes, red letters and sundry bits of paper, a stack of dog-eared copies of the *Racing Post* and a spiralling kennel bill. Oh, and I did have an over-the-top overdraft and half a dozen credit cards on meltdown too.

Over the weekend Baghdad had taken a pounding in Gulf War II: Return of the Fuckwits. I hadn't done much better at the track. I asked Dougie's sons what odds they'd give me on an Iraqi victory. Yeah, I'm a sucker for the underdog. They looked at me apologetically. Perhaps the joke was in poor taste. But it could've been worse. I once tried to get odds from William Hill on the Queen Mum and the Pope dying within twelve months of each other. Unsurprisingly they didn't take the bet. Thorstein Veblen wrote in *The Theory of the Leisure Class* that, 'We have a need to have entertainment during times of crisis.' I had a need for entertainment in my time of crisis. But as my crisis was financial I couldn't afford any bloody entertainment.

'So, are you going to open a casino here?' I asked Ann, dunking a digestive biscuit into my tea. I could always be guaranteed a cuppa in her office if I'd spunked my beer money at the track.

'I don't know. I couldn't say yes or no really. Why do you ask?'

'Well, it's just I'd heard a rumour that you guys were thinking of selling up, which seemed odd because this place is a licence to print money.'

'Selling up, eh? Where did you hear that?'

'Oh, just some fella at the track. You know, the usual gossip.'

'We get these rumours surfacing from time to time . . .'

There were always rumours going around, rumours about dogs, hot tips, the war. Most of them were bullshit. But if you were 'in the know' you might get wind of something special. I'd become so accustomed to people listening in or inviting themselves into my conversations at the track that I too was now in the habit of eavesdropping on every little piece of chitchat I could. If you were lucky you might get a tip or hear someone in the toilets talking about fake Rolex watches, hot mobiles or bank jobs.

I hung around the track until that evening's meet. Dog tracks are great places to simply hang around. I'd become good at that these days, hanging around. I often felt I was bringing up the rear in a futile race against time, despite harbouring a constant, nagging fear that I was wasting my time, my life, through disorganisation and poor 'time management', i.e. laziness. I popped over to the Popular Enclosure, hoping to catch Vince. I hadn't seen him for a while. I had a present for him.

'Sorry, I've been meaning to give this to you,' I said, handing over a video of Scurlogue Champ's greatest hits which Vince had lent me eight months earlier. He grinned, took the video and carried on looking at his race card. Neither he nor the Saints were having a good night.

'I'm going to see Chris Page in a minute,' I said.

'Oh really?' said Vince, animatedly. 'Ask him what's happened to the traps. They had three false starts last week. One of 'em even did a U-turn and started running in the opposite direction . . . never seen anything like it.'

Most punters would give their back teeth to get into a race manager's head, as his most important role as far as they are concerned is grading. On my way to see Chris, dark thoughts entered my mind. Maybe there was some way I could change his direction? No, not get him in a Ron Davies type moment of madness. I mean exploit his human frailties. What was his weakness? I wondered. What was his Achilles heel? Even a straight guy like him had to have a kink in his character some-where. Financial inducement would be far too tacky. That sort of move is best left to wealthy Arab shopkeepers and Tory MPs. Besides, I was skint. I couldn't afford the brown paper envelope, let alone the dough to put inside it. No, what I had in mind was more along the lines of the journalist's trusty manoeuvre: bad publicity. Maybe if I slipped into the racing office and caught them at it, whatever 'it' was, I could get an edge, maybe get Kevin dropped a grade or two or, better yet, matched against three terrapins, a tortoise and a dead cat.

During race meetings, once he had done the preliminaries, Chris lived up in the gods, in a little office high above the spectators, overlooking the finish line. From this vantage point he could see each race in its entirety and along with his two colleagues and a computerised timing and video recording system he compiled the necessary data that was circulated to the betting results services and used in future race programmes.

As fascinating as it was watching Chris spot minor infractions and incidences on the track and punch numbers into a computer, I didn't get any juice. Chris was so straight he was liable to snap in half. There were no drunken orgies going on up there, no lines of Coke on mirrors or gimps. Without the necessary leverage for blackmail I decided to let Chris and his fellow Honest Johns get on with it and took off. On my way downstairs I passed through the rather elegant Goodwood Lounge when someone cried out to me, 'Oi, Dave, over 'ere.'

His name was Michael Marks, David Stephens, Matthew Richards or some such doubled-up apostolic name. I had drunk too much that evening to think or care. Did we used to work on a building site somewhere together? Then it started coming back to me. I used to call him Rottweiler, because he looked like one and had a short temper.

'You don't remember me, do you?'

'To be honest, John, no.'

Rottweiler laughed. He didn't care that I couldn't remember him. Being a nobody was an occupational hazard. I knew that from experience. I didn't remember him at first because I guess it was easier to forget. Here's a tip: if you're ever in the East End and you bump into a fella but you can't remember his name, call him John. It's such a common name that at least 50 per cent of the time you'll guess right. And if you're wrong, keep calling him John anyway. It's a bit of an East End thing; like calling someone 'mate', 'china' or 'slag'.

'I heard that you're a journalist these days,' said Rottweiler.

'Yeah, for my sins. I'm actually writing a book on greyhound racing. I own a dog that I race over here.' Rottweiler looked at me dumbfounded, and laughed. I found it embarrassing meeting people from the past, people I had nothing to say to.

'Anyway, I've to go upstairs and interview someone right now. I'll see you on the way down.'

Got out of that one. Once upon a time I had another life, one not so far from the Stow. But despite my frequent visits to the track I seldom looked in on my old mates. A few were in jail, incoherently nuts or dead, so unless I found myself a good rope ladder, a lot of patience and a time machine, they were off the Sunday visit list. Most of my old school mates though I only saw at weddings, funerals and stag dos, which was just as well because we seemed to have so little in common these days. Many of them equated journalists with police informers and a few had actually grown to distrust me simply because of the (justifiably) bad reputation hacks have for selling their grannies to get a story.

Since the publication of my first book and the critical acclaim I got for it (ahem!) as far as the old school were concerned operating in the public domain meant exposure, and exposure was something many of my boys could do without. I felt sad at times that I had moved out of the loop and couldn't relate to people I'd known intimately since childhood. But times change and people move on. My idea of a great night out isn't smuggling ten kilos of coke in a camper van on a cross-channel ferry, thank you very much; and while I like a good drink as much as the next bad boy I like to keep my blood-alcohol levels with the balance on the blood side of the scales.

'I've got to go, mate. Got winnings to collect and all that. Be lucky.'

'Yeah, all the best.' John put his hand out. I shook it. It was clammy. Like he'd just been playing with himself.

I went back down to the betting ring. I had no winnings to collect, only thoughts. Why return to Walthamstow after all these years? What was the point in going back? I'd done so much to get the hell out of this crummy neighbourhood and a dog had dragged me back, and dragged me down too.

Down in the betting ring I ran into Ginger and his mate Phil. Phil had a touch of the Dirty Den about him. He was middle-aged, with slick, dark hair, lean and sharp features, always the geezer in slacks, loafers and open-necked shirts and leather jackets and jewellery, but nothing too ostentatious. He owned a mini-cab company. He turned over a lot of bread. 'They all know me down there,' said Phil, nodding towards the bookies, 'either as Phil or Romford Phil or Romford.'

Phil was a big punter. A thousand pound a race was nothing to him. Consequently, the bookies would run shy of him at times. 'It's all about beating them at their own game,' Phil would say. 'To beat the bookies you've got to think like them, bet like them.'

Like all big punters, Romford Phil had a system. Back in the main stand he explained it: it's what's known as 'hedging' or 'dutching'. 'What I do is play the bookies at their own game,' said Phil, 'it's the only way you'll get anything out of them. See, I don't like to have big single bets like these fellas.' He cast his eyes over Ginger and his pals and frowned. 'They think I'm mad doing it this way . . . too complicated for 'em. But the way that I look at it is, rather than put big single lumps on a dog, I'd rather spread the same amount of money across three dogs and increase my chances of winning. Look, this is how it works . . .'

Phil started scribbling figures on his *Racing Post*, outlining the level of stake to put on each dog according to its odds. The idea was to scrub out the two rank outsiders in the field and from that work out the likely winner from the remaining three or four runners. Phil would then hedge his bets by putting say £150 on one dog, £300 on another and £250 on a third, depending on the odds. Occasionally he'd back a fourth dog against the bookies.

'A punter doesn't have to bet on every race,' said Phil, pulling out a brick-sized wad of notes, 'but the bookies have to take bets, they have to take a risk or they won't make money. So you work the odds to your favour. You bet on what *you* want, not what they want. Patience is a virtue in dog racing.'

Like Ginger, Vince and every serious punter I'd come across, Phil had a highly developed level of mental arithmetic. But none of these guys were mathematical geniuses or even enjoyed maths at school. Many punters didn't even finish formal education. Even the larger than life John McCririck, ex-bookie and Channel 4's eccentric and bejewelled racing pundit, had said he 'couldn't even pass my Elementary Maths O-Level'. Being a mathematical whiz was not a prerequisite to being a bookie or gambler so there was hope for me yet.

What kind of cultural values are at play in a society where a largely working-class and moderate to poorly educated band of gamblers and dog fanciers can work out statistics, form and complex betting permutations that would challenge the average accountant but are incapable of going beyond comprehensive school education?

I had a degree in business, scored an A in my statistics finals and couldn't understand half the shit these guys spoke about.

But of course it didn't always go their way. Ginger lost £300 on a mutt called Toosey Magic in the last race of the evening. He'd waited all night for this opportunity. The others were so convinced by Ginger's predictive powers that they too laid several hundred pounds on the dog. Ginger had slipped down to the bookies and wagered what looked like a couple of grand in total. These guys could lose more in one night, individually, than I could *win* in a year. When I asked Ginger how he felt about losing big lumps of cash he simply shrugged his shoulders and said, 'Win some, lose some.'

The wads of cash that people handled at the track always

intrigued me: bulging doorstops of tens, twenties and fifties, thick juicy wedges of cash to be touched, to be won and lost. Forensic examination of the notes doing the rounds at the Stow would uncover traces of cocaine, carbon deposits from spent shotgun cartridges, blood . . . At a dog track there is enough dirty cash in circulation to make a Nigerian oil minister's eyes pop out. The obligatory wad of cash is always kept in mini wads of a hundred, preferably with four twenties back to back with another folded across like a money clip; that way one hundred pound batches can be conveniently removed from the pocket without the need to rifle through loose cash or count. Similarly, wads are always kept in the pocket, never a wallet, as nothing short of a handbag can accommodate £1000 plus in cash.

Of course, I didn't have the disposables to front it like Ginger, Romford Phil and the like, although I would occasionally, when I was flush, stuff several hundred pounds in my pockets, just so I could *feel* like a high roller in the betting ring.

According Dr Rebecca Cassidy, an anthropologist at Goldsmiths University, men, specifically, gamble because gambling evokes a sense of 'being a good bloke'. You are in essence defined by your wad. I could appreciate this notion, coming from a background where cash is king. Whether down the pub or the snooker hall, in the East End you are always armed with a wad of cash, good old working-class currency. Back in the day, credit cards were for fags. Real men eat cash, not quiche.

I think our relationship with cash comes from those afternoons way back in childhood spent playing Monopoly or 'shops', toying with wads of fake money as we dreamed of one day doing the same with the Real McCoy. 'Gambling money is play money,' Dr Cassidy told me. 'You don't use gambling money for practical purposes, such as paying the rent or the gas bill.' No, gambling money is special money, money for treats like booze, a good curry and more gambling.

Everybody's trying to beat the system somewhere, somehow. In boxing, beating the system means not being killed. Winning comes into it somewhere but the manner in which you win is more important than the pure statistical record of success. In greyhound racing, beating the system for the punter is beating the bookies and, given the state of my finances, it was time to start accepting that the system had perhaps beaten me.

chapter 27

Joy and love and carbon monoxide were in the air. Looking out of the window on to the Thames I had the kind of vista I had always dreamed of. Suddenly, to paraphrase Tony Montana in *Scarface*, London was 'one big pussy waiting to get fucked'. According to the *Sunday Times* my local Sainsbury's on the Cromwell Road sold more bottled water than any other super-market in Britain. Look Ma, top of the world! All I needed now was a Volvo, a set of golf clubs, and a prolonged course of psychotherapy and my embourgeoisement would be complete. Some money would help too. In fact, *a lot* of money would help.

One day, I pulled up to the front gates of the apartment block. I had never lived in a gated community before, well, not one that was as easy to walk out of as it was to walk into. I had left my remote control for the gate in the apartment so I idled in front of the gate, waiting for it to open. One of the concierges approached me. 'Good afternoon, Sir. Can I help you?' 'Er, no,' I said. 'I live here.' 'OK, right, er, that's that then. Have a nice day.' Bet he wasn't expecting that in his cheap suit.

'Getting on is the opium of the middle classes.' Walter James, b. 1912. If this was the case then gambling was the crack cocaine of the working classes . . . I had Spanish lessons and occasional massages and pedicures. I had membership to a private club and an exclusive health resort. I took black cabs instead of mini cabs

... I'd moved further from Walthamstow, Paddington and Harlesden both physically and metaphorically. If I migrated any further westwards I'd be chewing tobacco, wearing a ten-gallon hat, chaps and riding a bucking bronco.

On the surface I had moved up in the world. This had had a temporary effect on both Kevin's and my fortunes. Within days of moving into my new, riverside, gated home, I'd won a few quid on the old dog in a trifecta at the track. He then won the following Monday, his first victory in eight outings followed by a couple of second places.

After a succession of nothing but grey BAGS meetings I finally hit the track on an afternoon when the sun was out. Life was so much more bearable in the spring and the summer.

'He's got two chances,' said Billy, chalking up 7–2 next to *Zussies Boy*.

'Don't start,' I said. 'I was about to have a punt.'

'I'm kidding. He's a good dog, that Zussies Boy,' said Bill. I waited for the punchline but none came. 'Yeah, a good dog. Not bad. I've seen worse.'

'In that case I'll have a score on him.' I pulled out a twenty and handed it over. If Kevin didn't win it was a long way back to Battersea. In the event, I didn't need the exercise. The boy trapped real sharp, bumped the one dog but recovered to romp home in a personal best of 29.55. You beauty. When I went to congratulate him on his success, Kelly said she thought that perhaps he didn't like the cold weather and now the sun was out maybe, just maybe, he'd perform.

'Well done, mate.' Some guy called Pete introduced himself to me by the paddock and gave me a pat on the shoulder. 'Well done.' Pete kept on walking, going about his business, smiling. I'd never met the guy before. My win, Kevin's win, *our* win had put a smile not just on my face but also on somebody else's. In a world where praise is scant and recognition fleeting, being the best for most is never a prospect. At the coalface of society simple pleasures count. To win at something, anything was an achievement when the most you'd ever won before was a plastic gimcrack or a goldfish with a seven-day shelf life at the fair.

Maybe there was the outside chance that Kevin could turn the corner and make it. The statistics seemed to prove that he was a fair-weather runner. Out of forty-two starts he had won seven races, which meant he was maintaining his hit rate of one-in-six; not fantastic but not utterly hopeless.

After the BAGS meeting I took off for Walthamstow High Street to celebrate Kevin's success with plate of double pie and mash. Flicking through the *Racing Post* I noticed there were further BAGS meets at Monmore Green that evening so I finished up, went to the nearest cash till and strolled into Ladbrokes up the road.

'Hello, is that David Matthews?' You know you're in trouble with an introduction like that.

'Yes it is. What can I do for you?'

'Hi, my name's Mark. I'm calling from MBNA bank. You have an outstanding . . .'

'Hang on a second. Go on, my son, go on . . .'

'Yes, you have a payment overdue and . . .'

'Sorry. Yes, yes, yes . . .'

'You need to make a payment before . . .'

'Look, I'm kind of busy at the moment trying to win back that outstanding payment. Now if you just leave it with me I'll take care of business.'

'But . . .'

Who did these people think they were? Calling you up like that in the evening. There was no respect for time any more. The 24-hour society meant that banks, credit card companies and the like could call you after office hours and at weekends, hassling you for cash. Away with you! My attitude was, debt is a commercial thing and thus it only counts during nine-to-five office hours. The rest of the time I'm a debt-free citizen.

Two hours later I emerged, £75 lighter than I had been when I entered. The 10 to 20 per cent of the time that I actually won money the cash would slip into the shadows of my back pocket without a trace, then creep out moments later like a teenager on heat. Maybe I didn't want to win at all? Or had I formed an unhealthy relationship with losing? In Bill Bryson's charming book *Mother Tongue*, he wrote that dogs go '*ouâ-ouâ* in France, *bu-bu* in Italy, *mung-mung* in Korea and *wan-wan* in Japan'. For some strange reason when I backed them they seemed to go 'last-last'.

It was approaching time for me to start thinking about Kevin's future or, more importantly, how I was going to get rid of him. I'd been a real April Fool. What a month. I was approaching a grand in arrears over my kennel bill and had blown several thousand pounds more in betting. How I had amassed such a loss I couldn't tell but I seemed to be haemorrhaging money. I was living so far beyond my means we were in different time zones. Kevin had come second twice, third and fifth that month. He was going backwards. Soon he wouldn't bother coming out of the kennels, just kick back with a fag and say, 'Nah, don't fancy this one. I'm staying put.' As seasons changed I'd suffered my heaviest losses to date. Perhaps it was a sense of optimism that kept me going. But the gambling was starting to get out of hand. Perhaps I was giving my troubles too much thought.

I could feel the threads of life's rich tapestry slowly coming apart at the seams. It was Margot's birthday and cash was running low. At this rate the only present she'd get from me was a hard luck story. Still, it was a convenient excuse not to spoil her. She never appreciated my fucking presents anyway. I now had a budget of just fifty quid for presents and another fifty to keep me going. The plan was to go to the bookies and win her birthday present. I'd try Corals on Battersea Park Road for a change. I'd been lucky the last time I popped in. Yes, lucky. I'd managed to walk out with my shirt *and* pants intact. As soon as I doubled my money I'd walk away and go buy Margot a bag full of goodies.

Conveniently, where I lived was ringed by a number of bookies, enough to keep a compulsive gambler happy. There was the

Tote on Battersea Bridge Road, then Corals, William Hill and Ladbrokes on Battersea Park Road.

I thought I'd try out Romford Phil's hedge betting system, so I spread forty quid in the bookies on the 3.07 at Monmore by placing £10 on trap 1 at 4–1, £10 on trap 2 at 4–1 and £20 on trap 6 at 5–2. None of them came in. Stupid fucking hedge betting. Bollocks. So much for the *Racing Post* nap selection too. I should've stuck with my own bad judgement. I screwed up the slip and threw it dejectedly across the shop floor, hitting a guy in the side of the face. I then spunked another score or so on piddling forecasts, tricasts and video roulette. This didn't leave much for presents. I wound up buying Margot a dodgy picture frame and a book she's never read. It was after this maddening afternoon in the bookies that I decided to go to Gamblers Anonymous. Life had started to imitate art with treacherous consequences. All I had for chronicling the underbelly of British society were empty pockets and a stomach ulcer. In fact, as cliché no. 167 goes: if it weren't for bad luck, I'd have no luck at all.

What bullshit. Gambling to buy birthday presents. This was almost as absurd as gambling to pay my bills. What next, gambling to pay my gambling debts? It was getting so bad that I'd be in the pub and when one of those charity cases came in, you know, with the fake ID and the plastic egg-timer-shaped ponce box I'd say, 'I can't make a *donation*. But I bet you I can guess how much money you've got in there to the nearest pound. If I win I keep the money. If I lose I'll give you double the amount you've got.'

Of course they never went for it. They'd always say that it was 'illegal' or some silliness like that. Still, at least it got me out of a donation without ignoring the poor bastard or uttering some student union line about 'not believing in charity and it being the government's responsibility and nah, nah, nah-nah-nah . . .'

Margot had become concerned at my increasing interest in betting and my mood swings. 'You're not turning into a compulsive gambler, are you?' she asked one evening. 'No, of course not,' I replied. 'I bet you even money I don't have a problem with gambling.' She didn't laugh. Margot had seen me pouring over bits of paper and betting slips, scribbling notes and making various miscalculations night after night and I had acquired various books on gambling and statistics in the past few months. I'd got into this game for sport, comically thinking I could make a fast buck out of it: now I was on the brink of financial meltdown.

It almost goes without saying that greyhound racing, while an amusing pastime for the casual onlooker, is rooted in gambling. I was mad to have thought all those months ago that I could get into the dogs without gambling. Having something to lose, be it your pride, reputation or shirt, transcends the sport into another realm. It was the same thing I had found with boxing – what psychologists call the 'rollercoaster syndrome', the need to always be on the edge of potential or impeding catastrophe.

I needed the fix so instantly I couldn't waste time travelling to the track. I'd just go straight to the local bookies, another cauldron of testosterone, just like the betting ring at the Stow. Bookies stink of masculine deceit. The macho posturing and aggression in these environments partly explain why women are virtually non-existent in the betting ring, other than as curious onlookers to the antics of their menfolk; and the women in betting shops, a significant minority drawn largely from the white bread, twenty Silk Cut and a scratch card classes, are the kind of bints that used to give the January sales a bad name. In the bookies you get a few little old ladies wagering their pension books and the odd one or two on the fruit machines accompanying their compulsive partners, but it's certainly no pick-up joint.

If I were a new-age, born-again, revisionist, new-man psychologist I'd probably make a connection between cruising and men hanging around in betting shops, tracks, five-a-side football pitches and prison cells. Men like hanging out with each other, I suspect, more than women like hanging out with women. Men like hanging out with women when they're after something, nominally sex or food. The rest of the time we can amuse ourselves with a vast array of toys, inventions, machinations and the like. Women, by drawing attention to our anally retentive desire for such distractions, do not make convenient playmates in such games. Their need to probe, to investigate the statistical absurdity of the Goliath, the Heinz or the ITV Seven, to highlight the overstated importance of the off-side rule (a rule so simple to comprehend a marmoset could figure it out in thirty seconds yet a woman feels duty bound to 'not get it') embarrasses most men.

Men that have had the macho-guy hardwiring removed, or at least modified, tend to find female company easy. In essence those men have been feminised. Feminisation makes things work. The world doesn't work better through the masculinisation or retardation of women. You only have to look at Africa and Islamic states to realise that 'keeping women in their place' creates fascism and mayhem. Having only 49 per cent of the world's population, i.e. men, running the show is not the way forward. Britain would've been wiped out during the Second World War had women not gone to work in industry.

I had amassed a library of bits of paper with stats, facts and figures thrown together in the fantastical belief that somehow this information would lead me to the pot at the end of the rainbow. But to a gambler, the pot would only present another opportunity to test the boundaries of his failure.

'Go on trap two,' said the man, tapping the TV screen as if to gee on the dog. 'Go on, ya blood claat!'

What a clown; riding the betting shop pony was an exercise in dismay. The few spare coins I had left I threw into a video roulette machine. Clunk. Clunk. My money was gone. The screen seemed to turn black, as if to say, 'I don't play with broke-ass losers,' and I noticed my reflection in the glass. I looked pained, haggard. And all along there was I thinking I was having a great time shovelling fives, tens and twenties into the betting industry's coffers.

I had a problem. Not a major one, but a problem nonetheless. I had the Chinese water torture version of gambling addiction, a daily, constant drip drip of fives, tens, twenties, small change, credit card transactions, milk tokens, gift vouchers, anything. I had been consumed by my own artifice, exposed by reckless conceit. I had to do something about this before I was sunk. Something in the region of £15,000 had disappeared in under a year and I had nothing to show for it other than a collection of torn betting slips, sob stories and a dog that was worth more in cat food than kennel bills. Kevin was spoilt. A useful amount o' fleas is good for a dog – keeps him from brooding over bein' a dog.

I got some information about Gamblers Anonymous, just out of curiosity. The flyer said: 'Most compulsive gamblers will answer YES to at least SEVEN of these questions:

1. Do you lose time from work due to gambling?
2. Is gambling making your home life unhappy?
3. Is gambling affecting your reputation?
4. Have you ever felt remorse after gambling?
5. Do you ever gamble to get money with which to pay debts or to otherwise solve financial difficulties?
6. Does gambling cause a decrease in your ambition or efficiency?
7. After losing, do you feel you must return as soon as possible and win back your losses?
8. After a win do you have a strong urge to return and win more?
9. Do you often gamble until your last pound is gone?
10. Do you ever borrow to finance your gambling?
11. Have you ever sold anything to finance gambling?
12. Are you reluctant to use gambling money for normal expenditures?
13. Does gambling make you careless of the welfare of your family?
14. Do you gamble longer than you planned?
15. Do you ever gamble to escape worry or trouble?

16. Have you ever committed, or considered committing, an illegal act to finance gambling?
17. Does gambling cause you to have difficulty in sleeping?
18. Do arguments, disappointments, or frustrations create an urge within you to gamble?
19. Do you have an urge to celebrate any good fortune by a few hours' gambling?
20. Have you ever considered self-destruction as a result of your gambling?

I answered YES to eleven of the above questions.

chapter 28

The more I got into gambling, the less I saw the dogs as living, breathing creatures. Just as brokers do not care much for the physical, spiritual or philosophical nature of what they trade in, a gambler does not think too deeply about the welfare of the greyhounds he backs. I am not suggesting that gamblers wish harm on a dog, or any animal for that matter; gamblers are not necessarily barbarians. If anything, they believe deep down that good animal welfare is essential for the sports to survive and for them to have sufficient gambling opportunities. Ill-treatment of dogs also gives the sport a bad name and by implication gamblers too, which is why perhaps gamblers tend to be very charitable outside of the money markets of the races.

While I was at the track I ran into Ginger, who kindly reminded me what the root of my problem was.

'Yeah, get rid of him now while he's still winning. You'll get your money back that way. You keep him any longer, mate, and he'll be worth nothing, nothing, mate. Stick 'im in there.' Ginger pointed to a copy of the *Racing Post* on the table. I felt a bit sentimental. To people like Ginger racing dogs were just a commodity, a gambling chip. I told Ginger what a dead loss Kevin had been. ' 'Ere, Dave got into the dogs to write a book about it and now he's a compulsive gambler,' he joked with Romford Phil that night.

'Yeah, put an ad in there,' repeated Ginger, stabbing again at the *Racing Post*. 'He'll get two and a half for him, won't he, Phil?' Phil nodded his agreement. 'There's worse dogs going for more money at the moment,' added Ginger.

What to do now? I couldn't afford to keep Kevin racing, so I had to look at other options. Firstly, I could sell him for chump change, or chump meat. Secondly, I could do a deal with another owner and give him away on licence, as it were, to keep racing until his days were over. I'd retain ownership of him but I wouldn't have to maintain him. Nah, that would involve too much hassle. Thirdly, I could reform a syndicate and sucker some friends into financing his training fees, but given my friends' apathy in the first place it was highly unlikely they'd go for it now. Finally, if I couldn't sell him or give him away, I could offer him up for adoption. Short of shipping him off to Spain for the dreaded hare-coursing death sentence, there was one last option: I could keep him.

Somehow, though, this just didn't seem feasible. I didn't live in a home conducive to owning a dog. I should've had my exit strategy worked out a year ago when I first got into this mess. A greyhound can live to around fourteen years of age, which is ninety-eight in dog years, if you accept the notion that a human year is equal to seven dog years. That is a long time to be saddled with an animal. I couldn't even contemplate spending that long with a woman.

I started slowly, tentatively, asking friends if they knew anyone who might be interested in him. Margot implored me not to 'turn my back on him'. She pestered me constantly about Kevin's future, like a child nagging for a new toy. Or a pet. I told her that he had always been a commercial consideration, a movable asset, an investment. I didn't see anything intrinsically wrong with using animals as moneymaking tools. Margot and her friend Liz had met someone walking a retired racer in Battersea Park and she had told them that over nine thousand greyhounds are put to the sword each year. Here we go again . . .

'It'd be bad PR for you if you got rid of him,' she said. 'What you gonna do when people start asking what happened to him?'

'All right, all right.'

'Supposing he gets into the wrong hands? It could come back on you and your publisher.'

'But I can't afford to keep him and we can't have him in the flat.'

'But . . .'

'But what? I'll deal with it. Jesus. Give me a break.'

chapter 29

It was like a prison waiting room: sweaty, frowsy, the aroma of rancid hard-luck stories wafting through the air. Thirty compulsive gamblers, all men, no women, all fucked. This was the bad time. This is what they don't tell you about in the glossy promo brochures and the betting-shop posters. This is hell.

'My name's Terry and I'm a compulsive gambler. It's been six days since my last bet.' A smattering of applause and salutations greeted Terry, a weaselly cabbie in his mid-forties, as he sat in the hot seat in front of the group. Terry explained that he'd do endless night shifts to fund his gambling but would get so skint he couldn't put any diesel in his cab.

'Horses, football, dogs . . . anything . . . I'd bet on anything,' said Terry. Several members of the group nodded sagely. One or two rocked in their chairs. I could see a sliver of spittle running down the side of one old boy's mouth as he sat there agape. Young and old, rich and poor, what a band of brothers, what a fraternity of hard knocks and misery. One by one they sat in that rickety old chair and spilled the beans on a life of false expectations and failure. Jesus, this was so depressing. It was like being teleported into *One Flew Over the Cuckoo's Nest*. What a bunch of basket cases. I'd been to funerals that were more upbeat.

The methods of Gamblers Anonymous are simple. The programme of recovery is taken from Alcoholics Anonymous. The steps of recovery are read at weekly meetings and the chairman, one of the members, invites each punter to speak of his own experiences. This is called his therapy. He describes something of his gambling days and how great his life is now that he's addicted to group therapy rather than scratch cards or bingo.

As a new member I was meant to have an epiphany through self-recognition. The meeting, they say, is your 'mirror'. Christ, what a reflection. There was plenty of talk of new lives, sin, repentance and 'the truth'. The truth? *You can't handle the truth!* Another side of the evangelical nature of these twelve-step programmes is the, I feel, false supposition that once an addict, always an addict. Where is the hope in that? The line is that there is no cure for addiction so you come to the meeting to stop you from going to the dog track, amusement arcade or whatever tickles your fancy. I refused to believe that a twelve-month moment of madness slumming it at the dogs could result in a lifetime of addiction.

Tim broke down in tears, saying that he was lonely and that playing the slot machines in an amusement arcade in King's Cross helped him cope with his loneliness. Yeah, go Tim! Around a quarter of all GA members are addicted to fruit machines. Fucking fruit machines! Christ, if you are going to be addicted to something make it worthwhile, like cocaine or rich women. But fruit machines? These days you can be addicted to anything. You can even be addicted to being addicted to something. Now where was the goddamn help for these people? Since the introduction of the Lotto GA has seen a 17 per cent increase in calls, not just for Lotto, but across the board. What a sad bunch. Surely it hadn't come to this? I was here for research purposes only. Research. I heard awful stories of men rifling through their elderly mothers' handbags, lying, cheating and stealing in order to get cash to gamble with.

Halfway through the session I started to feel guilty; not just because the line between research and reality had blurred indistinguishably but because I was in an environment where, as the chair of the meeting had said, 'Anything that's said in here stays in here, so feel free to speak openly.' I had baulked at secretly recording the meeting but I still felt like a plant and I knew at some point I would regurgitate selected sufferings of the gamblers present on to the page. The only way forward was to protect the identities of those present by using pseudonyms. Everyone was referred to strictly by first name only and I don't doubt that some of those were *nom de plumes* anyway. But to be on the safe side I decided to change the identities of anyone who had a distinctive name and or stated occupation. So Ezekiel, the forty-something advertising exec and George Clooney look-alike from Kew, became 'John' just as Chad, the openly gay QC who I also noticed drove an aquamarine Aston Martin DB5, simply became 'Steve'. So that puts everyone in the clear.

Along with GA one man said he was also attending two NAs, an AA and Freudian psychotherapy. Such permutations of therapy gave me another blistering idea: how about an Anon Anon, or AA2 if you like – Anonymity Anonymous. *Hi. My name's David and I'm a compulsive group therapy attendee. My last meeting was two hours ago.*

What the GA meeting told me was that compared to the other patrons I had it easy. In fact, I didn't have a gambling problem at all. And to prove it, two nights later, I went to the track and duly lost £120.

'Mo' had got in the hot seat and compared gambling to taking narcotics, which he had also done. 'You start slowly, with small stakes, but you soon need a bigger fix to get you off. So you make more bets, for bigger stakes and it just goes on and on until all you can do is think about where to get money to gamble. Gambling is bullshit. It's fucking hell. That's all I've got to say.' Rapturous applause.

More than one gambler mentioned, in an aside, that at the height of their addiction they found gambling better than sex. Linda had said the same thing about racing greyhounds which prompted me to think what kind of sex were these people having?

I was intrigued at how so many of the guys could remember their first punt, as your first gamble isn't as memorable as, say, losing your virginity or passing your driving test. But nonetheless, it was eerie how many gamblers could remember their first bet, as though they were conscious at the time that they were undergoing some kind of initiation or rite of passage. Once you got on the bandwagon, it seemed, you were fucked. The bookies were in a win-win position: if you started your gambling career a winner you started believing you were lucky. If you started out a loser, then your ego made you want to start chasing your losses; you'd become obsessed with beating the bookies and they'd grind you slowly into the ground. And if you won a bit and lost a bit, on the dogs or the horses, well that just made you obsess about provenance, streaks, biorhythms and other superstitious claptrap.

It's easy to look at pathological gamblers as greedy, lazy, stupid. Because so many of them are. But what came out of my informal relationship with the gambling fraternity was that here are people, real people, who manifest the kind of compulsive behaviour that seems to be all-pervasive in Western society. It could be argued that our pathological behaviour only becomes a problem when money or other people are involved. But take away money and people from Western culture and what are you left with? Nature? Thin air?

At the very least gambling had greatly improved my powers of mental arithmetic.

And then *I'm* in the chair.

'Hi. My name's David. It's been forty-eight hours since my last bet. Jesus. I can't believe I just said that.'

I spent the next *twenty minutes* talking absolute bollocks about myself. I spilled my guts on how I had an ego problem, I overestimated my talent, I was arrogant, selfish, deceitful, conceited, disorganised, moody . . .

'Thank you for sharing that with us, David,' said the chairman before I'd even finished my monologue. I returned to my chair to several nods and screwed-up faces of encouragement.

As my father used to tell me, 'Experience teaches wisdom.' But was losing all of one's money necessary to learn the lesson that gambling doesn't pay?

My father. It was his fault. Well, you have to blame someone. And I was fed up of dumping it on Kevin. The most illuminating thing to come out of that balding fart of a poet Philip Larkin was 'They fuck you up, your mum and dad.' New research has found a genetic/hereditary rather than an environmental link in addiction between parents and offspring. Cackling round me like a group of harridans several GA members repeated the line that it was not gambling that was the problem but something in their nature – a pathological addictive or compulsive personality, laying dormant like a cancer, waiting for a trigger, the catalyst that would spur them into action. All addictions follow the same pattern and all have a human *and* financial cost. Even if the only financial cost is paying a Harley Street shrink to get you over your addiction to apathy, it costs somewhere down the line. So what was eating me; what was the root of my compulsive behaviour? Was it hereditary, something constructed or a combination of the two.

My father had, at various stages, been a heavy gambler. I wouldn't go as far as saying he had a problem, but then like most personal problems, if well concealed, they usually manifest themselves in an indirect fashion. For me this meant having Dunlop Greenflash instead of Adidas SL80s as a kid.

Having grown up watching my father slip-slide into hypertension, in part through thrombotic Saturday afternoon rituals like horseracing, I understand that gambling can seriously damage your wealth and your health. How can any activity that makes the veins on your neck bulge like mutant black pudding be any good for you?

'Go on, son, go on, son, go on, my boy . . .' the old man would yell at the TV while making like Lester Piggot with a severe case of whip fever. In between races he'd nip round the corner to the conveniently located bookies (next to the conveniently located off-licence) to place a bet, collect his paltry winnings and, more often than not, lose his mind.

Sometimes I'd look into his yellowing eyes as he worked himself into a lather in front of the goggle box, transfixed by the 3.15 at Kempton Park, and wonder what could possess someone to get so worked up about a financial proposition which they knew ultimately was doomed to failure. Usually the old boy lost. Not big money, but enough to deny me a pair of Levis or a Meccano set.

Other times he would despatch me to the bookies to lay a bet on for him. A bookmakers is a strange, intimidating place for a shy adolescent. I was always struck by the foul, manly smell of the place. The air thick with cigarette smoke and BO, the punters with their stinking alcoholic breath – it insulted my frail sensibilities. A bookie is one chronic case of halitosis. And thus I learnt that gambling, especially on animals, was bullshit. Nevertheless, we don't always act on what we know . . .

At the end of the meeting I hung around drinking tea and eating stale biscuits. One of the guys said if the gaming industry didn't get its act together and stump up an extra £2.2 million to fund treatment for gambling addicts, it faced a possible levy on its profits. The industry had failed to educate people about the dangers of gambling. Funding treatment was a key condition of the proposed deregulation of the UK's gambling laws.

Richard Caborn, the Minister for Sport and Tourism had warned gaming companies that they had to find £3 million to pay for care for addicts or the Government would introduce a levy on gross profits. So far the industry had raised only £800,000 to fund GamCare, which promoted 'responsible attitudes to gambling', and Gordon House, the country's only residential treatment centre for gamblers.

More than one of the speakers at GA spoke of walking into the bookies 'feeling confident'. What did this mean? Confident about what? I'd used this line before. Bullshit. We're kidding ourselves. See, that was the problem with us mugs, the ill-informed and feckless fools who spent too much time at the track and the bookies: we got off on *gambling*, not making money.

Statistically speaking, if you're serious about making money from gambling the best odds are to be found at a blackjack table. An astute player can average out a 10–15 per cent profit in the long term. Blackjack is the only game in town where you can consistently fix the 'edge' in your favour. Trouble is, to be good at blackjack, as I once learned to my cost in Las Vegas, you have to card-count, concentrate on sequences of numbers and percentages of high and low cards, alter stakes according to probability outcomes and all that bollocks, which is too much work for the average mug punter.

One punter once even said to me, 'If the dogs was so bent, people wouldn't bet millions on it, would they?' This kind of self-delusion is common amongst gamblers. It has to be to keep the wheels turning.

'If you ever fancy going to the dogs, I've got passes,' I said to the merry men gathered outside the meeting hall. They looked at me blankly.

'There's another meeting on Thursday,' said one character. 'You should come.'

'I'll think about it,' I said and walked off into the night.

chapter 30

Kevin was lagging. He came in fifth over the 640 trip, which was the second time he'd run the distance. He was simply making up the numbers. I didn't have a single bet. I decided to deal with my addictions and afflictions myself. Besides, I didn't have any money. I hung around for the last race, looked down at my watch to check the time and clocked the date. It was May 12th, my father's birthday. Where art thou, old man? I hadn't seen him in nearly three years. He'd just upped and gone. The last I had heard of him was a rumour that he had gone back to Guyana to sort out a retirement home and had been mugged and beaten to the ground by a couple of hoodlums. Jesus, why hadn't we spoken in all this time? He had my mobile number; it had been the same for ten years. All he had to do was dial and there I'd be. And even if he'd lost my number he could find me, it wouldn't take much. After all, I made enough of a cock of myself in the papers or on TV to get spotted. Surely someone who knew him would've said, 'I read some piece of shit by that no good son of yours . . .'

A slightly disconcerting recent observation was how I had started to become more like my father and less like myself. Age has a way of playing such tricks on you, like the way that as you get older your parents become proportionately less older than you, creating the illusion that if you keep on ageing *ad infinitum* you would both wind up the same age one day. (For example, when I was eight years old my father was forty, i.e. five times my age. When I turned sixteen, my father was forty-eight, i.e. three times my age. Now that I was thirty-six and he was sixty-eight, he wasn't even twice my age. The age gap between us was narrowing and so was the difference between us.)

Not speaking to my father had done me some favours. It made me feel a hell of a lot easier about being a shit dad to my own kid. It made me realise that being a 'good father' is not all it's cracked up to be. Being good at anything isn't all it's cracked up to be.

After a run of bad form at 640 metres Kevin finally returned to winning ways at 475 metres, leading from the off to record another decent time of 29:56. At 4–1 he would've made someone reasonably happy. As I was on the betting wagon I had to content myself with the knowledge that I had bagged the princely sum of £65 as owner.

For Kevin's arch nemesis, Twotone, things were also looking up.

So I'm slopping out the dog food at the kennels – the usual mix of hard biscuits, diced beef, chicken and minced lamb. Maybe Linda could give me a job to work off my kennel bill. She's looking at the weekly feeding schedule that outlines the weights of each dog and reels off their names as we hang around waiting to ferry an aluminium bowl to each hungry hound.

'Stinky,' she cries. 'Mary and Kevin . . .'

'Sounds like a good Catholic couple,' I say.

'Blackie.' Linda looks up at me. 'No offence meant.'

'None taken.'

'He's all right,' says Nan. 'He don't mind, do you, love?'

'To be honest with you I hadn't even given it any thought.'

'He's all right, Linda. He's one of us.'

What did she mean by that. One of us? What, was I a white man all of a sudden?

I hadn't even thought about the implications of a black dog named Blackie. It wasn't like calling a fawn dog 'Chinky' or a brown dog 'Paki'. And it certainly wasn't like the RAF hero (played by Richard Todd) Wing Commander Guy Gibson's Labrador in *The Dam Busters*, who was affectionately known as 'Nigger' which friends of pensionable age inform me was a common name for black cats and dogs in the 1940s. Every time I see that movie I can't help but marvel at the scene where the dog kicks the bucket after being run over by a car bringing Gibson, squadron leader of the historic bombing raid on the Ruhr dams in Germany in 1943 and wannabe Tory MP, to tears. (Gibson, incidentally, had requested that 'Nigger' be buried at midnight, the time of the unsuccessful raid, and that the word 'Nigger' be used as the codeword for the breaching of the Möhne Dam.) Some film historians and critics cite Nigger as being the conscience of the film. (ITV famously edited references to 'Nigger' from the film thus incurring the wrath of anti-censorship goons. And US TV networks even replaced the epithet with 'Trigger' when the film was shown across the Atlantic.)

'Right. This is Twotone's,' said Linda, giving me the eye. 'And watch it, you. No funny stuff in his food.'

'Don't worry.'

When I got back to the kitchen Linda was on her high horse.

'Someone ought to do something about what they're doing in Europe to the cats and dogs,' she said.

'Why, what's happened to them?'

'Didn't you see that programme on telly the other night? Oh, it was terrible. People are stealing them for their fur. Making Alsatian fur coats they were. Terrible business.'

Linda told me she had been on a disciplinary charge at Walthamstow Stadium for 'time finding', i.e. deliberately slowing a dog down for a trial in order to have it downgraded so it can run against inferior opposition. Was the old girl a bit tricky after all? Maybe her luck was changing too. She was down to third place in the Greyhound Trainers' Association rankings and the winners weren't coming in like they used to. Ultimately, she beat the time-finding rap. 'They couldn't prove anything one way or the other at the inquiry,' she said. 'I've been a good girl, David. It's just one of those things. They just gave me a slap on the wrist and said don't let it happen again. What can you do, eh?'

I told Linda I was wondering what to do with Kevin. I didn't want to tell her outright that I was planning to get rid of him. I managed, through circumlocution, to get round to the subject. 'So, er, ha . . . Twotone, eh? Be worth a few quid if he gets into the Derby?'

'That's right, David. Bundles.'

'Ha, dogs, eh? Who'd have 'em? So, er, what do you reckon, you know, I'm thinking about getting a few more people on board on the syndicate. Er, what do you . . .'

'If you wanna tell 'em what he's worth, say £500. That's what you'd get for him.'

Linda cut me a knowing glance and carried on divvying up lumps of beef and chicken. Five hundred pounds. Five hundred pounds for a life. It would hardly cover his kennel bill. Extricating myself from her and Kevin would not be easy without being mercenary. Since I'd had a child, and now a dog, I'd gone soft. Perhaps I could take Kevin on to the dog show circuit . . . after all a greyhound had won 2003's best of breed for hounds or Crufts.

Five days later Twotone entered the Derby trial at Wimbledon, his defining moment. He'd been saved for over a month for his big shot. A win would put him into the next round and ever closer to that £75,000 prize.

Before that, he'd won six out of his last ten races, an incredible strike rate. But then his luck changed. He was beaten into third spot. Only the first two from each trial could qualify for the heats. Ha! I never liked that dog's attitude from the off. That'll learn him for not taking a biscuit from me. Boy, did I know how to hold a grudge. What *Schadenfreude!* But look at it from my point of view: if Twotone had gone on to run and, heaven forbid, win the Derby I would've lost £75,000 for the sake of an extra 1500 quid.

In all honesty I wasn't crowing. One should never bask in others' misery. I'd heard too many punters cussing dogs in the stands, blaming their lack of judgement or just fate on a dumb animal. For all my lip, I did believe in the Corinthian ideal, fair play, being a good sport, 'it's the taking part that counts' and all that tosh.

Winning is great, but it's rare, a fleeting moment to be savoured, a dream. Losing on the other hand is a perpetual grind; it is the commute to work, the credit card bills, the failed exam, the wife walking out with the kids. It's the reality of everyday life. Four days earlier Kevin had come fifth; a week after that he won and I pocketed £65 in prize money. But the results didn't matter any more. They really didn't.

chapter 31

It was time to organise a 'testimonial' so the other silent partners of the Headline Syndicate could see the Boy Blunder run one last time before I sold him into medical research. It would be one last roll of the dice, his last opportunity to shine. If he impressed, maybe my friends and acquaintances would finally realise what they'd been missing and buy a share in him, that way I could keep him running until I figured out his fate, otherwise it was curtains. The expense of running a greyhound was more than I could shoulder on my own. I owed Linda so much in training fees, if I didn't get a handle on the money situation, I'd be washing dishes and slopping out at Imperial Kennels for the rest of my life. I would call the dog track, tell them I wanted to put on a bit of a do on a forthcoming Thursday night, sponsor a race and that'd be that. But there were complications, like rules.

'You'll have to talk to Chris about that,' said Ann. 'I can't get involved in all that. It could be a bit . . . tricky.'

'OK. By the way, I'd like to call the race the Zussies Boy Memorial Stakes.'

Ann wasn't too keen on the idea.

'David, please don't call it the Memorial Stakes,' she said, 'as they only do that when someone's dead!' There I go again. Thinking too far into the future.

Allowing owners to sponsor races in which they have a canine stake creates a clear conflict of interest. Imagine the hullabaloo if

I sponsored a race that Kevin actually ran in . . . and won? Questions would be asked. Eyebrows would be raised. In the event, I, I mean the Headline Syndicate wound up sponsoring, *for one night only*, the 'Headline Stakes' for the cost of a trophy and £290 in prize money.

A problem was the grade of Kevin's race. It was Chris Page, the Race Manager's responsibility to grade races according to ability, not wallet size, and Thursday nights were open race nights, which meant ordinarily Kevin would have no chance of running. However, as a one-off, Kevin was appearing in the following Thursday's 20:49 race – the Eric Burgess Retirement Stakes. On paper he wasn't the slowest dog in the field but the grade was a notch or two higher than he was generally used to and the competition was much more consistent with their times. All I could hope for was that he didn't embarrass himself or me in front of his new fans.

Come the night, I felt mildly nervous. For the first time in months, in fact ever, a substantial number of friends, acquaintances and colleagues had turned up at the Stow to see Kevin in action.

'The toffs get Ascot and we get Walthamstow,' said my friend Tam, looking round at the clientele. But so what? So what if the toffs had 'the season'? I had the 'counter-season'. Who needed Henley, Royal Ascot and Glyndebourne when you had the English Greyhound Derby, the National Lawnmower Championships and the All England Hod Carrying Finals?

But enough of the social commentary. Let's cut to the chase. When Kevin's race finally came around half my crew were too pissed to even notice. Having made a conscious effort to curb my gambling habits I made a concession for the Boy Blunder and stuck a token £10 on him at 10–1. Having studied the form in the race card I may as well have set a match to the money. By the time he came out the traps most were so far into their scampi and chips they didn't even see him get fried at the first bend. He didn't have a chance. Come the second turn he'd been well and truly muscled out of the game by the pack. At the third bend he was lagging, unable to contend with the superior opposition. Boy, the Stow had covered its arse all right. Unless he pulled a kalashnikov from out of his jacket and went postal on the other dogs he had no chance of winning. Coming down the home straight I could feel a year's work going down the toilet.

Kevin came last.

Not only did he lose, he lost spectacularly, crawling home last by at least six lengths. I felt sorry for the boy. Nobody gave a toss about him really. He was just a dog. All that stuff about us being a nation of animal lovers is romantic fantasy. People don't give a shit about animals. Like Ann had said, she loved her dogs but still ate steak. As if on cue, at a time when I assemble a decent crowd of people and after pulling strings to get him on the Thursday night card, Kevin comes last for only the second time in his career. At least everyone had a laugh at our expense.

But hey, if you are going to lose, lose in style baby. Everyone remembers Eddie the Eagle and Eric the Eel because they came last. Can you remember who won the 2000 Olympic downhill or 100 metres breaststroke? Exactly. Case closed. And what about that freak Tony Bullimore who tried to row across the Pacific in a bath tub or something? Everyone remembers that nut because he got within a hundred metres of the shore in Australia after an epic 900-odd-mile journey only to capsize the fucker. *Winner!*

Plucky Brits, just as we know it will rain at Wimbledon, know not to complain or try too hard or change things too fast. In this sense the plucky Brit has something of the Zen master about him, always guided by the middle way.

In the final analysis I could always console myself that I was simply following in the tradition of the Great British loser. Basil Fawlty, Rigsby, Steptoe and Son, Ian Duncan Smith . . . After all, there is a lot more to be said for being a loser than being a winner. Winning leaves little room for reflection other than the usual protestations of thanking God, Mum and the Academy. You only have to witness the fawning, gushing yak of Oscar winners, podium-traipsing Olympians and obsequious politicians to deduce that there is something vaguely tacky, slightly oily, about winning and winners. The conscious loser on the other hand is the second-rater's philosopher, the master of mediocrity, doyen of the dropout.

Well that's one way of looking at it.

After the race I led some of the troops over to the kennels. This caused a bit of a stir. I could see Patrick, Kevin's handler, doing the post-race honours, washing his feet and giving him a rub down. Eventually he brought him out to the expectant crowd. Kevin was panting heavier than I'd ever seen him. 'Aw, poor Kevin, you're such a loser,' came a voice from the crowd.

'No he's not,' I said, trying to stay cool and not take the slight personally. *It was aimed at the dog, not me.* I started babbling on again about him being overmatched and out of his depth etc. but my words fell on deaf ears. I carried on but the group just melted away into the mass of spectators in the stands with their beers and thoughts of dancing the night away at Charlie Chan's. Everyone was laughing. When I went to join the group in the club, the doormen stopped me and my friend Damian, who was dressed in an Hawaian shirt, khaki shorts and trainers. 'Not tonight, lads,' said one of them, looking at Damian's attire. I felt like a chump.

This had been Kevin's forty-third race and he'd won seven. He was the epitome of mediocrity. The little fella had really pulled the stops out in the race. And came last. Once again he'd tried his best. That's all a greyhound can ever do. But his best simply wasn't good enough.

chapter 32

'We've got a saying up here in Yorkshire,' said Old Man Dennis, leaning back in his chair. 'If you don't like someone, give 'em a greyhound.' Boy, did I know what he was talking about.

I ran into Dennis after dropping Margot off at her parents' house in Cheshire and heading across the Pennine Way to Sheffield. to see some of my boxing cronies. Dennis owned the gym I used to train at in my bad old days as a boxer. He claimed to have been the first man in Sheffield to own a Rolls Royce Silver Shadow and was a bit of a character. Now in his mid-sixties he was still stocky, still pugnacious, but a 'lovable rogue'. These days he ran a modest scrap-metal business, a couple of cafés and a sauna and massage parlour, among other business interests.

'I'd say I've done over a million pounds gambling over the years, Dave,' said Dennis, as we pulled up outside his old friend Walter Hesselwood's scrap-metal factory. Dennis had been a compulsive gambler with a bizarre set of superstitions to match. There was the usual stuff, like lucky socks and jumpers, but he'd also make his ex-wife wear any item of clothing she'd worn when he'd last had a big win. 'I even used to ask her where she was standing when such and such a dog or horse won,' said Dennis. 'And she'd say, "Over there" and point to a corner or other part of a room. I'd then tell her, "Go and stand in that fucking corner; the race is on in a minute and he's running again." I were fucking insane, Dave.'

Superstition had started to get the better of me too. I was convinced that Kevin was jinxed. For one, whenever I backed him he lost. OK, admittedly more often than not he lost regardless of whether I backed him or not. But he had, after all, brought me nothing but bad luck. I knew that protruding ribcage of his was an omen. Well, I couldn't put my failure purely down to my own incompetence, could I? Gamblers and dog owners are a superstitious bunch. Superstition gives you a sense of control by making you think you can work out what's going to happen next, a sort of adjunct to the 'locus of control' – the belief that you can control your destiny.

I didn't want to believe in luck any more. But somehow I couldn't help but think luck had played a massive role in my life of late . . . all of it bad. My foray into greyhound racing had been cursed from the start. Why hadn't I taken Vince's advice and bought a car?

Dennis eventually gave up gambling for four years following a course of hypnotherapy with a mutual friend called Paul Dorking. Paul had worked with me on mental techniques I had used in boxing training. But just as I'd started to pile on the pounds and lose the six-pack through lack of mental conditioning, Dennis had returned to his gambling ways.

'A million pounds. Lot of money innit, Dave?'

'It is, Den.'

'You think I would've learnt my lesson.'

'But you haven't, have ya?'

'I'm a fucking shit gambler as well. Waste of money. You know I used to have thirty-odd greyhounds.'

We strolled into Walter Hesselwood's office, an old school joint locked in a 1970s vacuum, and met the old boy sitting behind his desk. His secretary was shuffling files around and stapling bits of paper together. Walter had 'pillar of the community' written all over him. He greeted us and wasted no time with the nostalgia.

'Tell Dave how many dogs you had, Walter,' said Dennis.

'Oh, I couldn't say, Den. Loads. Loads. I used to buy 'em from a farm in Ireland. One week I bought forty different dogs for different trainers and I had up to thirty dogs running at any one time.'

Walter, now aged seventy-four, had owned the Duke of Alva who won the St Leger in 1957, which he said was one of the first greyhounds to earn appearance money 'without even putting a paw on sand'. The St Leger was the first ever televised greyhound race. Alva won every heat and then of course the final. He won seventeen consecutive four-dog races.

'I had so many dogs,' reminisced Walter. 'Tinryland Snowball . . . he were a winner at Hull, Bradford and Leeds in the *News of the World* Inter Track Competition 1956. Trained by Jack Brennan. I sold Newdown Prairie to Paddy Keane for stud in Australia. He had a hairline fracture and went lame. Then I had Shepherds Gold. He were a good hurdler, but he were vicious. Greyhounds are lovely animals but when they turn they don't bite, they chomp. Vicious . . . Jimmy Jowette was walking six dogs when one turned on him – never said which one it was – two hundred stitches he needed.'

Walter dropped names like they were out of style. His time had been about names, faces, big wins and championships. Mine had been about . . . well . . . fuck all really. We couldn't have been further apart on the greyhound scale.

'It were exciting in them days. It were good to take a dog anywhere, you know, and take on all comers. I suppose the kick were gambling. But I haven't had a bet in twenty years.'

Old boys make me laugh. They have the kind of patience I envy. Like a lot of the 'younger generation' I want everything yesterday, which means I often fall short today. Age slows you down for a reason; it forces you to stop wasting your time. My old man used to say, 'Youth is wasted on the young.'

'I've got some advice for you,' said Walter, leaning across his desk. 'Find someone you don't like, give that bloody dog you've got to 'em as a Christmas present, cos there's no future in it.'

Chance would be a fine thing. I couldn't even give Kevin away. There was always one last resort however.

'Aye, there's flapping near Barnsley,' said Dennis as we headed back into Sheffield city centre. 'I don't go any more but there used to be some right scams in the old days, Dave. People would rub Vaseline in dogs' eyes, dope 'em, dig holes in front of boxes, anything to nobble a race. A fella once got pulled for putting Formica in traps at one track.'

Flapping is the arse end of greyhound racing, the lowest of the low. Part sport, part fairground attraction, flapping is the bare-knuckle fighting of dog racing. One of the last surviving flapping tracks near Sheffield is Highgate Greyhound Stadium in a village just outside Barnsley called Thurnscoe. Thurnscoe is England's fortieth worst employment area. It's one of only four council wards in the Yorkshire and Humber Region which are in the top hundred of the most deprived out of 8500 wards in England. The unemployment rate is double the national average. This is a hidden Britain of burnt-out cars, a forgotten Britain of potholed roads and scallies on stolen mopeds.

The high street of boarded-up shops and smashed windows had had the guts ripped out of it and what was once a thriving community based on industry, coal and steel was now a wasteland. On the corner of Tudor Street, just off the main drag, was the Spit and Whisper, the Officials Club which promised 'New Members Welcome'. I bet if I went in and tried to get membership I'd be made welcome all right. In Thurnscoe it was an occupation for scrawny Reebok-clad youths to loiter on street corners and prepubescent girls to dress like whores. Kids without helmets or ambition raced up and down the high street on snarling motor-bikes. Everywhere I turned I was stared at. This was real white-boy territory. For many years I had embraced the spirit of multiculturalism but this was a bridge-building exercise too far. I'd ventured out into the sticks enough to know that feeling like a foreigner in your own supposed country was a damn sight more uncomfortable than feeling like a foreigner in a foreign country.

While the origins are unclear, I've heard it said that the term 'flapping' comes from the sound that the rag lures used to make in the old days. Regardless of historical pretensions, people in the BGRF/NGRC community take a dim view of the unregistered flapping track scene. The lack of regulation and casual philosophy of many flapping folk mean that, rightly or wrongly, it attracts the kind of bad press the mainstream industry is working hard to eradicate.

There are 27 unsupervised flapping tracks like Highgate in Britain, but since 1985 some 28 had closed, many of them in the north of England. Aldershot, Ashington, Barnsley, Barrow, Berwick, Bideford, Bolton, Carfin, Chasewater, Chester, Chesterfield, Clacton, Cleethorpes, Coatbridge, Deeside, Doncaster, Falkirk, Glastonbury, Hawick, Huntingdon, Preston, Skegness, Skewen, St Helens, Stanley, Westhoughton, Wisbech and Workington were all names consigned to the dustbin of greyhound racing. Maybe it was simply the case that public tastes and attitudes had become too sophisticated for the gritty reality of standing in a field with a pint of Smiths and a roll-up watching your sixteen seconds of fame whiz round a sodden field.

I paid my £3.50 entry fee and passed through a rickety turnstile. The track, situated in the middle of a field and surrounded by corrugated iron, was even grimier than I had imagined. The dogs weren't actually kennelled on site; people kept them in their vehicles – white vans, Astra estates, trailers or some just on the back seat of a car.

As soon as I set foot inside Highgate, typically, all eyes were on me. Every note I took, every observation I made, someone, somewhere was monitoring my actions. I felt uncomfortable, unwelcome even, although there was no open hostility.

I got myself a pint of Guinness from the bar, hung back and watched the goings on.

A black and white dog came out of the paddock reluctantly with its owner, a walking meat pie of a man. It was straining its lead as it stopped, shivering with fear, to take a shit on the sand.

'C'mon there,' said Meat Pie Man. The dog was a nothing more than a rasher of skin and bone. The crowd at the stand-side rails looked on dismissively.

I overheard an old boy giving a fella next to me some advice. I think his name was Alf. He was the only man in all the time I'd been to the dogs that I saw actually wearing a flat cap. Alf had a face like a fist, all gnarled and calloused. I asked him if he had a tip.

'Yeah, keep ya money in ya pocket. There's now't but rubbish here t'day.'

The last straw came when a black dog named 'Darkie' was paraded in the paddock. Its name was called out and I heard a few sniggers followed by furtive glances in my direction. Time to get the fuck out of there and get back to civilisation. Time to get back on the beaten track, forget about the dogs and end this cultural safari once and for all.

chapter 33

Weeks passed, then months and Kevin's performances got worse and worse. His stock value was nil. Selling was no longer an option. Apart from a small knock in December of 2002 which laid him up for three weeks, he'd been fit and healthy and a loyal, if mediocre, servant and was still running, but if he had ever had a best he'd long passed it. I had exploited him. That was the name of the game. But what could I give him in return? A home? The property company that managed the Norman Foster des res where I lived had other ideas. In a memorandum that was sent to all residents they reiterated *inter alia* their policy of 'no pets or animals allowed' in the building. Screw them and Foster anyway. Living in a million-pound pad overlooking the Thames wasn't all it was cracked up to be.

Margot and I returned to Barbados for our annual dose of winter sun. We paid a trip to the Garrison racecourse, had a great day out and a modest flutter. I'd managed to wean myself off compulsive gambling, not through group therapy or hypnosis but sheer willpower, which meant avoiding the Stow and my local bookies long enough to escape the lure. I had given up gambling, just as I had once given up smoking, being fat, lazy and a scallywag, simply by recognising the futility of what I was doing. It felt good being clean again, being free of an irrational compulsion.

Barbados was crying out for a dog track but I certainly wasn't going to measure it up for one. No, my days in the greyhound business were about to come to an abrupt end. Halfway through the holiday, one evening, while spraying mosquito repellent on my legs and knocking back an ice-cold beer, I got a voicemail message. It was Linda Jones. 'Can you call me, David?' she said. 'It's very important.' It was Thursday night, a race night, and around 11.30p.m. UK time. *My God. Something's happened to Kevin.* Linda and I hadn't spoken for a while, but not through a falling out. I just owed her a chunk of change in unpaid kennel fees. I had the matter in hand. I'm no deadbeat: I always pay my debts . . . eventually. But I was embarrassed at not sorting it out sooner and was caught in the ninety-day invoice trap by one of my paymasters. I called her back straight away.

'Hi, Linda, how's it going?' I said, fearing the worst. We talked small for a bit, about the kennels, performances etc. She'd been trying to contact me for some time she said. The bills never failed to get through though. I apologised profusely for my flakiness. Linda was cool. I felt better, temporarily. Getting into greyhound racing had always been a big risk. Not just financially but because a life was involved, a dog's life. For all my macho posturing, Kevin, in a small way, combined with my fumbling experiences in town and country, track and field, had taught me to give animals a bit of a break.

'OK. Give me the bad news.'

'Well, Kevin's been carrying a bit of an injury,' said Linda.

'His hock?'

'That's right,' she said. 'And he's not been doing too well. To be fair to him we put him out last week and he won.'

'That's great,' I said.

'But he's been struggling. We put him out again tonight and . . .'

He's dead.

'Well, he could hardly get round, David. I'm afraid we're gonna have to retire him. I think it's for the best.'

He's not dead.

'He's OK? I mean, he's all right in himself?'

'Oh yeah, he's fine. He's just struggling to make the grade.'

'But he's OK?'

'Yes, David.'

'Thank Christ. I thought you were going to tell me he'd snuffed it.'

'No, no. Don't be silly.'

Linda told me that she would make the necessary arrangements for him to go into the Stow's greyhound retirement scheme. All I had to do was pay a registration fee of £100 and they'd kennel Kevin until a suitable home for him was found.

'That's fine. I'll sort it out when I get back to London. And, er, I'll, er, take care of my bill too.'

'Don't worry, David. I know you won't let us down. And by the way . . .'

'Yes Linda?'

'Don't forget to bring us back some sunshine. The weather's terrible over 'ere.'

I put the phone down. Margot looked across the room at me, sympathetically. 'What's up, babe?'

I peered at the floor and shrugged my shoulders. What an anti-climax. 'It's all over, sweetheart. Kevin's done his hock in and Linda reckons it'd be best if we retired him now before it gets worse.' Kevin's career was effectively over. If ever I needed an ending to the story, it was now.

Epilogue

It was nearly noon, early spring, but the charcoal sky and driving rain betrayed the time of year. After four frustrating hours on the road I finally reached the tiny village of Lydney in the Forest of Dean, Gloucestershire, and my appointment with Ray Jones, a small-time trainer I had met through a tax exile from Barbados called John Watt. John, his estranged wife, their son, his wife's brother (also called John) and their cousin Ray had formed a syndicate in the late 1990s with a view to breeding and training open racers and perhaps, one day, an elusive Derby winner.

I pulled into the farmyard adjacent to Ray's kennels, over-steered, skidded, and then coasted into an iron gate. *Why me?* I got out of the car. *No damage, thank God.* I got back in the car, drenched, called Ray from my mobile and waited.

A minute later he appeared, all eighteen stone of him, dressed in waterproofs and a woolly hat, trudging through the mush. Ray, who had not long turned 40, had more than a passing resemblance to the former England cricket captain Graham Gooch, insofar as he had a thick handlebar moustache, dark hair and darker eyes. I wound down the window and a backhand of rain slapped me in the face. 'Hello Ray,' I spluttered, drying myself off. 'All right Dave,' he replied in his West Country twang. 'You'd better stay in the car cos these dogs go mad when they see a stranger. I'll give you a shout when I've finished sorting 'em out.'

I sat in the car, listening to the rain drumming on the roof. *Why me? Why the cats and dogs whenever I ventured into the countryside? What had I done to Mother Nature?* Gradually, the rain and sleet subsided and I could hear barking and empty buckets being tossed around outside. Ray soon reappeared with his cousin John, a wiry, unobtrusive character, and we all traipsed off to the kennels, the bulk of which had been fashioned out of a rusting corrugated transport container, home to a dozen or so dogs.

'Most of 'em are locked up now,' said Ray as we made for the rickety old caravan that served as his office. John mumbled something about pups and then scuttled off. 'I bet this ain't like Linda Jones's place, eh?' said Ray, laughing. 'It's not . . .' I said, looking round at the array of leads, collars, muzzles, bowls, grooming equipment and sundry crap. 'But it's not far off.'

Ray's 'home' track was Reading, a shack of a place compared to the Stow. He charged £2.50 a day in kennelling fees as opposed to Linda's £7 plus VAT. I had tried on more than one occasion to palm off Kevin on Ray, just for a couple of months, so I could buy some time and figure out what to do with him. But Ray wasn't having any of it. 'I ain't got the room, Dave,' he said, pottering around the caravan. 'I got too many here as it is.'

I sat in the caravan shivering. *Damn the countryside and everything in it.* 'Haven't you got a garden shed you could put him in, or a car boot, anything?' I pleaded. Ray laughed. With four retired greyhounds living at home he was already doing his bit for the greyhound welfare state. 'They put in the effort for us so we owe it to them to do the right thing,' he said, giving me a knowing look. 'I suppose we've got a duty to them.'

Now I felt even more guilty. I had failed in my 'duty' as an owner and now I was paying the price for it.

'Look, for a small outfit like us we've got to go for open racers,' explained Ray. 'If we don't get open racers, we sell them [the graders] and breed another litter. The first litter we bred, three of them were good open racers out of five and the other was an A1 track champion. When you get used to having good dogs, having mediocre ones after that isn't the same. I've sold pups to people who've been in racing 25 years with the aspiration of getting an open racer and they've never had one. We were in it a few years and got three in our first litter so you can see we were a bit fortunate.'

Ray showed me a litter of eighteen-week-old puppies that he had bred. They lived in their own private kennel, fenced off at the end of a field backing on to the main enclosure. *How cute. The little bastards . . .*

'There's a bias against English dogs,' said Ray as the little nippers jumped up excitedly at the wire mesh separating them from us. 'If you took an English dog to the sales you'd get laughed at.' Despite the prejudice, Ray only trained and raced dogs bred by his loving hand. This was mainly for the sense of personal achievement but also to protect the integrity of his bloodlines. Greyhound racing is certainly not a free-for-all when it comes to breeding – one cannot pair up any two mutts without the right official paperwork. But it is not controlled as rigidly as thorough-bred racing where, for instance, artificial insemination is banned. Thanks to the wonders of the internet, it is possible to buy frozen greyhound semen from a variety of sources. Take one bitch and a pipette and you're in business. *Now there's an idea.*

As I toyed with Ray's puppies, teasing out their natural instinct to chase, I thought of the thousands of animals that are culled every year because they'll never make the grade. I had to ask the obvious question.

'So what do you do if you breed a dog that's duff?' I said.

'Luckily we haven't been in that situation yet, but I have had one in a litter that wouldn't chase. Well, he'd chase, but he went after the lure and then started looking at me at the side of the track. I'd never seen anything like it. The Great White Hope he was called. If they do that . . . well, if you try 'em a couple of times and they're still not chasing you've got your work cut out. I gave him away I did. He was a beautiful puppy.'

After a greasy breakfast we headed to a schooling track in Kidderminster, Worcestershire to trial four of Ray's older puppies.

When we got there, several other owners, trainers and dogs were queuing at the side of the track, waiting their turn to pit their wits and bloodlines against the clock. A grey-haired trap steward in green overalls was standing on the track ready to hand slip a slightly bemused looking pup. His chubby owner stood on the sidelines with another pup, watching keenly as the hare came clackety clack round the track, travelling at half-speed to make pursuit that bit easier.

As an added touch, the trap steward made a point of showing the dog the hare until it rounded the bend and reached them, upon which he gave the dog a gentle push, as though releasing a dove from cupped hands, urging it to give chase. 'Go on boy,' cried the steward, but the dog remained motionless. It then sniffed the air nonchalantly before turning to the steward and jumping up, attempting to lick his face, leaving the hare trundling off into the distance.

'We've got no fucking chance with these two, have we?' said the chubby man to the steward in a broad west Midlands accent. *How did I ever get into this comedy of a business?*

'You see how that guy slipped that dog,' said Ray gesturing toward the steward, 'I don't like doing that, cos that's encouraging the dog to look behind for the lure. As soon as it comes by it's gotta be pretty dumb not to see it anyway.

'A lot of trainers will take pups for a walk to chase rabbits,' continued Ray, as we slowly advanced in the queue, waiting our turn to trial. 'The trouble is, the more kills they've had the more they figure out the lure is a dummy. I was talking to a trainer yesterday who has a ferret. He lets it run around free and gets the dog to sight it, just to liven it up. Anyway, the dog ran and won. But you can only do that once in a while.'

There are so many tricks and dodges in greyhound racing and even though I'd probably learnt more than the average punter I had only scratched the surface. To make it in this game, like any business, you need dedication. You have to live and breathe, eat, shit and sleep the dogs. You needed patience, money to burn and time on your hands. I had none of this left to offer. I was nothing more than a dilettante, and a failed one at that.

'At the end of the day they wanna get to that lure first,' said Ray, gazing at the conveyor belt of dogs going round the track in pursuit of a rag and a stupid cuddly toy thrown in for good measure. 'That's what it's all about – that's what the competition is. You do get some dogs that, after they've raced a while, get a little bit cunning and realise that they're just there for the night out!' *That'll be Kevin.* 'But they enjoy it . . .' Ray seemed almost hypnotised by the cyclical goings on. He is a dog man, all right. And I am a fraud. 'You see these,' he said, looking at the queue of dogs, 'when that hare comes round they wanna get on it. They're bred to do that, that's their instinct.' As if on cue, as an illustration of Sod's Law, at that point one of the next dogs to trial came to an abrupt halt halfway round the track and started sniffing the ground, the air and listening to the spring chorus of birds tweeting in the nearby woods. And to think I paid £2,500 for one of these idiot animals.

'We're up next anyway,' said Ray. 'This one's a bit nervous, the fawn one. She doesn't take to it.' The bitch was yelping and squeezing her tail firmly between her legs. Ray took her and a black dog through a small gate leading onto the track, where a steward was on hand to help them into the traps. 'This is the second time they're going in the boxes,' said Ray. 'As you school 'em, you do it a little different every time. First off, when you bring 'em here you start 'em just where that dog wouldn't run, straight around to the pick up over here – that's the first time. Then the second time you slip 'em by that tower further on and time 'em, so you've got half an idea then. Then the third time, hand slip 'em from here; fourth time out of the boxes for the first time; fifth time out of the boxes for the second time but with a muzzle on. And the next week, everything being OK, you start two dog trials and . . .'

Back in London, I still flirted with the idea of bringing the Boy Blunder home. Ever the nomads, Margot and I had recently moved to a modest but spacious new build opposite Battersea Park. Without a garden, the park nevertheless offered ideal dog walking territory.

'I could build a kennel and he can live on the balcony,' I'd suggested, trying like a desperate, bogey-nosed child to convince Mummy that I could, I would, I *should* have a dog of my very own. *Grow up man.* Margot almost bought the idea until a meddling French polisher and know-it-all ex-greyhound owner showed up one day to do some work and pointed out that a big dog could easily jump off the balcony if a passing cat took its fancy. Well, I guess he had a point. A thirty-two-kilo dog falling thirty feet would make a bit of a mess.

At one stage, an ex-girlfriend agreed to re-home Kevin, then changed her mind, then changed again on the basis that she would have him for a trial period, then reconsidered, then re-reconsidered and then . . . *whatever.* In the end I gave up and paid the £100 as Linda had suggested and Kevin went into the lottery that is the Walthamstow Stadium Homefinding Scheme.

Eventually, Kevin wound up in Whittingham Kennels near Waltham Abbey, on the edge of Epping Forest in Essex, where up to 48 retired dogs are cared for. As he bided his time here hoping that some poor sap, I mean *animal lover*, would come along with a new lead, a rubber bone and a cosy home, I all but gave up on him. I had become the epitome of the wretched, embittered, failed owner. *Why should I care anymore?* He was out of my hands and had served his purpose, albeit miserably. The retirement people could take care of him from now on. *Stuff him.*

Yeah, go on: boo and hiss and paint me the pantomime villain. But let's get it into perspective: I am a grown man and he a *dog.* I had other shit to deal with. For instance, in the time that Kevin had joined the retirement home, I had learned that my father, aged 69, had died the previous summer in Guyana. It had taken seven months for me to be informed. *Seven months.* But that's another story. Suffice to say, in the most anticlimactic way possible, the gambler, the raconteur, the drinker, the arrogant sonofabitch who had forged me was gone. There was no 'closure', no reconciliation, no Hollywood ending to the Great Man's demise. I felt empty for a long while. Empty.

I had to move on. I had to draw this chapter to a close. The time for wallowing in self-pity was over. And I'm talking about Kevin here, not my old man! On the page, if not in life and death, I *could* find reconciliation, I could be the architect my own destiny. Resolution: this was the key. Maybe I did have a heart after all.

'Zussies Boy?' said Johanna, who runs the Whittingham Kennel. 'Kevin . . . hmm . . .' Down the telephone line I could hear her flicking through the pages of a ledger. 'Kevin . . . that's right. He's with a lovely woman called Anna down in Surrey. Hang on a minute I'll give you her number.'

I arranged to meet Anna one Sunday afternoon near her home in Mogador, Surrey at the 'dog friendly' Sportsman – an archetypal isolated country pub on the edge of a snow-covered moor. I felt uncharacteristically nervous, like a father about to meet his long-lost son for the first time. As I crossed the threshold every one of the dozen or so patrons, to a tee, stopped talking, turned, gave me a cursory look, and then carried on with their business.

Having survived the entrance test, I scanned the bar for Kevin. I couldn't see him. I did a double take. *Am I in the right pub?* Suddenly, I clocked him snuggled up on a jacket on the floor next to Anna, who by this point had got up to greet me with a wide grin and a handshake, introducing herself and her younger brother, James. 'Hi Anna, James,' I said, beaming, before turning my attention, somewhat rudely, to Kevin who was now on his feet attempting to sniff my balls. At first he seemed apprehensive. Cowering ever so slightly, unsurprisingly with his tail between his legs, he gave a few more sniffs and calmed down. 'I think he remembers you,' said Anna. 'Maybe he thinks I've come to take him back to the track,' I said. I got myself a drink, sat down and couldn't shake him off.

We were like old swells again, Kevin and me, snuggling and cuddling. Anna, a petite twenty-six-year-old occupational therapist, explained that she had got Kevin six months earlier from Johanna after seeing several other greyhounds at a retirement home in Gravesend, Kent. 'A friend of mine has got one and it's such a beautiful, gentle dog I thought I'd get one,' she said. 'I purposefully went for a big dog because I know they're harder to home; and I like the fact that he's mature. He's already got his personality, so there are no shocks. He's so laid back he'd sleep for twenty-four hours if he could.'

Living at home with her family meant there were always people around to look after him, and he even got on with her two cats, although at a distance. Many patrons came up to pet Kevin. He was obviously a star in the local. A middle-aged couple in particular, who were sitting next to us getting slowly sloshed, were all over him. 'Ooh, he soooo beautiful,' cooed the woman. 'Do you wanna sell him? Only joking! No, I couldn't have another one. We lost a greyhound a few years ago.'

'Lost?' I enquired. 'What happened to him?'

'Died . . .'

'Oh, that sort of lost,' I said.

'Lovely dogs, lovely,' continued the woman. 'Custer we called him. Greyhounds are the Gerald Hadley of the dog world: cool, calm, self-assured. They've got a posh face, haven't they? They've got *class*.'

The couple were so fixated with Kevin and reliving their greyhound memories that it was becoming increasingly difficult to have a conversation with Anna without them butting in. This was my big reunion and they were screwing it up.

'So, Anna.' I said, trying to squeeze a word out through gritted teeth.

'He lived to about fourteen, didn't he love?' said the man, returning to the bar with what looked like a couple of double malt whiskeys. 'We used to dress him up at Christmas in a Santa outfit.'

'With little reindeer horns,' added the woman. *Oh the laughter!* 'Beautiful dogs, beautiful.'

Behind my bravado and insouciance and sneering cynicism I was genuinely happy that Kevin had found a good home. Seeing him leading a dog's life and not busting his balls on a track assuaged any guilt I had felt for exploiting such a graceful, peaceful animal for such a frivolous pastime as dog racing. In truth, I felt mildly jealous of Anna and Kevin as an 'item'. But at least I could take satisfaction in knowing that some good had come of my adventure, even if it was at my expense.

As we left the pub for a quick country walk and last goodbye, it started snowing again. 'He *loves* the snow under his feet,' said Anna, removing Kevin's lead. Unshackled and unrestrained I waited eagerly for him to take off into the distance at speed with gay abandon, chasing powdery snowflakes and dancing shadows. But he simply took a few steps, cocked his leg against a tree, relieved himself and ambled along sniffing the ground. Such is life.